CW01271596

NEW TERRITORIES

Laboratories for Design, Craft and Art in Latin America

NEW TERRITORIES

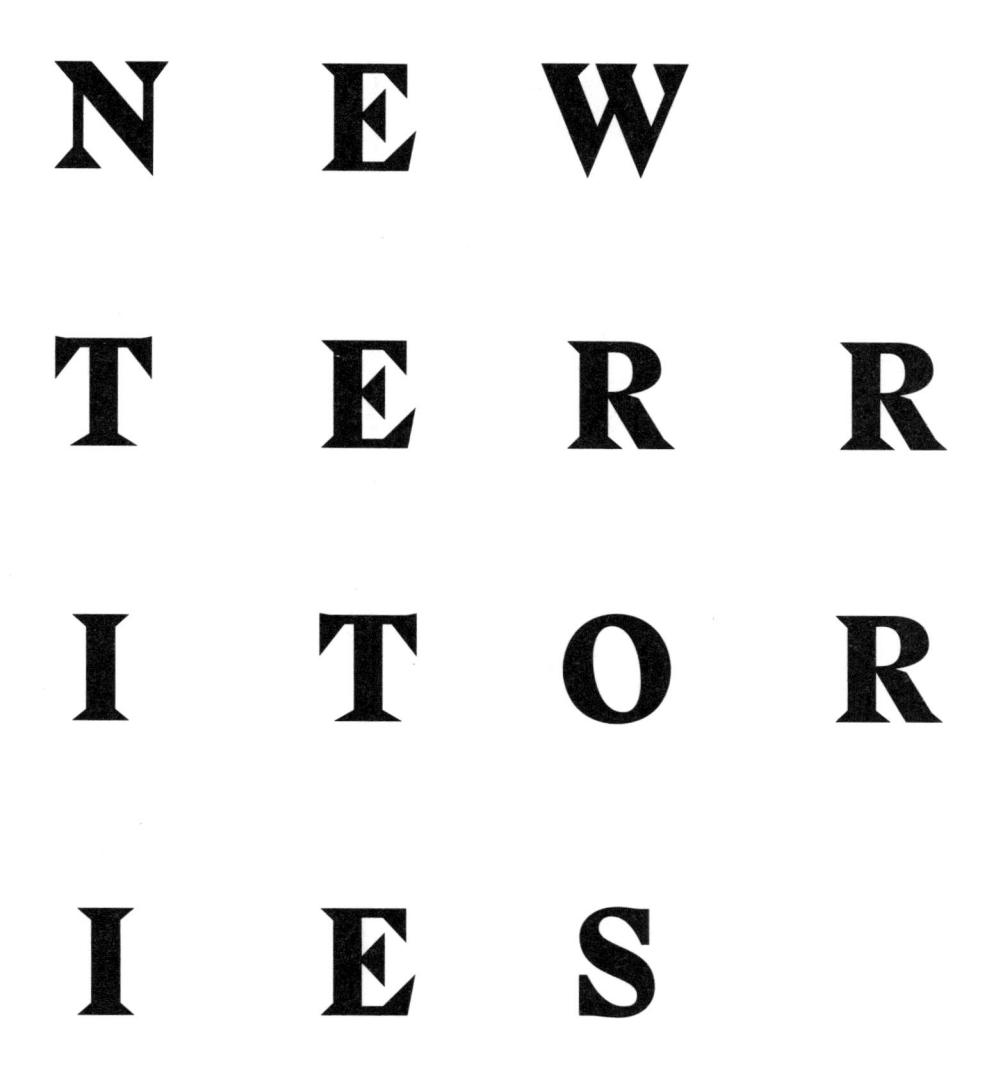

Laboratories for Design, Craft and Art in Latin America

Lowery Stokes Sims, with contributions by Mari Carmen Ramírez, Gabriela Rangel, Jorge Rivas Pérez, Regine Basha, Nessia Leonzini Pope and Fabiana Lopes, Antonio Sánchez Gómez, Adélia Borges, Ana Elena Mallet, Magdalena Grüneisen, Adriana Kertzer, and Marcella Echavarría.

Museum of Arts and Design
published in association with Turner
Madrid and Mexico City

Contents

Director's Foreword — 8

Acknowledgements — 10

A Report from the Field: — 12
New Territories in Design, Craft and Art in Latin America
Lowery Stokes Sims

Charting a "New Territory" for an — 33
Old Continent: Latin America as an Operative Construct
Mari Carmen Ramírez

Navigating the Past and Present — 38
in Latin America
Antonio Sánchez Gómez

Between Limit and Possibility: — 41
The Visual Culture of Bricolage in 1990s Cuba
Blanca Serrano Ortiz de Solórzano

Merging High and Low: — 46
Materials in Brazilian Contemporary Artistic Production
Nessia Leonzini Pope and
Fabiana Lopes

Productive Conflicts of Interest — 50
Interview with Jorge Pardo by
Regine Basha

Toys for Adults: Kawaii in — 54
South American Design
Magdalena Grüneisen

	Focus: Mexico City & Oaxaca *Moving Craft into the Future through Collaborations with Artists and Designers*	82
	Focus: Caracas *Conversations with Artistic Legacies*	118
Notes on Design and Material Culture in Latin America at the Global Crossroads Gabriela Rangel	56	
	Focus: São Paulo & Rio de Janeiro *Upcycling and Repurposing Objects*	138
The Nerve Center: Identity and Production in Contemporary Latin American Design Jorge Rivas Pérez	59	
	Focus: Santiago & Buenos Aires *Cultivating Collectivity and Experimentation in Design and Craft*	156
The Circulation of New Design: Trends in Latin America Ana Elena Mallet	63	
	Focus: San Salvador & San Juan *Developing New Markets for Design*	170
Designers and Artisans in Latin America: A Fruitful Collaboration Adélia Borges	68	
	Focus: Havana *Navigating Personal and Civic Space*	184
The Ethical Dimensions of Design: A Cautionary Note from Latin America Adriana Kertzer	74	Artist Statements	221
	Selected Bibliography	239
Rediscovering and Reinventing Latin American Food Marcella Echavarría	77	

Glenn Adamson
Nanette L. Laitman Director

According to the 1892 poem penned by seventeen-year-old Winifred Sackville Stoner of New York City: "In fourteen hundred and ninety-two, Columbus sailed the ocean blue." He sought and found a new territory, at least to his way of thinking.

Of course to those who lived here already, what was new was Columbus. He knew very little about the inhabitants of the Americas, and vice versa. The same was true of his colonial and imperial successors. From the very first moment and through to recent times, cross-cultural contact between Europeans, Africans, indigenous peoples, and Asians led to many misunderstandings and often this led in turn to exploitation and violence. Yet the cultural fruits of this exchange have been legion: in architecture, music, art, food, clothing, dance, and many other fields, the encounter between indigenous and immigrant populations in Latin America has produced miracles of invention.

In staging *New Territories*, we at the Museum of Arts and Design (MAD) knowingly reflect on this complex history. Our subject is emerging creativity in the fields of art, craft, and design across Latin America. Not a single contributor to the show, nor a single object featured in the galleries, is purely traditional. Yet neither are they completely divorced from the past. Latin America today is a vast fabric, shot through with threads of change and memory.

Resources and markets are sometimes (though not always) limited in comparison to European and North American contexts of creativity. The way that creative practitioners adapt and innovate in such circumstances is, most often, to rely on their own, or at least on local, capabilities: to make things well, and to work with those around them who do.

This makes Latin America a perfect subject for MAD circa 2014. We are an institution with a long history of commitment to craftsmanship. Today, we carry on that legacy by exploring contemporary cultures of making. This might involve advanced technology or long-established skills. It might take place in any discipline, or result in any type of object or experience. We are most attuned not to categories of things, but rather to the processes and people involved in creativity writ large. What the practitioners in *New Territories* have in common—apart from their geography—is the inspiring way that they go about their business.

And we do mean "business." Many museums tend to downplay commerce as a factor in creative practice, preferring to focus on ideas in pure form. We at MAD are hardly uninterested in ideas, but we tend to assume that really powerful, influential ideas involve entrepreneurial (not just conceptual) innovation. This project's focus on cities as laboratories of innovation is one signal of this emphasis. We are interested in the way that urban centers foster dynamics of collaboration, and the way that individual makers can prosper in cities, even as they shape the communities around them for the better.

The curator of our exhibition, Lowery Stokes Sims, has spent the better part of four years bringing it into reality—in collaboration with a generous group of advisors and supporters across Latin America. She was ably assisted in this task by curatorial assistants Magdalena Grüneisen and Adriana Kertzer, and interns Antonio Sánchez Gómez from the Bard Graduate Center and Alex Montane from Pratt Institute. Sims's previous major exhibition at MAD, *The Global Africa Project*, had a similarly ambitious scope and was also unexpected in its range and diversity of content. Like that project, *New Territories* is a revelation: it will introduce almost every visitor to exciting makers they have never seen before. It is as much a feat of investigative journalism as curating, and a testament to Sims's extraordinary gifts, not only as a museum professional, but also as a person who convenes the creative energies of others.

We are indebted to the supporters and sponsors of the exhibition. The Ford Foundation and the Robert Sterling Clark Foundation provided major initial funding that was crucial to the early planning for the exhibition, which included the meetings of the Curatorial Advisory Group in New York City and Mexico City. We are also grateful to Karen and Charles Phillips for their timely contribution, to the auction house Phillips for their support of the exhibition website, and to Furthermore: a program of the J.M. Kaplan Fund for its support of the exhibition catalogue. The Venezuelan American Endowment for the Arts and Ch.ACO, the Contemporary Art Fair of Chile supported curatorial research in Venezuela and Chile respectively, and we would also like to express our appreciation to Generoso Villarreal Garza, a member of MAD's International Council, who supported the curatorial visit to Monterrey. Additional support has been provided by The Louise D. and Morton J. Macks Family Foundation, the Mex-Am Cultural Foundation, and the Consulate General of Brazil in New York. Finally, we express our appreciation to all the designers, craftsmen and artists, galleries, and patrons who have provided loans to the exhibition.

Lowery Stokes Sims
William and Mildred Lasdon Chief Curator

While the genesis of the idea of the exhibition *New Territories: Laboratories of Design, Craft and Art in Latin America* grew out of the 2010 exhibition *The Global Africa Project*, its development took an entirely different track. As opposed to Africa, where design was at the time a nascent phenomenon, in Latin America design has been an organized discipline with strong theoretical and critical bases and organized pedagogical curricula. It was clear, therefore, from the beginning that the cogency of the proposal to organize an exhibition about Latin American design required careful consideration and consultation with colleagues in the field.

We received early and encouraging support from Mari Carmen Ramírez, Wortham Curator of Latin American Art and Director of the International Center for the Arts of the Americas (ICAA) at the Museum of Fine Arts, Houston, who joined the Curatorial Advisory Committee for the exhibition. This group eventually came to constitute a stellar group of curators, writers, academics, and experts on a range of matters related to artistic production in Latin America, whose input was essential to the vetting of issues around the exhibition, as well as selecting designers, artists, and craftspersons for consideration for the exhibition. They include: Regine Basha, independent curator and founder of Basha Projects; Marcella Echavarría, cultural entrepreneur, branding and marketing expert; Susana Torruella Leval, independent curator and former director of El Museo del Barrio; Ana Elena Mallet, independent curator specializing in Mexican design, and curatorial consultant for *Destination: Mexico* for the MoMA Design Store; Nessia Leonzini Pope, independent curator and journalist in the United States and Brazil; Gabriela Rangel, Director of Visual Arts, The Americas Society; Jorge Rivas Pérez, designer and former curator, Colección Patricia Phelps de Cisneros.

A special thanks is due to Glenn Adamson, the Nanette L. Laitman Director of the Museum of Arts and Design (MAD), who affirmed the Museum's commitment to this project when he assumed the directorship of MAD, and provided cogent and timely suggestions that resulted in the final organization of the exhibition. We would like to thank Barbara Tober, the force behind the MAD International Council; former director, Holly Hotchner; Cathleen Lewis and Jake Yuzna, our colleagues in Education; Alan Yamahata, Megan Skidmore, Sophie Henderson, Anna Starling, Rafael Flores, Tiffany Jow, and Georgia Wright in Development; Claire Laporte and Allie Underwood in Public Affairs; and Hendrick Gerrits, Elizabeth Kirrane, and Patrick Paine in Exhibitions. This project was also immeasurably served by our curatorial colleagues and project managers: Magdalena Grüneisen (April 2013–December 2013) and Adriana Kertzer, who in particular has been especially instrumental in conceptualizing the digital strategy for this exhibition. Adriana was ably assisted in this project by Luiza Brenner, curatorial assistant. Our interns Antonio Sánchez Gómez from the Bard Graduate Center and Alex Montane from Pratt Institute not only expertly coordinated the collecting of biographical materials and artist statements but also contributed to the conceptual development of the exhibition.

Essential components of the planning process took place during the meetings of the Curatorial Advisory Committee, which convened in New York City in October 2012 and June 2013 and in Mexico City in March 2013. In Mexico, Graciela de laTorre and Patricia Sloan at the Museo Universitarío Arte Contemporáneo (MUAC) were gracious hosts for our committee meeting, and we are grateful to our colleagues at MAD who participated in the New York City meetings. We would also like to acknowledge the assistance of numerous other individuals who supported this exhibition. Rocio Aranda-Alvarado, curator at Museo del Barrio, encouraged the first research trip to Panama to attend the 8th Biennial of Visual Arts of the Central American Isthmus (BAVIC), and Carolina Haussman facilitated the accommodations as well as contacts with artists there. Adriana Kertzer, as a consultant to MAD in 2013, organized the details of the trip to Mexico City and the curatorial research trip to São Paulo and Rio de Janeiro, Brazil. Veronica Liprandi, Gabriela Otero, and Carlos Hueck were able guides during the Caracas, Venezuela trip. Irene Abujadem and Elodie Fulton of AFA Gallery, Santiago and Eugenie Bertele of Ch.ACO, Contemporary Art Fair of Chile supported travel to Santiago. Studio visits with a number of younger Chilean designers were organized by Guillermo Parada and Eduardo Arancibia of the design studio gt2P in their Santiago offices. During her stint as a Fulbright scholar in Santiago, Chile, Julia Herzberg provided contact with Natalia Yañez Guzman and Jorge Morales Menses of the Universidad Diego Portales in Santiago, who offered information on key alumni of the program. Mari Carmen Ramírez connected us with Arturo Grimaldi, who offered an orientation to contemporary design in Argentina. Marilú Purcell-Villafañe was an invaluable resource for design in Puerto Rico and assisted with curating that section of the exhibition. Pablo León de la Barra has been a supporter from afar sending materials on artists he has encountered in his own curatorial work. We were also able to coordinate participation in a number of other cultural venues in New York City that helped to bring this project to potential audiences through the support of Tiana Webb, Laura Gonzalez, and Lauren Stafford at Phillips, New York and Odile Hainaut and Claire Pijoulet of the WantedDesign fair. In addition to the individual designers, artists, and craftspeople in the exhibition, we are grateful to so many others with whom we were in contact as we benefitted from our dialogues with them. We were fortunate to have been introduced to publisher Santiago Fernández de Caleya of Turner Libros by Marisa Bartolucci. He has not only been an engaged attendee in the Curatorial Advisory Committee meetings but, along with Donna Wingate of Artist and Publishers Services, has been an essential collaborator on the production of the catalogue. We thank those Curatorial Advisory Committee members who have also contributed essays to the catalogue, along with Adélia Borges, Blanca Serrano Ortiz de Solórzano, Adriana Kertzer, Magdalena Grüneisen, and Antonio Sánchez Gómez. As always, Martina D'Alton has sensitively edited this publication and we appreciate the design of Leftloft, which captures the spirit of the project.

Lowery Stokes Sims

A Report from the Field:
**New Territories
in Design, Craft and Art
in Latin America**

In 2013, Italian designer Gaetano Pesce observed that transcending the parochial notions of genres in contemporary creative practice created a "new territory."[1] His remarks inspired the title of this exhibition of contemporary designers and artists in Latin America who are finding myriad intersections between design, art, and craft in their practices. Latin American makers not only follow multiple directions in their careers and across genres, but also form strong alliances to "outlier" communities, such as traditional folk artists, indigenous craftspeople, and small artisan operations.[2] Even within their chosen fields, they are expanding habitual limits by drawing on their national heritages and cultural legacies, and engaging contemporary global trends in creative expression. *New Territories: Laboratories for Design, Craft and Art in Latin America* celebrates the commitment of artists and designers to deploying inventive and bold strategies, and developing local and global markets for production.

New Territories is organized around various urban hubs throughout Latin America and dominant themes being pursued by local artists and designers. A main feature of the show is its crosscurrents: themes identified in one city also extend to other regions across the continent. That means that a critical issue in one hub can also be a relevant factor in another. The model of the exhibition resembles a *biome*—a nexus of communities governed, in this case, not by climate but by culture.[3] Such a model effectively encapsulates the complex interactions examined in *New Territories* and allows the exhibition to focus on individual designers, craftspeople, and artists all over Latin America. The nomadic nature of their discourses is predicated on the vision and entrepreneurship of the individuals involved. Taking all that into account, the biome model allows the exhibition to focus both on individual designers, craftspeople, and artists all over Latin America and the relations between them.

The focus cities and themes featured in *New Territories* are Mexico City and Oaxaca, Mexico (moving craft into the future through collaborations with artists and designers); Caracas, Venezuela (conversations with artistic legacies); São Paulo and Rio de Janeiro, Brazil (upcycling and repurposing objects); Santiago, Chile, and Buenos Aires, Argentina (cultivating collectivity and experimentation in design and craft); San Salvador, El Salvador and San Juan, Puerto Rico (developing new markets for design); and Havana, Cuba (navigating personal and civic space).

The concept of centering on cities—as opposed to genres of creativity or general themes alone— is part of the current critical landscape in which hubs of creativity are explored.[4] Within these "informal" urban laboratories, *New Territories* focuses more on interpersonal relations than on infrastructural ones. In other words, connections are made on the grassroots level, revealing critiques of the status quo and addressing the aspirations of ordinary citizens outside the

---

Unless otherwise noted, quotations from and information on specific artists, designers, architects, and design studios derive from their websites or from artist statements on gallery websites.

1) Pesce's statement was part of didactic text at the Collective 1 Design Fair, New York, May 2013: "For over 50 years, I have firmly believed that if objects expressed values that were not exclusively utilitarian and that if the so-called work of art revealed its own functionality, as it did in the past, then the frontiers of artistic expression would open up to new territories, eliminating the barriers separating the various creative media and enriching the entire culture"; see Melissa Mazzoleni, "Collective Design Fair Opens with Gaetano Pesce's Art," *HOW magazine*, May 6, 2013, www.howdesign.com.

2) Malcolm Gladwell, *Outliers: The Story of Success* (New York: Back Bay Books, 2011).

3) For more information on biomes, see: http://users.rcn.com/jkimball.ma.ultranet/BiologyPages/B/Biomes.html.

4) See for example Antawan I. Byrd, et al., *Art Cities of the Future: 21st Century Avant Gardes* (London: Phaidon Books, 2013). In it, twelve curators discuss twelve prospective new hubs beyond the usual power nexuses of the art world; these are targeted as new centers for creativity to watch. Their selection was based on specific criteria: "a commitment to experimental art and an allegiance to their local milieu, support by a vibrant cultural infrastructure," be it organizations, private foundations, artist-led initiatives, influential dealers and curators, or individuals. Gareth Harris, "From Beirut to Bogotá: Art Cities to Watch?," *New York Times*, September 23, 2013). See also American Institute of Architects, *Cities as a Lab: Designing the Innovation Economy*, Local Leaders report (Washington, DC: AIA, 2013).

parameters of official policy. Cities "have always been centers of creativity and economic growth," but there is a caveat: "the reality in today's urban environment is that millions endure a daily struggle for survival and a barrage of additional risks."[5]

As noted in the essay by Jorge Rivas-Pérez in this volume, since World War II, there have been protocols and values for design that distinguished Latin American work within a global context. While respecting that past, many young creators are moving beyond a preoccupation with iconic, singular objects to an actualization of design—along with craft and art—as a social, political, and economic engine. Such strategies are similar to the rubrics of relational aesthetics and social production that dominate global creative discourses today—but, in Latin America, the specters of political instability and social inequality, the availability of abundant natural resources, and a sense of personal destiny coalesce to create a fertile context for a unique creativity.

Focus: Mexico City and Oaxaca
Moving Craft into the Future through Collaborations with Artists and Designers

The interface of design with traditional forms and craft achieves a particular resonance in cities such as Mexico City and Oaxaca. A number of resident artists and designers have sought to collaborate with folk and artisan communities not only to effect production of their own designs but also to help move traditional craft skills into the future. Such collaborations engender an acute awareness of the challenges and pressures that inexpensive production elsewhere, in countries such as China, can put on local workers. In Mexico, this has led designers and educators to emphasize their commitment to the country's especially rich craft scene.[6]

Since the moment its founders were led to the site on Lake Texcoco in the fourteenth century, Mexico City has been the economic, social, political, and cultural hub of its eponymous country. Because many of the products sold or promoted throughout the region are collaborative efforts between designers and indigenous/traditional artisans, there is a new examination of the concept of "making" as a process that is intertwined with makers' lives under the rubric of social production and economic development. This trend in Mexico is representative of a global ethos among designers and artists worldwide who are inspired by a new sense of social engagement on various levels. As detailed by Ana Elena Mallet in her essay in this volume, the recent design and craft scene in Mexico has been catalyzed by events in Mexico City, such as Design Week Mexico and the addition of the design section of Zona MACO (México Arte Contemporaneo). These venues, along with others in the city, have provided exposure for both national and international design and craft promoters who have helped establish contemporary Mexican design, such as Casa Gutiérrez Nájera, Esware Gallery, Studio Roca, Rococo Gallery, Nouvel glass studio, and Design Within Reach in Mexico City.

Meanwhile, Oaxaca has always been an important center for pottery in Mexico. There, several designers have established a working relationship with the inhabitants to create new products made with traditional techniques. Liliana Ovalle, for example, worked with local ceramic artisans from Colectivo 1050º, located in Tlapazola, Oaxaca, to catalogue the repertory of traditional forms and update traditional fare. This collaboration provided a platform for Ovalle to create her series *Sinkhole Vessels* (see pages

---

5) Integrated Regional Information Networks, *Tomorrow's Crises Today: The Humanitarian Impact Of Urbanization*, In-Depth Report, UN Office for the Coordination of Humanitarian Affairs, 2007.
6) Sebastian Ocampo, Director of Product Design at the Centro Advanced Design Institute, Mexico made this comment at a panel on design in Latin America at WantedDesign, 2013.

94–95), black containers of Oaxacan ware that evoke the sinkholes that have appeared in Mexican streets, set within an architectural framing. The vessels' shapes are composites of familiar forms recombined to demonstrate new approaches to traditional ceramics, while suggesting in title and concept certain physical problems inherent in the infrastructure of Mexico City.[7]

The Venezuelan-born designer Raul Cabra has also located his project Oax-i-fornia in Oaxaca, bringing students from the California College of the Arts, San Francisco—where he teaches design—to Oaxaca to work with local artisans and "broaden creative opportunities" for them "through multidisciplinary and collaborative work with other professionals in visual and creative fields." Like Colectivo 1050º, Oax-i-fornia moves ancestral traditions into contemporary world markets, searching for "new methodologies for the use of design and creativity as tools for social change and cultural engagement."[8] The lamps showcased in *New Territories* (see pages 84–86), were created by three teams of students in collaboration with artisan families who have worked with carrizo cane for generations. For the *Blowfish Lamp*, artisan Lander Cruz created the shape by "[i]nverting a typical weave used for ornament ...The lamp's shape emerged from the hands of someone who has never seen the ocean, but imagines the blowfish as a creature that must glow with magic."[9]

While all of these examples focus on the direct translations of traditional craft skills into contemporary production, back in Mexico City, DFC (Distrito Federal Casa)—a collaboration between Tony Moxham (born in Australia) and Mauricio Paniagua (born in Guatemala)—enlists these skills more obliquely to create signature Postmodern interpretations of iconic Mexican images, objects, and myths (see pages 88–90). In their words, their work is a combination of "a romanticized vision of pre-Columbian life and design with references to contemporary and modern art, pop culture, sex, science fiction, and modern savagery." Collaborating with a wide network of artisans (whom they know personally) from the states of Oaxaca, Michoacan, Morelos, and Sonora, they create decorative and functional ceramics and glassware, furniture, décor, and incidental sculptures, adhering to labor practices that include pay above national wage rates and a focus on sourcing production locally whenever possible.

Jorge Lizarazo established Hechizoo, an atelier in Bogotá, Colombia, that has a similar model of collaboration with local craftspeople. Lizarazo brings a contemporary nuance to traditional craft methods by combining organic materials with microfilament and metallic fibers to create hangings, rugs, incidental pieces, and lighting characterized by a distinctive use of color and sheen (see page 131). As Lizarazo insists on the highest level of craftsmanship, Hechizoo textiles require months of collaborative work and dedication. As a political gesture of reclamation and cultural defiance, Lizarazo and his collaborators produced beaded versions of canoes that, in the past, were used to transport people and goods in the Amazon interior but now are often commandeered by law enforcement and criminals. Hechizoo's beaded incarnations (see page 114) from the Putumayo region of Colombia reassert the vessel's relationship to the communities that depend on them, also highlighting the particular local beading techniques and designs.

The work of José de la O mirrors any number of examples of designer-artisan collaborations in Latin America. In 2010, the Mexican designer founded his creative agency in the Dutch city of

---

7) Andy Butler, "Sinkhole Vessels by Liliana Ovalle and Colectivo 1050º," DesignBoom, newsletter, September 19, 2013, www.designboom.com.

8) Raul Cabra, project description for *New Territories*, January 24, 2014, Museum of Arts and Design archives.

9) Ibid.

Eindhoven, and later relocated to Mexico City in 2014. He initiated a collaborative project that brought together artisans of Tlacotalpan, Mexico, and contemporary designers, producing the rocking chair *Sillón Tlacotalpeño* (Fig. 1). The goals of this project were familiar and paradigmatic: to rescue and preserve local crafts and techniques, to reactivate the local economy, and to foster "designer tourism" in Tlacotalpan, where "creative professionals can learn a new craft, produce new work, and exchange knowledge with local craftsmen."

This notion of new production out of traditional craft skills also motivated Mattias Rask and Tor Palm of the Swedish design team Glimpt to establish a working relationship with the artisans of the venerable organization Artesanos Don Bosco in Peru. Founded in the 1960s by the Italian priest Father Ugo, this nonprofit organization is dedicated to training people and creating economic opportunities in woodworking, masonry, glass making, textiles, and metalwork. The result was the series of furniture dubbed *Prehistoric Aliens* (see page 113), which features the fine handcarved faceting and detailing that characterized Artesanos Don Bosco's more traditional products. The cast of players in this production demonstrates how the concept of what is specifically "Latin American" increasingly is being called into question.

When choosing groups of skilled artisans as collaborators, many designers and artists single out indigenous communities on the periphery of society to work with. Many designers, such as Natalia Yañez Guzman, a professor in the design department at Universidad Diego Portales in Santiago, Chile, have focused their practice on working with rural indigenous and other marginalized groups, such as prisoners. The Chilean-born, Los Angeles–based artist Guillermo Bert has been working on a series of tapestries encoded with computer symbols and prompts in collaboration with members of the Mapuche community of southern Chile. He incorporates themes from their traditional stories, poems, and self-narratives using software that translates this information into QR codes. The resulting imagery is developed into a prototype that Bert created with Mapuche weaver Anita Pailamil, and the tapestry is then woven by the Chol-Chol Weavers Cooperative.

In 2010, Brazilian designer Marcelo Rosenbaum launched the ambitious program A Gente Transforma, which takes groups of designers to communities such as Parque Santo Antônio (a *favela* [slum] in São Paulo) and Várzea Queimada, in the town of Jaicós in northeastern Brazil. Rosenbaum and the program participants worked with community members and artisans to create products from local materials such as straw and rubber. André Bastos e Guilherme Leite of Nada Se Leva joined the group that worked with the Yawanawá people in the villages of Nova Esperança and Amparo in the Brazilian state of Acre, and made lamps reflecting the tribe's myths and ideas about the Amazon environment. The Yawanawá artisans embellished the designer-conceived lamps with beading typical of the region.[10]

In a parallel project, designer Pedro Barrail in Asunción, Paraguay, works with the Pai Tavytera people who live in the country's Amambay region. Barrail is dedicated to preserving the tribal artisans' pyrogravure techniques by

Fig. 1 Sillón Tlacotalpeño from *The Chair that Rocks* project by Studio José de la O
15.75 x 47.25 x 23.6 in. (120 x 40 x 60 cm)
Red cedar and natural wicker
Photo: José de la O

commissioning them to "tattoo" pieces of furniture he designs and builds in his studio with patterns chronicling both traditional mythology and contemporary motifs (see page 105). This type of primary relationship with the symbols and signs of indigenous culture also exists in the work of Sheroanawë Hakihiiwë, who records the life and beliefs of the Yanomami people of Venezuela in his drawings and books (Fig. 2).

In Caracas, designers Mária Antonia Godigna and Anabella Georgi, working under the brand MáximaDuda, have conceived furniture and apparel designs with the Warao people. Their now-signature chair *Miss Delta Amacuro* (see page 115) is draped with a weaving of *moriche* palm fibers that is typically woven by Warao women. Another Caraqueño, Pepe López, works with groups such as the Guahibo, Ye'kuana, and Yanomami. In his *Guapísimas* series (Fig. 3), he grouped baskets known as *guapas* and *manares*, which are customarily given to women by their suitors, and substituted symbols from the traditional myths with logos from contemporary fashion, consumer society, and Japanese *anime* cartoon figures known to these communities through television, reflecting the global transmission and exchange of cultural values and signifiers.[11]

Indigenous basketry and weaving techniques are also featured in the works by Rio de Janeiro–based artist Maria Nepomuceno, who developed her technique alongside artisans from the northeastern region of Brazil.[12] In the summer of 2013, she began working with weaver Dona Dalva (Fig. 4) and, using traditional methods of rope weaving and straw braiding as well as techniques of her own design, she creates sculptural installations (see page 117) that usually consist of abstracted elements referencing baskets, mats, and other forms, collaged together—or, occasionally, evoking the prototypical form of the hammock. Venezuelan designer Anabella Giorgi also draws inspiration from this form in her *Silla Fuga Kids Policromatica* (see page 128), as does Brazilian designer Rodrigo Almeida, whose hammock converts into a garment (see page 96) that, conceptually, is meant to function as a "transcendental cocoon vestment" that reflects "atavism/transcendence/protection/rituals."[13]

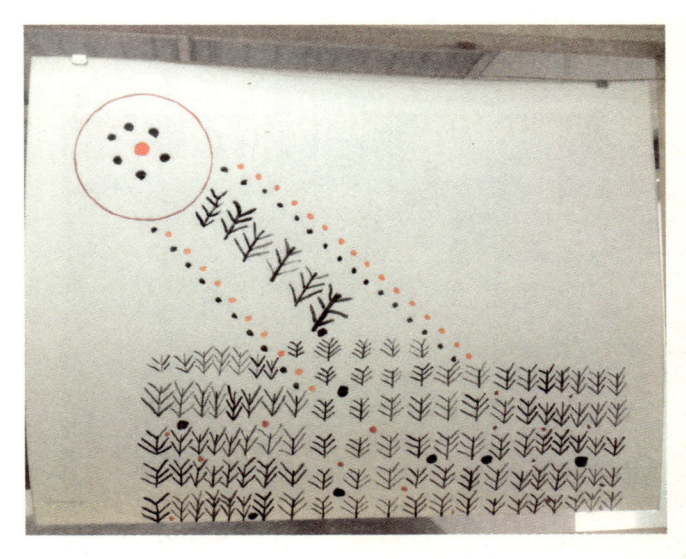

Fig. 2 Sheroanawë Hakihiiwë
Image from the series *Porerimou at the Galeria Oficina #1*, Caracas, Venezuela, July, 2013
Photo: Lowery Stokes Sims

There is no doubt that textiles are a preeminent expression in Latin American design. Over the last four centuries, contacts among indigenous, African, and European cultures have resulted in a rich legacy in various media, including natural fibers, feathers, and grasses. Perhaps the most

---

10) Winnie Bastian, "As luminárias da coleção Yawanawá," *Casa Vogue*, April 2, 2013.
11) López observed that television and the international migration of programming has has led indigenous peoples to syncretize their traditional roster of deities with characters from Japanese history and culture as viewed in contemporary television programs, such as Dragon Ball, the anime series by Akira Toriyama. Pepe López, in conversation with Lowery Stokes Sims and Veronica Liprandi, Galerie ArtePuy Caracas, Venezuela, July 4, 2013.
12) Nepomuceno notes that she meets these artisans through SEBRAE (Serviço Brasileiro de Apoio às Micro e Pequenas Empresas). Maria Nepomuceno, in conversation with Lowery Stokes Sims and Adriana Kertzer, Rio de Janeiro, May 3, 2013.
13) Rodrigo Almeida, "Body Object of the Soul," PDF file, e-mail to Lowery Stokes Sims, May 5, 2013, artist files, Museum of Arts and Design, New York.

prominent practitioner is the Colombian artist Olga de Amaral. Over the last six decades, she has explored the possibilities of traditional techniques within a contemporary practice (Fig. 5), working with women whom she has described as contributing their spirit as much as their skill to each of her pieces.[14]

Silk, which has a surprisingly robust cultivation in Latin America, is the medium of María Eugenia Dávila and Eduardo Portillo, working under the label Taller Morera in partnership with an Andean community in Mérida, in the Venezuelan Andes. Their story demonstrates personal passion, determination, and entrepreneurship. They traveled to India, China, and Japan to learn about silk cultivation and production, then audaciously smuggled a seminal group of worms back into Venezuela to start their industry.[15] Today, Dávila and Portillo raise and harvest silkworms to produce their fabrics and tapestries within an art context. Their locally based shop features yard lengths of silk patterns (see page 108) through which they explore local resources such as indigo dyes. As a new experiment, the couple has recently begun to experiment with casting weavings in bronze (see page 109) to extend the expressive potential of their work.

What is patently clear in various investigations throughout Latin America is a focus on women. Carla Fernández has worked for more than a decade as a designer, researcher, and social activist with local textile weavers to create contemporary interpretations of traditional Mexican clothing (see pages 91–93), adapting the "elaborate system of pleats, folds, and seams that construct a vast array of garments using squares and rectangles only for a modern fashion market."[16] With her traveling studio and virtual laboratory Taller Flora, Fernández has researched, collected, and catalogued garment designs that "were at risk of extinction." She pays the weavers not only for their manual labor but also, commendably, for "the intellectual property of their designs."[17] Her social commitment to these communities helped bring their craft into the international marketplace.

In Latin America, other domestic needlework techniques—knitting, crocheting, hooking, quilting, and piece work such as *fuxico* are present in the design and art spheres. *Fuxico* (fashioning circles from squares of fabric) found new life in *Fuxico Design*, created by women of Santa Luiza do Itanhy, Brazil, for the São Paulo-based design studio Nada Se Leva (see page 116).[18] Such techniques also trace patterns of immigration into Latin America: vibrant manifestations of European lace-making traditions, for example, can be found all over

Fig. 3 Pepe López
Guapísimas, 2011; mixed media
Photo: Courtesy of the artist

14) Olga de Amaral, artist's statement, artist files, Museum of Arts and Design.
15) Eduardo Portillo, in conversation with Lowery Stokes Sims, Museum of Arts and Design, New York, August 13, 2013.
16) "People: Carla Fernandez," Creative Economy program of the British Council, n.d., http://creativeconomy.britishcouncil.org.
17) Ibid.
18) Guilherme Leite Ribeiro and André Bastos, in conversation with Lowery Stokes Sims and Adriana Kertzer, São Paulo, May 1, 2013.

Bahia.[19] Irish lace maintains a strong presence in Rio de Janeiro, in the form of bulbous light fixtures, the signature product of Cooperativa de Trabalho Artesanal e de Costura da Rocinha Ltda. (Coopa-Roca), a women's collaborative founded by Maria Teresa Leal in the Rocinha *favela*. Leal has fostered projects with world-renowned designers such as Tord Boontje, who conceived of *Chandelier* for Los Angeles-based Artecnica (see page 106), the Campana Brothers, and Carlos Miele, among others. These collaborations have cemented Coopa-Roca's international reputation and, in 2012, they opened a retail store at the prestigious Fashion Mall in Rio de Janeiro.[20]

The modalities of "women's work" also provide an interesting context for *La ciudad frondosa* (see page 110–111), a large-scale hand-embroidered wall hanging by Buenos Aires-based Leo Chiachio and Daniel Giannone. Over the last decade, they have created autobiographical and topical compositions, often depicting themselves in various guises as indigenous people among outsized panoplies of flora and fauna native to Latin America. While destabilizing the gendered associations of embroidery (see Antonio Sánchez Gómez's essay, pages 40–42), their choice of method allows them to transcend the tempo of contemporary life for a more meditative approach to their work.

In sum, all of these different strategies practiced throughout Latin America by young and socially concerned designers and artists effectively provide labor for production, encourage and engage artisan skills, and help to celebrate and preserve traditional techniques while, at the same time, moving them into the future.

Focus Caracas: Conversations with Artistic Legacies

Despite the movement of Latin American design and artistic pedagogy away from models based in Europe and the United States, young designers continue to have a particular infatuation with, and affection for, classic icons of modern design such as the bentwood chairs of Michael Thonet (1796–1871), furniture by Charles Eames (1907–1978) and his wife and partner Ray Eames (1912–1988), Eero Saarinen's (1910–1961) Panton, and designs by Ettore Sottsass (1907–1977). Venezuelan artist Alessandro Balteo Yazbeck

Fig. 4 Studio of Maria Nepomeceno, Rio de Janeiro, May 3, 2013
Photo: Lowery Stokes Sims

captured the spirit of Postmodern homages to contemporary art and design in his *Eames Derivative* (see pages 120–121), an installation created in collaboration with Media Farzin that features a timeline tracing design and

---

19) Michele Y. Washington, in conversation with Lowery Stokes Sims, Museum of Arts and Design, November 7, 2013. See also Michele Y. Washington, "Festa de Nossa Senhor da Boa Morte," *Cultural Boundaries* blog, August 18, 2010, http://culturalboundaries.com/wordpress/tag/bahia-2/.

20) Flávia Ribero, "Coopa-Roca: Favela Cooperative Opens Mall Store," *Infosurhoy*, August 31, 2012, http://infosurhoy.com/en.

technology in the twentieth century, and "portrays the dominant influence of modern technology and the fragility of the financial systems that keep the world going."[21]

Caracas is a vibrant city of designers, artists, and museum curators who cope with economic challenges and restrictions with a remarkable spirit and aplomb, embracing an improvisational approach in their work. Some of this energy is fueled by the chaotic—yet oddly rhythmic— organization of the city's poor areas known as *ranchos*, which dominate the hills rising above the city and influence Venezuelan artistic production. The *ranchos* have inspired the work of artists such as Pepe López, whose almost algorithmic patterning of the buildings in the ranchos found expression in his wall works and tapestries. He grafted different photographic views of the *ranchos* for compositions such as *Geometrías marginales* (see pages 124–125), a wall installation that isolates the geography of these poorer neighborhoods in Caracas, thereby dealing with social and political developments in the city through minimal, geometric expressions. This urban segmentation also became the basis for *Panton Catuche* and *Panton Vias* (see page 123 and 122), part of a series in which Deborah Castillo[22] and Carolina Tinoco transformed a series of repurposed chairs in the style of the classic *S Chair* conceived in 1960 by Danish designer Verner Panton (1926-1998) into an installation in shades of white, black, and gray, and decorated them with linear patterns based again on diagrammatic views of the *ranchos*.

Via the topography of Caracas and its interaction with its citizens, López, Tinoco, and Castillo navigate the strong legacy of geometric art by such famed modernist artists as Carlos Cruz-Diez (b. 1923) and Gego (Gertrude Goldschmidt, 1912–1994). In the 1940s, Cruz-Diez documented his own interest in rural and vernacular culture in black-and-white photographs, while Gego's abstract, linear drawings and prints echo in the work of later artists.[23] The works of Cruz-Diez and Gego may be said to have effected a realization—or reaffirmation—of the initial idealism of the Russian Constructivists, the Dutch De Stilj group, and the German Bauhaus. The presumed nonspecific, nonobjective nature of the geometry they pursued moved toward a universal idealism, beyond any national boundaries. That this style might be an alternative signifier of Latin American art—in opposition to fantastic surrealism—is an irony

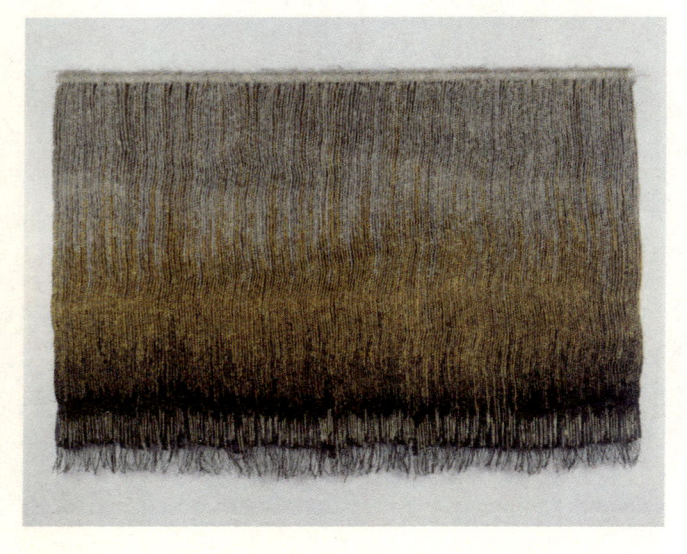

Fig. 5 Olga de Amaral
Alquima #76, 1989
Linen, gesso, gold leaf paint
47 x 71 in. (111.8 x 180.3 cm)
Museum of Arts and Design
Gift of Arlene and Harvey Caplan, 2010
Photo: Ed Watkins

---

21) Alessandro Balteo Yazbeck, "Modern Entanglements," *NY Artbeat*, Events, November 2012, www.nyartbeat.com.
22) Soledad Erdocia, for example, a professor of sculpture in Buenos Aires, organizes group activities around crochet and embroidery, which she chronicles on her blog [Bricollage] http://mibricollage.blogspot.com. Deborah Castillo further reports meeting women in Buenos Aires who taught her the technique of *tortora* or *trapillo* that originated on the Pampas of Argentina. It consists of weaving strips of cotton cloth with thick wooden needles (Deborah Castillo, e-mail to Lowery Stokes Sims, Museum of Arts and Design, March 10, 2014).
23) Carlos Cruz-Diez and Edgar Cherubini Lecuna, *Cruz-Diez en Blanco y Negro*, exh. cat. (Paris: Cruz-Diez Foundation, 2013).

not lost on López, Tinoco, and Castillo, and other contemporary makers, who are creating a hybrid expression through modifications of classical modernism with local nuances.[24] What connects the generations in this engagement with everyday culture is a lingering commitment to projecting a national image embodied in the vernacular as well as in indigenous and working-class life.[25] Hints of Gego's legacy can be seen in the networking of Rodolfo Agrella's *Isidora* hanging system (see page 127), which also references the biomorphic shapes of acoustic panels by American sculptor Alexander Calder (1898–1976). Designed in 1952–53, Calder's panels are installed in the Aula Magna auditorium at the Ciudad Universitaria de Caracas.[26]

Another aspect of homage can be seen in the furniture of Venezuelans Bernardo Mazzei and Jorge Rivas. These designers have married modernist vocabularies to narratives in the history of their home country. Mazzei's *Anauco Aalto* (see page 126) references both a signature chair by the Finnish architect and designer Alvar Aalto (1898–1976), and the *butaca*, a low-seated, often foldable chair whose history reaches to precolonial Venezuela. In this one form, Mazzei mediates the principles of modernism and celebrates the heritage of the Cumanagoto people. Rivas' own *Banco* (see page 128) alludes to the traditional form of the Ye'kuana culture. In his work, Rivas links Venezuelan material tradition and modern design with references that include pre-Columbian cultures, the art of the colonial period in Latin America, Venezuelan design of the mid-twentieth century, geometric abstraction, and modern design. He is also one of the many designers for whom the Casa Curuba workshop in the small city of Quíbor, Venezuela (under the ownership of Dennis Schmeichler) served as a conduit between designers and small artisan communities.[27]

Compelling examples of the next related biome on the theme of conversations with artistic and design legacies can be found in Mexico, where sculptor Edgar Orlaineta translates his fascination with twentieth-century design into sculptures that both reconstruct and re-present the works of designers as Charles and Ray Eames (see page 134), Thonet, and Sottsass (see page 135). Like his contemporary Courtney Smith (Fig. 6), who works between Brazil and the

Fig. 6 Courtney Smith
Vanité, 2000
48 x 36 x 15 in. (122 x 91.4 x 38 cm)
Antique Brazilian vanity, hinges, and hooks
Photo: Fausto Fleury

24) This point was made by Jorge Rivas Pérez, *New Territories* Curatorial Advisory Committee teleconference, Museo Universitario arte Contemporáneo, Universidad Nacional Autónoma de México, Mexico City, April 15, 2013.
25) The context for Cruz-Diez's photographs was discussed in conjunction with the exhibition, *Within the Light Trap: Carlos Cruz-Diez in Black and White*, Americas Society / Council of the Americas, New York, February 4–March 22, 2014: "Gallery Talk: Cruz-Diez's Ethnographic Eye with Gabriela Rangel [curator] and Iliana Cepero-Amador," Americas Society, March 5, 2014.
26) For Calder's "acoustic clouds," see Dawn Ades, ed., *Art in Latin America: The Modern Era, 1820–1980* (New Haven: Yale University Press, 1993), 254, Fig. 12.4. Multiple images can be found on the Internet.
27) Martiza Miménez, "Jorge Rivas y el alma de la madera," in *Maderas de Jorge Rivas: innovacion en la tradición* (San Joaquín, Venezuela: Casa Alejo Zuloaga, 2004), n.p.

United States, Orlaineta uses existing furniture as templates for investigations on the meaning of form in the context of modernism. The forms provide vehicles for postmodern explorations through parody, pastiche, alteration, and assemblage.

Cogent homages, references, and remakes of iconic modern designs are also apparent in the works of Brazilians Leo Capote, Lattoog, Guto Requena, and Studio MK27. Through Postmodern elegies, they make historical forms irrevocably their own. Capote revisits the design of *Tulip Chair* (1956) by Saarinen, as well as Panton's *S Chair* (see pages 129–130), reconstructing them in upcycled hardware. Similar to Tinoco and Castillo, Lattoog (led by Leonardo Lattavo and Pedro Moog) pays homage to Panton and Charles Rennie MacIntosh (1868–1928) in *Pantosh Easy Chair* (see page 132). The *Giraffe Chair* (1987), designed by Italian-born Brazilian architect Lina Bo Bardi (1914–1992) with Marcelo Ferraz and Marcelo Suzuki, has been given a digital update through 3-D printing by Guto Requena in his *Nóize St. Ifigênia* chair (see page 136), whose forms are derived from the sounds of the Grajau, Tiradentes, and Santa Ifigênia neighborhoods of São Paulo.[28]

Another nod to the vernacular forms that attracted Bo Bardi can be seen in *Prostheses and Innesti* (see page 143), a series of furniture by São Paulo–based Studio MK27 (founded by Marcio Kogan) in collaboration with Milan-based Manuela Verga and Paolo Boatti. The pieces of furniture were appropriated by the designers from the restoration work site located in an Italian castle. For each piece in this series, Studio MK27, Verga, and Boatti made minimal "gentle interventions," changing an element while preserving imperfections in the materials, or adding ironic embellishments such as gold leaf or blown glass. This project was inspired by Studio MK27's earlier series *Prostheses and Grafts*, in which furniture from the construction site of the firm's building for the furniture store Micasa in São Paulo were modified through similar interventions and later exhibited in the store once construction was finished. Created by construction workers, the furniture is "predicated on speed and available material."[29] Interestingly, despite the pride of craftsmanship, most makers of the original furniture were reluctant to take individual credit for their creations. In a spirit mirroring his contemporaries in Caracas, Kogan saw no reason to deny his elders by noting the similarities between these projects and Bo Bardi's work, thereby showing his willingness to "pay homage to their work while moving forward."[30]

Focus: São Paulo & Rio de Janeiro
Upcycling and Repurposing Objects

Brazil is a thriving center of modern and contemporary design, rich in natural resources and its cities home to art galleries of international repute. The country has spawned modernist design pioneers such as Sergio Rodrigues and Joaquim Tenreiro, as well as promising newcomers. Yet, perhaps the most intriguing aspect of contemporary design in Brazil is the widespread upcycling of objects, particularly in São Paulo and Rio de Janeiro, where the brothers Fernando and Humberto Campana have been key influences both as teachers and exemplars.[31] The upcycling and repurposing of objects mirrors environmental concerns—particularly over the deforestation of the Amazon region—that have been fodder for the various celebrity-backed global initiatives around ecological sustainability. The destruction of the very resources that made Brazilian design—particularly furniture—so famous is a terrible irony but, at the same time, has also

---

28) Emilie Chalcraft, "Nóize Chairs by Estudio Guto Requena," *de zeen magazine*, July 13, 2013, www.dezeen.com.
29) Marcio Kogan and Mariana Simas, in conversation with Lowery Stokes Sims and Adriana Kertzer, Studio MK27, São Paulo, May 1, 2013.
30) Ibid.
31) This term was coined by Reiner Pitz in 1994; quoted in Thornton Kay, "Salvo in Germany: Reiner Pilz," *SalvoNEWS* 99 (October 12, 1994): 14, available online.

disrupted any number of cultures, particularly the poor, disenfranchised, and indigenous.

In order to provide alternative means of production that may lessen their reliance on limited resources, several designers have stepped into the fray. Hugo França's distinctive design practice involves upcycling felled pequi wood (Fig. 7) through collaborations with local communities in Trancoso, Bahia. In urban areas, there is a focus on municipal garbage dumps, which serve as resources for the poor. Such waste sites in Brazil were chronicled in *Ilhas das Flores* (1989), a documentary by filmmaker Jorge Furtado and, more recently, in *Waste Land* (2010), a collaboration between filmmakers Lucy Walker, Karen Harley, and João Jardim with artist Vik Muniz, that depicts the conception of Muniz's series *Pictures of Garbage* (see page 150). Working with Brazilian "trash pickers," Muniz renders art-historical masterpieces in the garbage collected.

A direct engagement with the detritus of contemporary life is also the focus of São Paulo–based Coletivo Amor de Madre, dedicated to supporting "work that pushes boundaries through the use of recycled materials [and] technological exploration led by social inspiration and incorporating craft and handmade techniques."[32] A signature project was their collaboration with the English-Japanese team of Studio Swine (designers Alexander Groves and Azusa Murakami) on *Can City* (see page 145), an endeavor that upcycled discarded aluminum cans. The process was integral from start to finish: the cans collected from bars or trash around São Paulo were melted down in improvised furnaces fueled by cooking oil collected from eateries and street food vendors. The melted cans were then transformed into furniture like the *Mangueira Stool*, *Roda Stool*, and *Cesta Stool* (see pages 144–145).

Rodrigo Almeida bridges art and design by remixing preexisting and found elements into new forms. His *Servant Lamp* from the *Slaves Series* (see page 140) gives a poetic new life to found objects, with brushes symbolizing the menial tasks performed in any society. Almeida's bespoke approach to design has been associated with the Tropicalism movement, which celebrated the fusion of Brazilian and non-Brazilian cultural elements through the process described by José Oswald de Souza Andrade as "antropofagia" or "cultural cannibalism."[33] That

Fig. 7 Hugo França
Chara bench, 2007
Pequi wood
91.4 × 56 × 40.5 in. (232 × 142.2 × 102.8 cm)
Courtesy of R 20th Century, New York
Photo: Tuca Reinés

"cannibalism" is evident as Almeida draws from a wide range of sources—from Art Deco to the Memphis Group to the work of Brazilian artists Tunga and Adriana Varejão.[34] Zanini de Zanine

---

32) Oliva Fassudo Faria, in conversation with Lowery Stokes Sims and Adriana Kertzer, Coletivo Amor de Madre Gallery, São Paulo, April, 29, 2013; and at Miami Art Basel, Miami, December 6, 2013; e-mail to Adriana Kertzer, Lowery Stokes Sims, and Cathleen Lewis, Museum of Arts and Design, February 12, 2014.
33) Tropacalism emanated from Bahia, from musicians such as Caetano Veloso and Gilberto Gil, who were committed to presenting the harsh reality of Brazilian life under the military from 1964–85, and the social and economic disparities that existed in tandem with one's racial background. See Christopher Dunn, *Brutality Garden: Tropicália and the Emergence of a Brazilian Counterculture* (Chapel Hill: University of North Carolina Press, 2001).
34) Christopher Turner, "Feature: New Brazilian Designers," *ICONEYE*, no. 123 (September 2013), www.iconeye.com.
35) Sergio Zobaran, "Sem título/Untitled," *De Zanine*, exh. cat. (Rio de Janeiro: MeMo—Mercado Moderno Gallery, 2012).

also explores the repurposing of preexisting materials that would otherwise be discarded in his *Moeda Chair* (see page 149), made from sheet metal "rescued from the Brazilian mint." Perhaps best known for his craftsmanship in wood, Zanine demonstrates a willingness to experiment with materials and shapes that he connects to Brazilian culture.[35]

Carioca jewelry designer Mana Bernardes has a particular gift for repurposing plastic in imaginative ways, as seen in her *Môbiluz* series of lamps (see page 141). The discipline and formalism of her products brings upcycling to a high level of achievement. A comparable finesse marks the chandelier fashioned out of plastic bottles by the Mexico-based French designer Thierry Jeannot (see page 153). His practices merge design, architecture, and social commitment as he works closely with craftspeople in France and Mexico City to convey "high added value to recycled materials through design." His work for *New Territories* involved developing a new prototype for a table made from ubiquitous plastic bottles (see page 154).

In a parallel manner, Spanish designer Alvaro Catalán de Ocón recruited the indigenous Guambiano and Eperara-Siapidara communities in Colombia to create lamps by applying traditional weaving techniques to vertical strips of plastic PET bottles.[36] Thousands of miles away, in Fortaleza, Brazil, PET bottles also played a role in the making of *U Rock Chair* (see page 142), a project proposed by Davi Deusdará, Érica Martins, Rafael Studart, and Tais Costa for The Battery Conservancy outdoor seating competition in New York. Conceived as a reversible seating unit that can either rock or be stationary, the form is to be produced out of PET bottles collected as waste in the park.

The idea is to make the "owners" of the bottles "directly responsible for their future seats" and "connect with them through the design and recycling."[37]

An important aspect of upcycling is the revelation and exploration of the psychic, emotional, and existential associations of materials. The ubiquitous oil barrel, for example, has been often exploited by artists and designers, particularly in West Africa. Since Venezuela is a global oil-producing country, Caracas-based artist Rolando Peña was inspired to make furniture out of oil barrels (see page 155). These became an integral part of his larger enterprise of paintings and performances, in which he conjures the inescapable impact of the oil industry in oil-rich Venezuela. Another Venezuelan designer, Daniel Reynolds, engages in what he calls "contemporary archaology," casting mundane objects that would otherwise be discarded in bisque porcelain and glazing their insides so they can continue being used as vases (see page 147).

Mexican artist Abraham Cruzvillegas explored individual identity and a sense of place in his *Autoconstrucción* series, assemblages made of found objects. *Low Budget Rider* (see page 152) was created in collaboration with students in San Francisco in 2009 and first exhibited as part of a bike parade. The improvisational aspect of this piece and this type of cross-cultural intervention is characteristic of Cruzvillegas, who once described himself as "intergalactic indigenous."[38] It represents a global phenomenon of mechanical improvisation involving cars, trucks, or cycles.[39]

---

36) José Roca and Alejandro Martin, *Waterweavers: The River in Contemporary Colombian Visual and Material Culture*, exh. cat. (New York: Bard Graduate Center; London: Yale University Press, 2014).

37) *U Rock*: project description, "Draw Up a Chair Design Competition," Battery Conservancy, n.d., www.thebattery.org.

38) Arden Decker-Parks, "Interview with Abraham Cruzvillegas," *Museo Magazine*, 2009, www.museomagazine.com.

39) Cholo culture has even invaded Asia where trucks are decked out in a style the Japanese have dubbed "Dekotora." Kathleen Gasperini, "Japanese Dekotora Subculture of Illuminating Trucks Gives New Meaning to Pimp My Big Rig," *Label Networks: Global Youth Culture Intelligence*, Arts and Events, October 1, 2008, www.labelnetworks.com.

Focus: Santiago & Buenos Aires
Cultivating Collectivity and Experimentation in Design and Craft

Design is a flourishing academic arena in the colleges and universities of Chile and Argentina, but designers in Santiago and Buenos Aires continue to be challenged by a scarcity of local patronage and clientele. As the design theorist and educator Carlos Hinrichsen has noted, part of the solution to this issue is for Chilean and Argentinian design "to cease to be an 'academic curiosity'" and "to become a part of […] the region's social, productive and economic structure."[40] It is by working collectively in studios and engaging in experimentation with strategies such as upcycling that designers have found a way to move forward. In Santiago, Pro2Design, Studio Bravo, Modulab Ecodiseño, and We Say design studios represent designers who have chosen this path.

Satorilab is an experimental laboratory founded in Argentina by Alejandro Sarmiento and Luján Cambariere that explores design as a transformative element in Latin American societies. They use primarily discarded materials and promote the notion of creative play that stimulates the imagination. In one project, a collaboration with an individual of the Instituto Correccional de Mujeres Nr. 3 de Ezeiza (a women's correctional facility), Satorilab transformed packaging remains from the eco-conscious, Brazilian cosmetics company Natura into whimsical robot figures (see page 166–167).[41] This project is an example of playful design and reflects the emotional state of a younger consumer market that is design savvy, thanks to the impact of the marketing of socially conscious products by large mainstream retailers, yet at the same time is sentimentally detached from the images and objects from their childhoods.[42]

The influence of the young consumers was also noted by Charly Gonzalez Fernandez and Matías Fernández Moores of the Argentinian collaborative vacaValiente. They noted that their clientele includes tribes like "comic geeks" and young people who are moving from their parents' to their own homes (which often means small apartments). While seeking to maximize their living space, these consumers carry an emotional attachment to objects and images, yet without the sense of long-term ownership.[43] For their designs (which are mainly made with leather scraps), vacaValiente also upcycles materials and reduces forms to "minimal geometric expression," based on the structural principles found in nature, using themes that "create space for the user to participate." As in the case of many younger designers, they have found that a hands-on involvement in production and distribution allows them to insure a market share that is consistent and reliable.[44]

Fabián Bercic and Angello García Bassi are two designers who cement the connection between a segment of the creative sector in Argentina and Chile, respectively, to the global Art Toy movement. Known for the playful character of his installation and wall pieces, Bercic recently explored biblical themes in his *Eva* and *Conviértenos Dios, el nacimiento de Eva* (see page 158).

---

40) Carlos Hinrichsen, "The Impact of Design in South America: Emerging Vision with Global Perspective," International Council of Societies of Industrial Design / International Design Alliance, paper presented ca. 1990s. Hinrichsen is director of international affairs and former director (1992–2010) of the School of Design, Departamento Universitario Obrero Campesino, Universidad de Chile (Duoc UC).
41) Paula Avarado, "Satori: Two Pushing for a Conscious Design," *Treehugger*, January 30, 2007, www.treehugger.com.
42) This heightened awareness of the production and marketing of design and craft in all levels of society is the result of marketing and production initiatives aimed at a newly emerged global middle class. As commercial entities such as Design Within Reach, Crate and Barrel, Ikea, and Home Depot embrace, remix, and sell global trends to a constituency newly focused on lifestyle and personal expression, retailers like J. C. Penney, Kmart, and Sears are establishing design components. In Latin America, regional retailers such as Sanborns and The Home Store in Mexico, Firma Casa and DPot in São Paulo, and Airedelsur in Buenos Aires also cater to this trend. Designers and design entities have opportunities to colonize retail spaces worldwide, and local designers and makers may find their work filtered through a corporate lens and reframed as belonging to the global village.
43) Charly Gonzalez Fernandez and Matias Fernandez Moores, in conversation with Lowery Stokes Sims and Adriana Kertzer, Museum of Arts and Design, New York, April 14, 2014.
44) Ibid.

The figures are similar to the wooden Kokeshi dolls of northern Japan, with their simplified stylized bodies and relatively large heads painted with a few lines that suggest facial features. Bercic's work relates directly to the Japanese concept of *kawaii* (cuteness), which is addressed by Magdalena Grüneisen in her essay in this volume (see pages 54–55). It also demonstrates, as scholar Ami Kim has noted, that the "cuteness fervor is no longer limited to Japan or East Asia [...] It is a very transnational phenomenon."[45]

In a related vein, Santiago-based designer Bassi creates complex paper sculptures as part of his design conceit *Cubotoy*. The *Cubotoy* characters were invented by Bassi from a world of heroes and villains, while evoking figures reminiscent of "it's a small world," the Disney theme park feature.[46] The paper toys are intended as a design tool for students and professionals to use in advertising, animation, video, and television and are given form through folds and precise scissor cuts.

The Chilean design collective gt2P (Great Things to People) is conducting perhaps the most audacious experiments with design and craft in Latin America today. Its designer-members Eduardo Arancibia, Victor Imperiale, Guillermo Parada, Tamara Pérez, and Sebastian Rozas experiment with new paradigms for the interface between traditional crafts and digital design. In their project *Losing My America*, realized in collaboration with Estudio Guto Requena and Ariel Rojo (see pages 97–104), gt2P investigates a hybrid production between "crafts related to pottery, wood carving, and metal casting in Latin America" and a scanned 3-D element that is meant to suggest "that crafts mixed with new technologies can become the link between mass production and mass customization."[47] As *Losing My America* reveals, despite the impression of Chile and Argentina as European-focused, indigenous cultures continue to prosper even if on the periphery.

This link between "mass production and mass customization" was also achieved in *12 Shoes for 12 Lovers* (see pages 168–169), a series conceived by New York-based Chilean designer-artist-catalyst Sebastian Errazuriz. The series of shoes features twelve sculptural evocations of relationships that Errazuriz had with twelve former lovers. Each pair is distinguished by its particular form or the character of the heel and was produced in the artist's MakerBot Replicator 2X Experimental 3-D Printer. The shoes were sourced from digital drawings constructed on a CAD program and are accompanied by a photograph and text that reflect the nature of the relationship. Each pair embodies romance, pathos, and even vengeance that could come out of only a specific attitude, worldview, and gender experience. This project exemplifies, in the words of Riya Patel, the potential for product design to function in the future "as a form of personal expression and art."[48]

**Focus: San Salvador & San Juan
Developing New Markets for Design**

Latin American designers are actively promoting their work inside and outside of their countries of origin. They recognize the ongoing need to participate in global forums such as the International Contemporary Furniture Fair (ICFF) and WantedDesign in New York City, Salone del Mobile in Milan, Design Days Dubai, and the Guild Design Fair in Johannesburg, in order to showcase their work to the international public. The nascent design scenes in San

---

45) Ami Kim, "As Cute as It Gets: Kawaii Aesthetics of Japanese Contemporary Visual Culture and Art," PhD diss., New York University, forthcoming [2015]. I thank Adriana Kertzer for sharing this with me.
46) Bassi frames this conception within the realm of discovery of "a world of paper" and runs competitions for new personifications of the character on the *Cubotoy* website.
47) gt2P, project description of Losing My America, PDF file, 2013, artist files, Museum of Arts and Design.
48) New York, January 12, 2014. For Léon de la Barra Riya Patel, "12 Shoes for 12 Lovers by Sebastian Errazuriz," November 28, 2013, http://www.frameweb.com/news/12-shoes-for-12-lovers-by-sebastian-errazuriz.

Salvador, El Salvador, and San Juan, Puerto Rico, are based largely on collectives aiming to create a local and international market for Salvadoran and Puerto Rican design through exhibitions, marketing, education, and social interaction. The collaborative The Carrot Concept in San Salvador, the promotional initiative Design in Puerto Rico, and the collective Two Squared Studio in Puerto Rico are made up of designers who work to create new business opportunities for their members. The products they present reflect the ambition and vibrancy of emerging design centers, while drawing inspiration from quotidian life.

The Carrot Concept is a physical space that serves as a common home for art and design. It provides a space for the exchange of ideas and trends among local designers and a commercial outlet for Salvadoran products. There are many crosscurrents of local and international influences in the collective's design work: Roberto Javier Dumont found inspiration in Japanese origami for the faceted geometry in his *Fold Chair* (see page 175); in describing their *Ikono Chair* (see page 179), Claudia and Harry Washington reference mid-twentieth-century chair designs by Hans Wegner and Yngve Ekström; and José Roberto Paredes's *Canasto Lamp* (see page 174) evokes the woven frame for traditional baskets. As their overarching objective, The Carrot Concept aims to "transform Salvadoran design into a disciplined and systematic method for developing projects" and to "elevate local manufacturing by involving producers in the design process."

In San Juan, members of the creative sector have been moving through the global art market rather than leaving the island altogether.[49] While this sounds an optimistic note for the arts of Puerto Rico, the recent economic downturn caused a movement of middle and professional class Puerto Ricans from the island, exactly the base that would be expected to support local arts.[50] This indicates the fragile contexts within which designers and artists work in various locales. Puerto Rican designers still forge a strong connection to the island, however, in a design scene that reflects the fluctuation between local, national, and global aspirations, largely because of Puerto Rico's particular relationship to the mainland United States. The organization known as Design in Puerto Rico, under the leadership of Carlos Bobonis (see page 173), has become an important nexus for designers, manufacturers, and distributors. Bobonis came up with the idea for a collective after visiting WantedDesign in 2012 and seeing how other Latin American countries had presented their designers. One year later, Design in Puerto Rico presented its first joint exhibition at the fair. According to their website, "Design in Puerto Rico is a business platform for Puerto Rican designers to develop, promote, and export their products. It seeks to identify the best that Puerto Rican design talent has to offer and strengthen relationships between those designers and their potential manufacturers, distributors, and customers around the world." Vladimir García Bonilla, a member of Design in Puerto Rico, created *Meteoro* (see page 172), a hanging planter that pays homage to the residential steel planting ornaments typical of Puerto Rican mid-century modern house-patio décor. Mexican Cecilia Leon de la Barra's works (see page 178) also recontextualize garden accessories from a design perspective.

The embrace of everyday life and celebration of the quotidian can also be seen in the designs of another Puerto Rican, Eddie Figueroa Feliciano,

---

49) San Juan was somewhat paradoxically positioned as an emerging art city in Pablo Léon de la Barra, "San Juan," in Byrd et al., *Art Cities of the Future*. Léon de la Barra, the Guggenheim USB MAP Curator, Latin America, part of the Global Art Initiative at the Solomon R. Guggenheim Museum, New York, further analyzed San Juan's creative scene in a panel discussion cosponsored by the book's publisher and New Art Dealers of America (NADA) at CANADA Gallery, New York, January 12, 2014. For Léon de la Barra, the commitment to a local scene in San Juan mirrors the sentiment expressed by young designers in Mexico. He noted that, as of 2000, Puerto Rico looked to Mexico as a model of change and globalization.
50) Lizette Alvarez, "Economy and Crime Spur New Puerto Rican Exodus," *New York Times*, February 8, 2014.

a member of the collective Two Squared Studio. His *8 Lamp* (see page 174) references the "exterior lighting solutions found in the Caribbean region." The lamp's design can be adjusted depending on the necessities of the space in which it is used and allows for the incorporation of more than one bulb. Figueroa's *Zanco* (see page 176), an object that can be modified to become three different pieces of furniture, references the informal building systems of the slums that dot Carribean islands, including Puerto Rico. Figueroa focuses his research on identifying original Puerto Rican craftsmanship techniques in order to incorporate them into the industrial production of useful objects. *La Alfombra* (see page 177), the result of a project done in collaboration with students of the Escuela Internacional de Diseño y Arquitectura, Universidad del Turabo, in Caguas, Puerto Rico, consists of a modular tapestry, fabricated along with artisans at V'Soske (a company that has been based in Puerto Rico since the 1930s and has a long history of collaborating with artists).[51] Much like The Carrot Concept and Design in Puerto Rico, Two Squared Studio relies on international fairs to reach a larger audience. Its other three members, Ana Cristina Quiñones, Joel Álvarez, and Elia Barreiro, together with Figueroa, represented the Escuela Internacional de Diseño y Arquitectura at the 2013 Salone del Mobile and 2014 WantedDesign.

Focus: Havana
Navigating Personal and Civic Space

The works under this theme address the process of reclaiming civic spaces and personal integrity within the ever-shifting Latin American political climate. Both the formal and informal design solutions pursued throughout Latin America exemplify any number that can be found in the rest of the world, wherever people respond ingeniously to needs that are not met by official channels. Nowhere is this clearer than in Havana, Cuba. Cuban photographer Ernesto Oroza's series *Architecture of Necessity* (see pages 191–193) documents how individual citizens have retrofit existing structures and objects to address common quotidian needs. Similarly, in a process documented in a video created by the Colombian Ministry of Culture, Colectivo Cambalache from Bogotá have organized and presented found elements according to museological methods. Also featured in this section are *La Plaza Vacia* (2012), a video by Cuban artist Coco Fusco, Carlos Garaicoa's *Fin de Silencio*, an installation of floor tapestries woven in pavement patterns and videos, and clothes that explore narratives of gender by Peruvian clothing designer Lucia Cuba.

Oroza's photographs of what he has dubbed the "architecture of necessity" captures the ingenuity in and around Havana, where ordinary citizens have modified existing structures to provide for their needs, adding barrels for water, exterior stairwells, and even heating, ventilation, and air-conditioning systems. Oroza's work substantiates Garaicoa's reflection that Cuban cities represent "idyllic and nostalgic ruins from the colonial and first republic periods [...] The encounter with these buildings produces a strange sensation; the issue is not the ruin of a luminous past but a present of incapacity [...] I call these the Ruins of the Future."[52]

Garaicoa and Fusco examine architecture and space as specific modalities for political comment. Fusco has often described her video *The Empty Plaza* (see page 186) as a "meditation on public space, revolutionary promise, and memory." Presenting an empty Plaza de la Revolucíon, Fusco demonstrates its deficits outside of its function as a site of mass assembly. She focuses our attention on "a stark, inhospitable arena where all the major political events of the past half-century have been marked by mass

---

51) In the early 1940s, V'Soske collaborated with the Museum of Modern Art, New York, to produce a series of tapestries based on work by Stuart Davis, Charles Howards, Loren McIver, and Arshile Gorky, among others. These were exhibited in *New Rugs by American Artists* at MoMA in 1942.

52) Achim Drucks, "Carlos Garaicoa: Ruins of the Future," *dbArtMag*, no. 65 (June 2011), http://db-artmag.com/en/65/.

choreography, militarized displays, and rhetorical flourish. [She] decided to create a piece about that legendary site—an empty stage filled with memories, through which every foreign visitor passes, while nowadays many, if not most, Cubans flee."

For Garaicoa, the street becomes a vehicle for social commentary simply by naming it for a person, date, or event. Such tributes encourage civic pride and memorial sentiment. Garaicoa's large tapestries, which comprise *Fin de Silencio* (see pages 187–190), have textures mimicking cement or asphalt street surfaces. Their embedded slogans, however, comment on the state of pedestrians who live under a specific political system: "Cambio" (Change), "La General Tristeza" (The General Sadness), and "La lucha es de todos, de todos es la lucha" (The fight is all and everyone is fighting). The accompanying video projections show the movement on various streets, viewed from the pedestrian's perspective.

In contemporary cities, the ever-present threat of domestic or international terrorism has spawned constant surveillance. In addition to cameras, there is now the fast-developing technology of drones. This provides an appropriate context for Mexican designer Gilberto Esparza's drone-like sculptures that first appeared in Mexico City. His *Urban Parasites* (see pages 206–210, 212–213) confront us with notions of biomechanical survival dependent on the exploitation of sources of power that fuel our daily functions. As the artist has noted, his interest in more exploitative devices has evolved as he became aware of "research projects using microbial fuel cells." This inspired him to think of developing "a project that would engage with the issue of pollution in rivers" in sites such as El Salto Jalísco, Mexico, a community greatly affected by this problem.[53]

Meanwhile, in Brazil, the seizing of proprietary control of public space has become a particularly contested issue in cities such as Rio de Janeiro. The residents of Rio's *favelas* have been displaced by development as the city prepared for the arrival of tourists attending the 2014 World Cup and the 2016 Olympic Games. The issue of political, social, and economic hegemony in the *favelas* has been the focus of Projeto Morrinho (see page 216), a collective of youth from the *favela* Vila Pereira da Silva, in Rio de Janeiro. Their installations and videos chronicle the community's daily lives while commenting on the failure of municipal groups to curb crime and provide infrastructure services for marginalized communities. Their work has gained international attention and may be credited with increasing global awareness of conditions in the *favelas* over the last decade, but, with the recent economic problems in Brazil, these conditions threaten to resurface.

This type of youth-oriented navigation of personal and civic space can also be identified in the improbable popularity of street art, otherwise known as graffiti. This art form —largely considered a destructive element in the United States—has flourished and drawn sightseers from all over to neighborhoods such as Vila Madalena, in São Paulo. Brazilian William Baglione has been a godfather figure for a group of graffiti artists working in the city, including his brother Herbert, Felipe Yung (aka Flip), Thais Beltrame, and Alexander Cruz Sesper (aka Sesper). The group collaborated with Les Crayon Noirs, in Paris, to produce a series of aerosol cans made of porcelain from Limoges known collectively as the *Bombe* series (see page 198), featuring an image by each artist. Not only does this project represent a step into the modern world for a traditional French technique, it is also a vibrant crossing of societal lines in terms of signifiers of the luxurious and the proletarian.

---

53) See "Urban Parasites and Nomadic Plants," posted on Eyebeam, April 9, 2010, www.eyebeam.org.

54) See Michael Kimmelman, "A City Arises with Its Hopes," *New York Times*, May 18, 2012.

In Colombia, the quashing of drug cartels in the early 2000s led to dramatic reclamation of civic spaces. Medellín, for example, once a center of drug trafficking, was reclaimed through the work of the mayor Sergio Fajardo and architect-designers Alejandro Echeverri and Giancarlo Mazzanti.[54] The promise and vibrancy of community engagement is evident in the video *Capítulo 4 la conquista del espacio: Arte Público* (see page 215), produced by the Colombian Ministry of Culture and El Vicio Producciones. It features a medley of collaborative works: the *Venice Biennial*, a street festival in the Venice neighborhood of Bogotá; *Ciudad Kennedy*, a merging of memory and reality by artist Miler Lagos; the *Museo de la Calle*, a traveling museum by Colectivo Cambalache, where goods and services are bartered; and the *Bricolage Project* that encourages the use and reuse of objects in unsuspected ways in both the domestic and the public spheres.[55]

Interpersonal encounters and the choreography of inhabiting space inform projects by Argentinian designer Diana Cabeza in Buenos Aires. Her infrastructure designs include bus shelters, street gratings, and public seating. One of the latter, *Lace Cloth* (see page 194), a series of seating forms, encourages interaction among people by substituting the usual linear form with a face-to-face arrangement. She notes: "As Latin Americans we have a finely tuned sense of the communal character of public space and look for appropriate solutions to the massive scale of different places. Our elements are supports that qualify the community rites promoting social integration. The particular character of the surfaces of this series is also taken into consideration in order to serve the ideals of place and identity."

Artists and designers in Latin America have questioned the navigation of personal and civic space by addressing the theme of violence in contemporary society. At times, the expression is almost uncomfortably ironic, as in Jorge Diego Etienne's gun-barrel pencil holder *Choose Your Bullets* (Fig. 8), which the designer describes as "[responding] to the current situation in Mexico, where violence seems to have taken over our life." This seemingly innocuous desk accessory is sculpted out of aluminum by artisans in Monterrey, Mexico, and each piece is engraved with a serial number. Etienne's project can be seen as an attempt to co-opt and thus nullify the effects of guns. Pedro Reyes, who is also from Mexico, pursues the same goal: engaged in a long-term collaboration with the police department in Mexico City, the artist refashions confiscated guns into musical instruments, such as *Guitarra* (see page 217). Another Mexican artist, Teresa Margolles, incorporates jewelry and trophies that belonged to the victims of crime—policemen, government officials, and civilians—in her installations.[56]

Turning to the power dynamics and dysfunction in the border zone between the United States and Mexico is the subject matter of Eduardo Sarabia's ceramic work *A Thin Line Between Love and Hate* (see pages 218–219), which draws on the convention of Talavera blue and white pottery. Sarabia sought to present the "other side of Mexican culture" as an antidote to the "drug-war imagery [that] had become such a deeply embedded piece of that culture." He decorated the familiar Talavera ceramic form with contemporary Mexican images (such as marijuana leaves and scantily clad women), creating an effective vehicle to engage a dialogue about these issues.[57]

Surviving drive-by shootings is the subject of Monaco-based Brazilian designer David Elia (Design de Gema) in his somewhat macabre *Stray Bullet Chair* and *Bulletproof Side Table*, in which stainless-steel eyelets approximate bullet holes

---

55) Antonio Sánchez Gómez, e-mail to Lowery Stokes Sims, Museum of Arts and Design, May 17, 2013.
56) See Alpha Escobedo, et al., *Teresa Margolles: Frontera*, exh. cat. (Kassel, Germany: Kunsthalle Fridericianum, 2011).
57) Alex Greenberger, "Eduardo Sarabia on Confronting Mexico's Underbelly with Art," *Artspace*, November 7, 2013, www.artspace.com.

(see pages 204), and shell casings decorate a glass top (see page 205). São Paulo–based architect-designers Marcio Kogan and Isay Weinfeld created a totally enclosed and secured city in their installation *Happyland I*. In *Happyland II*, they presented accoutrements and accessories that would help a citizen survive urban danger: a suitcase was packed with necessities in case of a kidnapping, while specialized architectural elements included *Gradil*, a spiked fence with pistol crowns (see page 211). These designers are not working from a merely superficial sentiment: a 2013 study on global homicide conducted by the United Nations Office on Drugs and Crime identified eleven of the top thirty most violent cities in the world as being in Brazil.[58]

Notions of personal space and identity assume a particular importance in a world where group uniformity has dominated. Individuals with African ancestry have a singular sense of identity in societies that purport to suppress ethnic difference in the service of national harmony. The mechanisms of class and race, however, are still all too evident in the lives of these individuals. Liliana Angulo Cortés's documentation of designs for Afrocentric braided hair in Colombia and other parts of Latin America, as well as in the United States, tackles imagery and design items that often feature stereotypes of black people. *Project Quieto Pelo* (see page 197) demonstrates a global sense of identity on the part of African-descendant peoples, uniting them despite linguistic and cultural differences imposed by their history as slaves and colonials. The Panamanian artist José Castrellón documented another kind of challenge to uniformity in a series of photographic portraits of men and their "priti baiks" (see pages 195–196). Castrellón is interested in the personal ways in which a collective sensibility is manifest. In this series, the artist focuses on how young men throughout Panama use their limited resources to transform their only vehicles for transportation into something unique, reflective of their individual identity.

The dynamics of class and race are also explored by Peruvian designer and activist Lucia Cuba in *Articulo 6: Narratives of Gender, Strength and Politics* (see pages 199–203). Her line of dresses, masks, aprons, and shoes documents the forced sterilizations implemented during the government of Alberto Fujimori in Peru between 1996 and 2000. Cuba conceived new designs for traditional Andean *polleras* (fiesta skirts), printed with the names of victims (mostly indigenous women), texts of the legislation, and portrait medallions of Fujimori and the USAID logo (US Aid for International Development, an organization Cuba implicates in this policy). Fashion and politics have a long association

Fig. 8 Jorge Diego Etienne (with industrial artisans in Monterrey, Mexico)
Choose your Bullets, 2011; sculpted aluminum engraved with unique serial number
3.6 x 1.4 in. (9.2 x 3.8 cm)
Photo: Arturo Lozano

---

58) Statistics on guns are taken from the Global Homicide Book (2014 edition) on the website of the United Nations Office on Drugs and Crime.

throughout history, and Cuba's project brings to light a history of severe violation of personal rights.

If *New Territories* has opened the door to explorations of Latin America's nexus of design, craft and art, much is left to be discovered. Meanwhile, we can note that of the many revelations to emerge from the organization of *New Territories*, the most prominent was the widely shared notion of engaging regional/local/national artisan skills in the mainstream, international, and creative scene in order to preserve a sense of national pride. The limitations of the resources for this project did not allow for the full inclusion of material on various Latin American–based cultural expressions in the United States. One example would be a work that represents the theoretical concept of "rasquache" or "rasquachismo,"[59] which encompasses the celebration of upcycling in the Mexican American community that parallels what has been observed all over Latin America.

What we hope to communicate in *New Territories* is the varied and, at times, contradictory manifestations that convey a sense of Latin Americanness in the arts. We are grateful to have multiple points of view on this issue expressed in the essays in this volume by Mari Carmen Ramírez, Jorge Rivas-Pérez, and Antonio Sánchez Gómez. At the same time, the specifics of creative practices in countries such as Mexico, Argentina, Paraguay, Cuba, Venezuela, and Brazil are detailed in texts by Ana Elena Mallet, Magdalena Grüneisen, Adriana Kertzer, Blanca Serrano Ortiz de Solórzano, Gabriela Rangel, Marcella Echavarría, and Nessia Leonzini Pope with Fabiana Lopes. By including these different perspectives, *New Territories* not only embraces the contradictions and controversies over the designation "Latin America" but, above all, demonstrates that contemporary designers are forging personal and working relationships that cross borders as they search for ways to be meaningful in the pursuit of their work.

---

59) Tomás Ybarra-Frausto, "Rasquachismo: a Chicano Sensibility," *Chicano Aesthetics: Rasquachismo*, exh. cat. (Pheonix: MARS, Movimiento Artiscico del Rio Salado, 1989), 5–8, online at the International Center for the Arts of America at the Museum of Houston, ICAA record no. 845510.

Charting a "New Territory" for an Old Continent: Latin America as an Operative Construct

Mari Carmen Ramírez

Latin America as a regional concept can be merely nominal—an *operative construct*—but even then, it remains embedded in the history of the European discovery of the so-called New World.[1] This discovery generated utopias galore for those who took advantage of their amazing findings and engaged in an overt criticism of Old World societies. In this context, the notion of Latin America as virgin terrain—a brave *new world*—of expansive possibilities and rich, untapped resources looms over any attempt at interpretation of unprecedented artistic movements in the region. This fact transforms the category of the "new" into a highly problematic one. The "new" at stake, indeed, is only a matter of perspective, relative at best, but nothing else. To avoid any appearance of naïveté, we must pay close attention to the parameters into which the concept is being employed, or better, updated.

The Old Fallacy of "the New"

Originating in the mind-bending discovery of previously unknown lands and peoples by Christopher Columbus in 1492, the notion of "the new," continues to be associated with the vast geopolitical enclave that has come to be recognized as the Americas. In this case, as highlighted by this groundbreaking exhibition, the "new" subject at stake is the extraordinary explosion—since the beginning of the twenty-first century—of cutting-edge laboratories for Latin American craft and design in key cities of Mexico, Central and South America, and the Caribbean. Considered until very recently as marginal, virtually invisible areas of cultural activity, these locales have surged into the spotlight of the broader political and economic forces of globalization. The modes of expression employed illustrate the significant and timely role played by Latin America in the worldwide expansion of contemporary art and design since the 1990s. The "innovation" at play, however, may allow us to downplay more serious concerns about the applicability of the "new."

And yet, for those steeped in the study of twentieth-century Modernism and Postmodernism, and their aftermath in Latin America, the uncovering of this *new territory* of artistic production raises a familiar set of questions: Is there anything really "new" in this phenomenon? Does "the new" here point toward a truly uncharted territory of artistic creativity in Latin America, one where, as Lowery Sims's reading of Gaetano Pesce's notion of "new territory" suggests (see page 13), the boundaries between artistic media are not only breaking down but also opening the way for unfettered creativity? Or is the term merely a euphemism for a more serious condition affecting the region as a whole? As was previously (and until very recently) the case with the visual arts, does the overlooked situation of design in Latin America signal that the continent is about to be "rediscovered" once again? At the crux of this situation lie the paradoxes posed by the problematic categories "Latin America" and "Latin American art."[2] Do these terms apply to particular traits of a culturally defined yet extremely heterogeneous region? In other words, is there such a thing as "Latin American art"—and by extension "Latin American design"—or is the subject matter one more manifestation of universal art? Furthermore, to what extent does the increasing incorporation of Latin American art in the global arts mainstream invalidate these questions? Engaging these issues demands elucidation of the true meaning and function of such vastly overused yet frequently misunderstood terms.

---

1) See Guy Martinière, "The Invention of an Operative Concept: The Latin-ness of America" [1978], reprinted in Hector Olea and Melina Kervandjian, eds., *Resisting Categories: Latin American and/or Latino?*, Critical Documents of the Twentieth-Century Latin American and Latino Art, vol. 1, organized by Héctor Olea, Mari Carmen Ramírez, Tomás Ybarra-Frausto (Houston: The Museum of Fine Arts, Houston / International Center for the Arts of the Americas, 2012), 164–77, doc. I.2.10. See also ICAA doc. No. 838531 in http://www.icaadocs.mfah.org.

2) For a discussion of the historic and ideological evolution of these categories, see Olea and Kervandjian, eds., *Resisting Categories*.

Two Operative Contructs

From the very outset, the "discovery" of Latin America led to all sorts of geographic blunders (the belief that India and China were part of the same continent) and biased misinterpretations (that the natives were Indians and constituted an untapped labor force). Compounding the legacy of that involuntary discovery is the history of evangelization and colonialism that branded this semicontinent from day one. The term *Latin America*, indeed, was first introduced in France in 1862 to refer to the Spanish-speaking—or Latin—countries of the region.[3] What may appear as a simple nominal, if patronizing gesture, however, was actually a means to implement the imperial (political, religious, economic, and commercial) ambitions of Napoleon III in the area. This broad task began with the "big stick" invasion of Republican Mexico and the five-year ordeal (1862–67) that resulted from that imperialist aggression.[4] Added to three centuries of colonial domination by European nations (namely Catholic), the strategy of lumping together such a complex continental region into a seemingly homogenous bloc only continued to perpetuate its unequal—subordinated—footing vis-à-vis the metropolis. This practice continued with the new world order that came into place in the post–World War II period, marked by the political economic ascendancy of the United States. The US-driven notion of Pan-Americanism,[5] set in motion during this period, represented yet another attempt to erase English, Portuguese, French, and Spanish specificities into a homogeneous geopolitical bloc. Hence, in politics as well as culture, the exchange between Latin American countries and the centers represented by Europe and the United States always implied a unidirectional flow from there to here. The persistence until today of this unequal axis of exchange explains what Cuban critic and curator Gerardo Mosquera calls the "neurosis of identity"[6] that has dominated debates about the arts and culture of this region from colonial times to the present.

At another level, the ontological potential opened by Columbus's accidental discovery of the New World led to the "invention" of America as an open field of spiritual, cultural, and intellectual potential.[7] The idea of an artificial whole precariously held together by the utopian longings of generations of *pensadores*,[8] art critics, and cultural producers thus lies at the root of the terms that have come to define this geopolitical enclave. Such terms also pose difficulties for a critical understanding of the issues at stake. Since the nineteenth century, if not earlier, there have been consistent attempts to think about the culture and artistic production of the region in transnational, continental terms. The quest for common ground blanketing the vast political and cultural differences encompassed by Latin America was a recurring argument introduced to counter the perception of a fragmented continent comprised of individual nations. From this point of view, the project of thinking about Latin America as a comprehensive whole has nothing to do with a return to essentialism, but rather with the rightful search for bona fide autonomy and legitimate differentiation from hegemonic rule. Period.

At the same time, such an artificial if not outright misconstrued history, explains why, from their inception, the terms *Latin America* and *Latin American art* have been the object of heated debates over the geopolitical and sociocultural specificity they are presumed to represent or convey. The intrinsic paradox that they hide becomes clear when we consider that, contrary to what they imply, there is no such thing as "Latin America" (in the sense of a homogeneous geopolitical unit) or "Latin American art" (in the sense of a readily codified and identifiable artistic style or language). Instead, there is only art produced by individual artists in more than twenty countries and a plethora of diverse communities and ethnicities that extend from Tijuana to Tierra del Fuego. From the indigenous peoples who survived the colonial onslaught to the scores of slaves brought in from Africa and the waves of immigrants who arrived from Europe and Asia, this region embodies a true melting pot of races and cultures whose presence is alive in the multifarious fabric of its densely populated urban centers. The paradigm of intermingling, or *mestizaje*, serves, in turn, to convey the complex interaction—or active blending—of races and cultures throughout the region. Despite the importance of a widespread, shared language, Latin Americans are not

---

3) Charles (Carlos) Calvo, "Letter to His Majesty, Emperor Napoleon III," [1862]; "Letter from M. Thouvenel, Minister of the French Foreign Office to Charles (Carlos) Calvo," [1862]; Charles (Carlos) Calvo, "Latin America," [1862] Michel Chevalier "Ancient and Modern Mexico" [1863], in ibid., 105–17, docs. I.2.1–2. See also ICAA doc. no. 839365 in http://www.icaadocs.mfah.org.
4) Michel Chevalier "Ancient and Modern Mexico" [1863], in ibid. See also ICAA doc. no. 839365 in http://www.icaadocs.mfah.org.
5) See the extensive discussion in Tomás Ybarra-Frausto, "The Good Neighborhood and Bad Times" in ibid., 435–583. Chapters include documents on: (I) "The Monroe Doctrine: A Precursor of Pan Americanism;" (II) "Half-Words in Conflict;" (III) "Insights from Latin America on U.S. Art and Society;" (IV) "The United States 'Presents' and 'Collects' Latin American Art."
6) Gerardo Mosquera, "From Latin American Art to Art from Latin America" in ibid, 1123–31.; see doc. no. 1065622 in http://www.icaadocs.mfah.org.
7) Edmundo O'Gorman, *La invención de América* [1958] and "The Invention of America" [1961], in ibid., 95–104; see doc. no. 839287 in http://www.icaadocs.mfah.org.

"Hispanics." They are white, black, mulattoes, mestizos, indigenous peoples, and so on.

From this point of view, the terms *Latin America* and *Latin American art* can only function as operative constructs that duly serve to identify a broad ensemble of countries and cultures united by the common legacies of religion, language and, most importantly, a history of utopian aspirations and colonial domination, whether of Spanish, French, British, Lusitanian, or another origin. The persistence until today of the structural imbalance that articulate Latin America's relationship to the rest of the world, in turn, justifies the continued use of these terms as markers of resistance to present-day homogenizing tendencies represented by market forces in particular and globalization in general.

The Playing Field

Despite its built-in paradoxes and the difficulties of apprehending its vast heterogeneity, the field of Latin American art has grown exponentially over the last thirty years as a result of complex political, cultural, and economic forces that have altered the perception and status of these artistic manifestations worldwide. After 1979, for example, the establishment of a specialized market for Latin American art in the form of public purchases sponsored by the leading auction houses of Sotheby's and Christie's created a more stable niche for this eclectic art in the United States. This factor coincided with two key economic trends: on one hand, the surge of neoliberalism and the return to democracy in major countries of the region previously under military rule; on the other hand, the intricate phenomenon of globalization itself. Understood as the dynamic flow of financial capital and people across borders, globalization not only activated the financial and cultural circuits between the United States and countries in Central America, South America, and the Caribbean, but, in the process, contributed to the consolidation of the budding US market for Latin American art. This development, in turn, led to the first of various market-driven and exhibition "booms" of this art. The 1980s and early 1990s, indeed, saw a spate of shows that brought Latin American art to the attention of the US mainstream.[9] Both the intensity and pace of these transformations intensified over the last few years as a result of the rise of the art markets globally. In this context, Latin American art has been transformed from a marginal, risky investment into a strategic economic resource. Thanks to the activities of private and institutional collectors, this multifarious art has thus become an attractive commodity in art markets in both Europe and the United States.

As a result of these developments, what began as a mere descriptor of the underappreciated visual arts expression of a marginal (notwithstanding continental) region, became synonymous with a vibrant, rapidly expanding field of visual arts and its production, scholarship, and collecting—one that encompasses artists, museums, galleries, universities, private collectors, and exhibitions. This process was significantly spurred by the entrance of major art museums in the Latin American art playing field, as well as the increased professionalization of the agents in charge of researching, promoting, and displaying this art.[10] Not surprisingly, the last decade also saw the increased "mainstreaming" of the art of the region as more institutions and collectors sought access to its first-rate (yet underrecognized) artists. The enhanced presence of Latin American artists in today's global exhibition circuits and institutional collections attests to a belated evolution that is nevertheless producing the long-awaited consolidation of Latin American art as both a global exhibition and collecting phenomenon.

An Incomplete Narrative

Far from an eccentric indulgence or a faddish trend, the field of Latin American art in the United States and elsewhere has continued to evolve and mature at a steady pace over the last thirty years. Such a process of growth—combining producers, agents, and institutions—entailed a move away from market-generated reductive stereotypes embodied in the problematic

---

8) The term *pensador* is emblematic of the Latin American intellectual tradition. It refers to a "man of ideas" who writes about topical issues from the perspective of an erudite generalist or even a scholar. See ibid., 43.
9) Exhibitions ranged from the highly reductive and criticized *Art of the Fantastic* (Indianapolis Museum of Art, curated by Holiday T. Day and Hollister Sturges, 1987) to the more tempered *Latin American Artists of the Twentieth Century* (Museum of Modern Art, New York, curated by Waldo Rasmussen, 1993), among others. For introductions to these exhibitions, see Tomás Ybarra-Frausto, "Destabilizing Categorizations," in Olea and Kervandjian, *Resisting Categories*, 859–78, V.1.9 [1987], V.1.10 [1993], (2012), 859–78; see doc. no. 1965330 and doc. no. 1065350 in http://www.icaadocs.mfah.org.

10) These museums include the Museum of Fine Arts, Houston; Tate Modern; Museum of Modern Art, New York; Los Angeles County Museum; Centre Georges Pompidou, Paris; Museo Centro Nacional Reina Sofía, Madrid; and, more recently, The Metropolitan Museum of Art, New York and the Solomon R. Guggenheim Museum, New York.

notion of "the fantastic,"[11] toward previously overlooked or ignored areas of artmaking in the countries that comprise the region. The gamut of exhibitions, publications, and collection-building activities taking place since 1990 concentrated, above all, on two areas: the multifarious manifestations of the pre- and post–World War II avant-gardes (particularly those embodied by constructive and geometric art tendencies) and contemporary artistic practices. The current pervasiveness of geometric and constructive art in public and private collections as well as market circuits—including the emergence of a highly specialized niche reserved for galleries and curators dedicated to Latin American abstraction—signals the consolidation of a new canon for modern Latin American art. At the same time, the surge of contemporary art from this region in global markets beginning in the 1990s coincided with the opening up of Latin American economies as a result of neoliberalism and, again, globalization. This situation provided an unprecedented platform for contemporary artists in global circuits that resulted in the almost instantaneous rise in recognition of the generation who emerged on the scene during this critical decade.[12] Unlike those associated with the fantastic, these artists were no longer forced to carry their identity on their lapels. Seemingly liberated from the weight of the colonial legacy, they emerged onto the international scene as "global" artists.

Despite such significant advances in display, circulation, collection building, and scholarship, the narrative of modern and contemporary Latin American art, however, remains incomplete. The number of artistic movements and tendencies encompassed by such a vast region is, indeed, not only ungraspable, but also impossible to synthesize into a seamless account. In such a context, another question is timely: what can *New Territories*, an exhibition of contemporary art, craft and design, contribute to our current understanding of broader artistic practices and cultural developments in Latin America? The current explosion of experimental design in Latin America did not emerge in a vacuum. Understood in terms of the production of functional products for everyday pleasure and consumption—from furniture and ceramics to fashion—modern and contemporary design has had a rich history in Latin America, one that went hand in hand with national industrialization and modernization projects that began in the 1920s and intensified in the post–World War II period. As Jorge Rivas Pérez notes, the diverse manifestations of design in Latin America were not exempt from the same dynamic of assimilation/subversion of European avant-garde tenets that characterized other artistic movements in the region (see pages 59–62).[13] And, like these artistic movements, design production also incorporated key elements from the indigenous and vernacular traditions of their native countries. While pointing to one of the most exciting chapters of Latin American art, this phenomenon, however, not only remains a largely virgin territory of art historical and curatorial inquiry, but also has yet to produce its own cadre of professional experts and art historians.

The boom experienced by the field of design worldwide in recent decades, in turn, is grounded in one of the most paradigmatic utopias of the twentieth-century avant-garde. I refer to the desire to dramatically enhance the lives of ordinary individuals through the merging of *art* and *life*. Beginning with the nineteenth-century Arts and Crafts movement and extending through Russian Constructivism, De Stijl, the Bauhaus, and the Ulm School of Design, avant-garde artists set out to rethink the parameters of painting and sculpture beyond traditional formats and to introduce design and craftsmanship that reenvisioned the individual's everyday environment. Although significantly underappreciated and underrecognized, this tendency had a significant impact in Latin America where, beginning in the 1940s and '50s, avant-garde groups like the Taller Torres-García (Montevideo), Arte-Concreto-Invención (Buenos Aires), Concretismo and Neoconcretismo (São Paulo and Rio de Janeiro), as well as independent exponents of Constructivist and Geometric tendencies working in Caracas, Buenos Aires, and Paris, engaged in theoretical as well as practical incursions into the fields of architecture, craft, and design. Horacio and Augusto Torres, Gonzalo

---

11) See Mari Carmen Ramírez, "Beyond 'The Fantastic': Framing Identity in U.S. Exhibitions of Latin American Art," *Art Journal* 51, no. 4 (Winter 1992), 60–68. Doc. No. 1065386, in http://www.icaadocs.mfah.org.

12) This was the case with Alfredo Jaar, Doris Salcedo, Gabriel Orozco, Guillermo Kuitca, Ernesto Neto, and many other artists who have become staples of the international circuits.

13) For the dynamics that helped shape avant-garde movements in Latin America, see Héctor Olea and Mari Carmen Ramírez, *Inverted Utopias: Avant-Garde Art in Latin America, 1920–1970* (London and New Haven: Yale University Press, in association with The Museum of Fine Arts, Houston, 2004).

Fonseca, Julio Alpuy, and Francisco Matto—all members of the Taller Torres-García—produced ceramics, furniture, mural paintings, architectural designs, and even jewelry. In a similar vein, in São Paulo, leading members of Concretismo, such as Waldemar Cordeiro, Geraldo de Barros, and Alexandre Wollner set out to design gardens (Cordeiro), furniture (de Barros), or books and graphic materials (Wollner). Around the same time, in Rio de Janeiro, Lygia Clark constructed small architectural models for total environments. Among the Venezuelan constructive artists, Gertrude Goldschmidt (Gego) turned linear geometric designs into rugs and textiles while Carlos Cruz-Diez took his experiments with color to fashion and jewelry design. Gego, Cruz-Diez, and Jesús Soto, in turn, worked with architects to produce large-scale sculptures that remain as extraordinary examples of plastic integration. In the contemporary area, artists such as Jorge Pardo have reintroduced the notion of the total artwork, producing monumental environments that merge sculpture, architecture, and furniture design. Old and new examples thus abound in a history that is not only far from written but, least of all, exhausted.

In this context, the surge of design that we have witnessed since 2000, both as a singular practice and as an ongoing dialogue with contemporary art, is not an isolated phenomenon, it is the continuation of a line of artistic experimentation deeply entrenched in the utopian ideals of avant-garde movements in Europe and in Latin America. What is "new" in this case, however, is not only the intensity but the broad range, experimental impulse, and momentum through which this global trend is both manifesting and transforming itself across the region. Eschewing the exhausted parameters of the nation-state, Sims has identified hubs of radical creativity in key cities, the majority of which had never stood out for any type of contemporary design activity in the past, especially San Juan in Puerto Rico, El Salvador, Santiago de Chile, and Havana. Taken together with better-known hubs—Buenos Aires, São Paulo, Mexico City, Oaxaca, and Rio de Janeiro—these cities configure a vibrant network of young, experimental designers intent upon merging craft and vernacular traditions with the latest developments in technology, materials, and product design. Their existence today points to the activation of a complex area of transnational and interdisciplinary production that in its sensitivity to the social and political environment from and for which it operates frequently coalesces with contemporary artistic practices. As noted by Sims and other essayists in this catalogue, despite the precarious infrastructure that supports these designers, the outstanding feature of their production is the way it moves beyond the merely functional, engaging instead with social and cultural issues grounded in regional, national, and local contexts. The results are practices bent on having a transformative impact on the everyday environment.

From this point of view, the organization of *New Territories in Design, Craft and Art in Latin America* can be seen as the first step in correcting the glaring invisibility of design practice in the history of Latin American art; it signals that this region has indeed entered into a "new territory" of artistic practice—one that clearly escapes both the hegemonic stranglehold as well as the stereotypes with which the region was cast in the past. This is a bold, groundbreaking step that undoubtedly will stimulate further interest as well as new scholarship. We need many more exhibitions of this nature to duly grasp the complex and original contributions being made by contemporary designers from Latin America to the history of twentieth- and twenty-first-century art.

Navigating the Past and Present in Latin America

Antonio Sánchez Gómez

In his 2000 article "Coloniality of Power, Eurocentrism, and America Latina," Peruvian sociologist Aníbal Quijano explores how colonialism created a structure that far outlasted the independence processes and creation of states in Latin America.[1] For Quijano, the constitution of America created long-lasting space-time values sustained along two basic axes: "the codification of the differences between conquerors and conquered in the idea of 'race'" and the "constitution of a new structure of control of labor and its resources and products."

According to Quijano, the character of the newly discovered continent relied on the establishment of Europe as a modern force of global power. For that reason, the differentiation between Americans and Europeans was crucial. The author shows how, in a complex structure without precedent in its scale, all nonwhite Europeans and their descendants were meticulously categorized, defined, and introduced into a form of labor that replicated slavery and serfdom in the New World. Under this discourse of inferiority, nonwhite, non-Europeans were perceived as part of the past on an evolutionary timeline. In turn, Europe, and later the United States, become inheritors of the values of the future. Quijano observes how these values, established on the basis of race and control of labor, are still influential today in Latin America.

In this context—that of an imposed past that has remained as a deep structure in Latin American society—the present, as both an awareness of the now and the act of being present, acquires a revolutionary nature. Under these circumstances, the work of artists becomes crucial for evidencing the prevalence of the values of the past while creating a space for the manifestation of the present. A good example of this is Leo Chiachio and Daniel Giannone's work, which reveals nothing less than the structures of the world in which we live. The Argentinian artistic duo known as Chiachio & Giannone has become prominent in the last decade for their large-scale embroidered self-portraits, in which they embrace a traditionally feminine technique, while becoming performers of their own fantasies. Chiachio & Giannone have depicted themselves as geishas, indigenous people, and witches among many other roles, with Piolín—their dachshund who usually plays a central role in their compositions (Fig. 1). The patterns of the embroidered fabrics often feature anachronistic details purposely integrated into the pieces. As seen in *La ciudad frondosa* (2011–2012) (see page 110–111) these men are willing to traverse the globe, oscillating between the past and imaginary or mythical worlds, using the ancient skill of needlework rather than cutting-edge technology to capture the moment. By representing themselves in such a way, Chiachio & Giannone question the place of embroidery as a "minor art". They dismantle conventional images of manhood and family and blur the boundaries of time, space, and reality.

When questioned about the painstaking act of embroidering these large-scale pieces, Daniel Giannone forthrightly responded, "We are recovering time."[2] This response contradicts the assumption that by embroidering their images, the two artists deliberately slow their pace of production. In fact, for them, embroidering reconnects the act of creating the piece with the act of conceiving it. They have described their creative process as dry painting, and by stitching each brushstroke, the process becomes a conscious performance of elongating time while being inexorably present through it. Time, then, is a major theme in their work, both in the deconstruction of their own images through anachronistic compositions and in the needlework that allows the makers to be present in both a visual and temporal sense of the word. This time layering, so intensely complicated in Chiachio & Giannone's pieces, is a remarkable example of the new territories this exhibition explores through the work of artists, designers, craftsmen, and entrepreneurs in Latin America.

---

1) Aníbal Quijano, "Coloniality of Power and Eurocentrism in Latin America," *International Sociology* 15, no. 2 (2000): 215–32.

2) Leo Chiachio and Daniel Giannone, interviewed by the author, July 31, 2013.

Fig. 1 Chiachio & Giannone
Nacimiento, 2010 (detail)
Handmade embroidery with cotton thread,
lurex, and glitter on camouflage fabric
55 x 64.20 in. (139.7 x 163 cm)
Photo: Daniel Kiblisky

Fig. 2 Pedro Barrail
Stool/Table, from the *Castor* series, 2002
Cedar burned with hot tool, glass
Seat height: 20 in. (60 cm); seat width and depth: 14 in.
(35.6 cm); backrest height: 27 in. (68.5 cm)
Photo: Pedro Barrail

Welcome Home

Based on the large-scale model of differentiation presented by Quijano, we can infer a spatial distance between those in the past and those in the future, between the "white" and the "other," wage earner and servant. Although this separation is sometimes based on physical distance, in the domestic sphere, differentiation is implemented through other strategies as well.

In *House Maids* and *Maids' Rooms* (Figs. 3–4), the Peruvian artist Daniela Ortiz shows how the strategies of differentiation consist more of schemes of invisibility than a hermetic separation. For *House Maids*, Ortiz collected hundreds of images posted by Peruvian users of Facebook in which their maidservants were included. What the artist found was that these women appear as blurred figures in the background or as images edited in such a way that parts of their bodies are cropped in order to privilege a central figure like a baby. In *Maids' Rooms,* another aspect of the cohabitation of domestic servants with employer families emerges: the distribution of space in houses. This series gathers images and floor plans of houses built for wealthy Peruvians in Lima between 1930 and 2012 in Lima. Ortiz observes the relatively small spaces assigned to domestic workers, providing information about their exact dimensions. In a visual assembly, the artist displays a photograph of the building's facade, comparative dimensions of the space assigned to the domestic worker versus areas occupied by family members, and the resumé of the architect who designed the house.

By collecting and subtly commenting on the images fabricated by others, Ortiz makes a strong statement about the place of these "other" women in the domestic realm. By revealing strategies of invisibility, the artist subverts the formula and uncovers the permanence of the relationship between race and structures of labor. In Ortiz's work, the images are not created by the artist but by the architects and users of social media. In her sharp observations, the shared space of a house or a photograph becomes another form that brings us from the past to the present, both in the sense of time and presence.

Designing a Present from Images of the Past

In their work, Chiachio, Giannone, and Ortiz make important references to the fields of design and craft. In *Maids' Rooms*, Ortiz uses architectural design to point out the persistence of past structures in Peruvian architecture. In *Enlazados*, *Enmarañados*, and *Nacimiento*, among others, Chiachio & Giannone turn to the craft of embroidery applied to industrial textiles. They often depict themselves wearing ancient or traditional designs ranging from textiles to tattooing and body painting. Just as these artists cite design and craft, craftsmen and designers share similar concerns and have adopted comparable strategies.

In *El Castor*, from the *Darwin* series of furniture forms, Paraguayan designer Pedro Barrail (Fig. 2) displays elements that correspond to Chiachio & Giannone's interest in body ornamentation and their dialogue between ancient traditions and contemporary imagery. Barrail, however, focuses on a utilitarian object and a whole other world of visual references. He initially conceived these forms as an exchange between contemporary design and the "primitive"

Fig. 3 Daniela Ortiz, *97 House Maids*, 2010
Book (printed paper), 5.11 x 7.8 in. (13 x 19.8 cm)
Facebook images: 3.9 x 5.9 in. (10 x 15 cm), each
Installation: 49.2 in. (125 cm)
Photo: Xose Quiroga

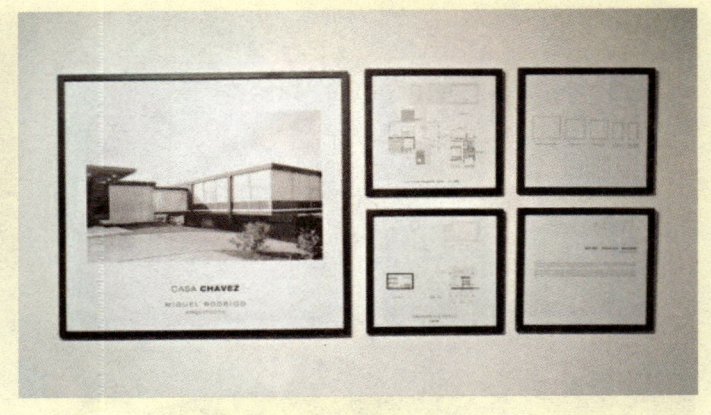

Fig. 4 Daniela Ortiz, *Maids' Rooms*, 2012
Printed paper
Series of 16 houses; detail: 23.6 x 23.6 in. (60 x 60 cm)
Four images: 12.9 x 12.9 in. (33 x 33 cm)
Photo: Xose Quiroga

forms and tattoo designs of the indigenous Pai Tavytera people. Later in his process, he based the shape of his table-chairs on anthropomorphic forms; referencing the painted bodies from his urban world: ordinary people with tattoos. The chair's removable back can be vertical or repositioned horizontally to become a side table. The two positions also symbolize an alert man (chair) or a submissive one (table). This contemporary "body" was then covered with motifs burned into the surface by members of the Pai Tavytera community. The meaning of the motifs is the product of conversations between Barrail and the tribesmen. In *Castor*, they decided to illustrate accounts of fantastic battles "between beasts . . . things trying to gobble each other up."[3] In the final product, this table-chair recalls the blurred boundary between oppressed and oppressor, as encountered in our daily lives.

Taking a cue from an evolutionary model, Barrail designed other pieces in the *Darwin* series, which were conceived not as individuals, but as an urban gang. Barrail conferred on them a symbolic power to rebel against their owner and the ability to escape, as if in response to the evolutionary values described by Quijano.

By incorporating such associations into his pieces, Barrail gives a whole new meaning to placing the object in a private space. The designer goes as far as to challenge the value of owning the furniture while pointing out the privileged position of the owners in a deeply unequal social structure.

The disruption of the conventions in Pedro Barrail's designs relate to the disruptions of time and space in the artworks of Daniela Ortiz and Chiachio & Gianonne. The significance of these creations may contain the seed of what Alejandro A. Vallega has called the "displacement of the images of coloniality."[4] This is achieved by altering the inherited boundaries of what we think is possible, so that "we are left with the possibility of looking for new configurations of images." We are also left with the chance of creating first the immediacy and then the *present,* which is the space and the time of the new territories for which some have vocally yearned for so long.

---

3) Pedro Barrail, e-mail correspondence with the author, July 14, 2013.

4) Alejandro A. Vallega, "Displacements: Beyond the Coloniality of Images," *Research in Phenomenology*, 41, no. 2 2011): 206–27.

Between Limit and Possibility: The Visual Culture of Bricolage in 1990s Cuba

Blanca Serrano Ortiz de Solórzano

Cardboard furniture, rice-peel bricks, a grapefruit "steak," and a fan built with the engine of a washing machine. These are among the do-it-yourself goods one can find in *Con Nuestros Propios Esfuerzos: Algunas experiencias para enfrentar el Periodo Especial en Tiempo de Paz* (With Our Own Efforts: Some Experiences to Face the Special Period in a Time of Peace), a book published by the Cuban government in 1992 (Fig. 1).[1] Seven years later, in a performance piece by the collective Desde Una Pragmática Pedagógica (DUPP) at a Havana department store called La Época, the artists mingled their art with the store's merchandise. Inside the display window, two women wearing clothing and accessories of recycled plastic posed dramatically next to store mannequins in suits (Fig. 2). These two examples—a book of instructions and a performance piece—demonstrate the Cuban bricolage phenomenon, a repurposing of material to create whatever is needed. *Con Nuestros Propios Esfuerzos* is a virtual manual on do-it-yourself—how to manufacture almost anything, from machinery to medicine, toys to musical instruments—a compilation of the myriad domestic tricks that Cubans have used to survive with a severe scarcity of resources.[2] And DUPP's performance piece called attention to the increasing economic divide between the Cuban people and foreign tourists (La Época's typical customers). The relation between art and the culture of bricolage in 1990s Cuba is evident in these and other exemplary works from the period.

In 1991, after the dissolution of the Soviet Union (Cuba's main ally and source of economic and military support), Cuba sank into a dramatic economic crisis that lasted almost a decade.[3] These years of hardship became known as the Special Period in Time of Peace.[4] Survival was challenging, and the aggravating shortages of virtually everything forced people to repurpose and reuse their possessions in imaginative ways that drew on a long-established mind-set. Since the beginning of the United States embargo in 1960, Cuba had not only learned how to adapt to its isolation, which meant an almost total exclusion from international trade, but had also prepared for an eventual attack from the United States by training engineers and mechanics.[5] The circumstances had equipped the population to handle potential threats, and perhaps because of this, the Cubans responded to the lack of goods with creative and efficient solutions. Havana became a cityscape of incongruous houses and extravagant objects that defied regional, temporal, and stylistic categories. The homemade items of this wide-scale, spontaneous phenomenon were all functional and visually compelling testaments to the citizens' response to political failure. Moreover, the worn-out aspect of Havana during this period, and the efforts by the people to increase the longevity of their belongings—rarely discarding them for new ones—inspired many Cuban artists of that generation, in both the form and content of their work.

---

1) All translations are by the author unless otherwise noted.
2) This book was published in response to the great success of a similar volume, edited by the army in 1991, titled *El Libro de la Familia*.
3) In 1989, the exchange with the USSR accounted for 85 percent of the island's trade, with 80 percent of Cuban food supplies coming from Eastern Europe. From 1991 to 1994, the Cuban GDP decreased 36 percent, and consumption in the island dropped by 40 percent. Shortages of food, water, medicine, electricity, and fuel were also dramatic. See Joseph S. Tulchin and Elizabeth Bryan, *Cambios en la sociedad cubana desde los noventa* (Washington DC: Woodrow Wilson International Center for Scholars Latin American Program, 2005), 99.
4) The Communist Party first used this cryptic designation for a series of austerity measures in *Cuba en el mes*, August 1990, 27.
5) Inspired by Ernesto Che Guevara's slogan "worker, build your machine," the Communist government encouraged the Cuban people to learn to repair their own machinery, spawning a movement called National Association of Innovators and Rationalists.

Using the urban environment as site, source, and idiom, Cuban art of the 1990s responded to the problems of Special Period Cuba. The artists' engagement with the architectural and material ruins of Havana was twofold: on one hand, it responded to the crisis of the socialist project in Cuba (and therefore also to poverty and emigration), and on the other, it valued the way these transformations of buildings and objects pointed to positive, alternative economic systems and represented a powerful civic initiative. Up until the present day, artists such as Ernesto Oroza, Carlos Garaicoa, and Los Carpinteros—almost all represented in *New Territories*—have remained mesmerized by the manipulation of objects and buildings accomplished by the Cuban people.

Oroza's interest lies in the different transformational strategies (such as reparation, repurposing, and reinvention) that Cubans developed to overcome almost all the limitations of a given object in order to make its use more economical.[6] He researches, collects, and documents vernacular designs from all over the island, and studies their diversity and significance. The photographic series *TV Aerial* (1999) is part of his larger project, *Objects of Necessity* (1997–2006), which parallels his *Architecture of Necessity* project, also included in the exhibition. In these photographs, he highlights the ingenuity and efficiency of an object alteration that could be found on almost any Cuban roof: TV aerials made with metal food trays from cafeterias, such as those in hospitals, schools, and prisons (Fig. 3). The antennas illustrate not only the standardization of most commercial goods in socialist Cuba (in this case, cafeteria trays), but also the rapidly growing popularity and widespread practice of similar strategies of modification on the island (here, the extended use of trays as satellite dishes). Another item that represents a milestone in what Oroza refers to as the "technological disobedience" of the Cubans is the "rikimbili" (Fig. 4).[7] Rikimbilis are extremely popular yet illegal motorcycles that are constructed by adding the engine from a different machine to an existing bicycle. According to the artist, these motorcycles represent the courage of the people to face complex technology and to flout the object's authority.[8]

In the mid-1990s, Carlos Garaicoa developed his series of imaginary architecture, which includes *La Maravilla* (1995–96) and *Hotel Rivoli, A Place Where the Blood Flows* (1993–95), based on the decrepit buildings of Havana. In these works, he reflects on the concepts of utopia and dystopia in relation to the ruins of the capital, while he "attempted to correct the city's history."[9] *On the Construction of the Real Tower of Babel* (1994–95) consists of a photograph of the wood scaffolding that shores up the corner of a majestic yet decaying arcaded colonial building, and an ink drawing of the same setting (Figs. 5–6). In the drawing, Garaicoa modifies the original image by adding three fantastical pyramidal protuberances to its roof. He also handwrites a verse from the Bible: "Come, let us build ourselves a city with a tower that reaches into the sky" (Genesis 11:4).[10] In this work, Garaicoa draws attention to the fragility of architecture and ideology, while also proposing a delirious construction that seems as sterile as the original, despite overcoming its deficiencies. He also ponders the subjectivity of landscape as a traditional genre of art history.

---

6) For Oroza's understanding of these concepts, see Ernesto Oroza, "Desobediencia tecnológica: De la revolución al revolico," last modified June 6, 2012, www.ernestooroza.com/?s=refuncionalizacion&search-submit=.

7) Ernesto Oroza, *Statements of Necessity* (Miami: Alonso Art, 2008), 4.

8) Manuel Cullen and Ernesto Oroza, "Revolución de la Desobediencia," *Hecho en Buenos Aires* 14, no. 161, (December 2013): 9.

9) Alma Ruiz, *Carlos Garaicoa: Capablanca's Real Passion* (Los Angeles: Museum of Contemporary Art, 2005), 14.

10) In Spanish on the artwork: "Y dijeron, vamos, edifiquémonos una ciudad y una torre cuya cúspide llegue al cielo."

The artist collective Los Carpinteros adopted their name from the way they first worked, using wood and carpentry tools. The name also makes a statement about their interest in the collective authorship of crafts.[11] Before their oeuvre of nonfunctional Duchampian hybrids, such as a humorous fire-extinguisher Christmas decoration and *Trash-Shopping Cart*, Los Carpinteros executed works that commented on the past of Cuba in relation to its present, and paid homage to traditional cabinetmaking techniques.[12] *Marquilla Cigarrera Cubana* (1993) is an oil painting with a monumental woodwork frame that purposefully brings to mind a large-scale cigar box (Fig. 8). This piece alludes to the history of the tobacco industry on the island, while it also harks back to the craftsmanship from those earlier times. Executed with pieces of wood found by the artists in the abandoned mansions of Havana, the ornately carved frame is decorated with a heraldic symbol composed of two hammers and a paintbrush. The small painting—a humorous scene that portrays two of the artists naked—ironically references the picturesque genre scenes that adorned traditional cigar boxes.[13]

The worn-down nature of Havana during the Special Period is subject to ambivalent yet complementary readings in the work of these artists. Oroza underlines the role of necessity as the motor behind the people's creations, Garaicoa stresses the frustration and helplessness generated by buildings falling into disrepair, and Los Carpinteros emphasize the absurdity of the waste inherent in the system. However, these artists also value the creative inventiveness of civic reformatting initiatives in Cuba, and they see a hopeful and promising force for change in the spontaneous and collective reshaping of the cityscape, and the alternative modes of consumption this phenomenon indicates. Thus, they read the bricolage culture in Cuba as both "limit and possibility."[14] Today, the work of these artists is less closely tied to the local context of 1990s Havana, than to the global interest in recycling and sustainable architecture. Yet they still share a preoccupation with the boundaries between art, crafts, and design, and they celebrate internationally the popular saying "Every Cuban is a mechanic."[15]

---

11) For Los Carpinteros explaining the origin of their name, see Gudrun Ankele, Daniela Zyman, Francesca von Habsburg, and Paulo Herkenhoff, *Los Carpinteros: Handwork—Constructing the World* (New York: Distributed Art Publishers, 2010), 16–17.
12) Los Carpinteros collective was founded in 1991 in Havana by Marco Antonio Castillo Valdes, Dagoberto Rodríguez Sánchez, and Alexandre Arrechea Jesus Zambrano. Arrechea was part of the group until 2003.
14) Oroza, *Statements of Necessity*, 18: "The house is limit and possibility. It's a prison and, at the same time, an asset. Havana's transformed houses adjust themselves to legal, economic, cultural and physical limits. These very limits enunciate/articulate the city's architecture. Architecture is limit and possibility."
15) See Rachel Weiss, *To and From Utopia in the New Cuban Art* (Minneapolis: University of Minnesota Press, 2011), 1.

Fig. 1 Covers of the books *El libro de la Familia* and *Con Nuestros Propios Esfuerzos*
Photo: Ernesto Oroza
Courtesy of Ernesto Oroza

Fig. 2 Beverly Mojena
Beverly top plastic, 1999
Performance at the department store La Época in Havana, 1999
Photo: René Francisco
Courtesy of Galería DUPP

Fig. 3 Ernesto Oroza
TV antenna made out of metal trays from public diners, 1999
Photo: Ernesto Oroza and Penelope de Bozzi
Courtesy of Ernesto Oroza

Fig. 4 Ernesto Oroza
Rikimbili, 2005
Photo: Ernesto Oroza
Courtesy of Ernesto Oroza

Fig. 5 Carlos Garaicoa
On the Construction of the Real Tower of Babel, 1994-1995 (detail); color photograph
19.68 x 23.62 in.
(50 x 60 cm)
Courtesy of the collection of Saul Dennison, New York

Fig. 6 Carlos Garaicoa
On the Construction of the Real Tower of Babel
1994-1995 (detail)
Ink on architecture paper
98.42 x 60.62 in.
(250 x 154 cm)
Courtesy of the collection of Saul Dennison, New York

Fig. 7 Los Carpinteros
(Marco Castello, Dagubetro Rodriguez, and Alexandre Arrechea), *Marquilla Cigarrera Cubana*, 1993
Wood, oil, canvas
65.35 x 84 x 3.15 in.
(166 x 213 x 8 cm)
Courtesy of the collection of Morris & Helen Belkin Art Gallery, Vancouver, Canada; University of British Columbia, Vancouver, Canada

ESSAYS

Merging High and Low: Materials in Brazilian Contemporary Artistic Production

Nessia Leonzini Pope and Fabiana Lopes

The use of everyday objects has been a strategy in contemporary art on a global scale frequently associated with the introduction of the readymade by Marcel Duchamp in 1913. However, the relevance of this strategy in specific cultural contexts is informed by cosmologies that do not necessarily correspond with the European tradition. In Brazil, such an undertaking is often connected to elements of the *cultura popular* (popular culture), yielding to a rich dialogue between contemporary and traditional, local and global.

Since the mid-1950s and 1960s, when Lygia Clark and Hélio Oiticica transformed common material into spaces of physical expression, their conceptual approach has become a cornerstone for subsequent generations of artists. With a series of sensorial experiences Lygia Clark dissolved the boundaries between art and life, redirecting the focus of her investigation toward the body. She deployed this strategy by using "relational objects"—objects she created with a range of everyday materials, including plastic bags, air, water, stones, shells, seeds, pantyhose, ping-pong balls, and sand, to name but a few.

Cildo Meireles's oeuvre takes on the legacy of materials and the tactile world of commonplace motifs to build on a closer relationship between spatial perception and physical engagement. With native objects, Meireles constructs a powerful symbolic system with dense political charge. For example, *Através* (1983–89) is a monumental installation that includes a collection of quotidian materials and objects, such as iron gates, shower curtains, and shattered glass, among various other domestic and industrial materials (Fig. 1). The work presents a striking perception of space and provides an immediate tactile experience associated with fragility and pain, as if walking on broken glass. Through this work, the artist confronts his moment in time[1] while raising questions related to social inequality, censorship, and historical legacies.

If Cildo Meireles's day-to-day vocabulary establishes a system with political density, Rivane Neuenschwander's syntax elevates the language she creates into a heavily metaphorical position. Using garlic skins (glued together to form a quilt), fruits, talcum powder, and other mundane materials, Neuenschwander suggests a reflection on the brevity of life. In one of her most memorable works *Continente/Nuvem* (2008), installed in a traditional farmhouse-style dating from 1874, the artist brings into play tiny Styrofoam balls that are propelled by air and graciously float on a semitransparent ceiling structure covered by fabric (Figs. 2–3). This random, poetic dance of monochromatic shapes that mediates the space between the viewer and the outside world provides an enchanting experience, one that lingers, revealing new aesthetic meanings with the passage of time.

In the 1980s, when young artists from Brazil began exhibiting in galleries and museums worldwide, critics endeavored to label their art with a "Brazilian character," usually defined as exotic, happy, and saturated with local flavors, their work, however, was far from being random iterations of a national voice or simplistic representations of the *local*.

Fig. 1 Cildo Meireles, *Através*, 1983-1989
Various materials; dimensions variable
Courtesy of the Inhotim Collection,
Minas Gerais, Brazil

Fig. 2 Rivane Neuenschwander, *Continent-Cloud*, 2007
Correx, aluminum, Styrofoam balls, fluorescent lighting, electric fans, timers; dimensions variable; photo: Steve White Courtesy of Stephen Friedman Gallery, London, United Kingdom Inhotim Collection, Minas Gerais, Brazil

Fig. 3 Rivanne Neuenschwander, *Continent-Cloud*, 2007
Correx, aluminum, Styrofoam balls, fluorescent lighting, electric fans, timers; dimensions variable; photo: Studio Hans Wilschut; courtesy of Museum Boijmans van Beuningen, Rotterdam, Netherlands; Inhotim Collection, Minas Gerais, Brazil

The application of humble everyday materials is widespread in Brazil and is related to the notion of *cultura popular*. Cultural theorist Jesús Martín-Barbero defined the concept of *popular* as not solely related to a rural past but rather with boundaries that extend to the present context—a present informed by modernity, tinted by *mestizaje*, and framed by urban complexities.[2] In this same context, Cuban art critic Gerardo Mosquera pointed out that in Cuba the relationship between the "popular" and the "cultured" can be intricate, giving rise to a creative process in which refined work can be constructed out of popular values and perspectives. Mosquera cautioned, however, that the vernacular is not "inspiring the 'high'," but is "*doing* the 'high'."[3]

The work by Marcos Reis Peixoto, known as Marepe, is deeply rooted in popular tradition. Informed by his experiences in his small hometown of Santo Antonio de Jesus, Marepe repurposes *stuff* that is typical of native households—brooms, plastic buckets, ceramic water filters, ironing boards, musical instruments, and pots and pans—into striking sculptural works that transcend their vernacular sources to acquire universal meanings (Fig. 4). While Duchamp's transformative gesture may be hovering over the work, Marepe's concerns form an intrinsic dialogue with the fragile economy of subsistence in rural Brazil through a direct appropriation of its system of language and symbols.

The practice of weaving within many indigenous communities is a collective activity undertaken exclusively by women who share meanings and symbols derived from social, educational, and ritualistic contexts. Their weaving results in aesthetic objects that also have a defined function within the social system (food container, bed, rug, and so on).[4] Maria Nepomuceno employs craftspeople who use methods directly inspired by the indigenous traditions and craft techniques of weaving and straw braiding. Her vibrant sculptures made of ropes and straw, beads, ceramics, and other found objects crawl on the floors, go up and down the walls, sneak onto outside surfaces before inching back to their starting points. Nevertheless, Nepomuceno appropriates the skill and relocates it within the context of individual creativity. The results of her artistic efforts are purely aesthetic (see page 117).

Nepomuceno's forms take the notion of sensory perception to the next level as she has an athletic, immersive relationship with the material, using strength to weave and pull the fibers, twisting them around into shapes recalling Jean-Paul Gaultier's cone-shaped bras. She lies on the floor to adjust a knot, or crouches down to sew on a bead or place a pearl necklace on a bed of woven straw. The work is usually distinguished by forestlike lush volumes, sensual forms, and bright colors—features that are often (and misguidedly) read as essentially Brazilian. The intriguing aspect of Nepomuceno's practice, however, rests not on such features or even on her borrowing from ancestral traditions, but on what remains, what is transformed, and on the implications, if any, of these operations.

For Rodrigo Almeida, material appears as a synthesis of a given culture, yet it is not articulated as essential or authentic. It does

1) Framed by twenty-one years of dictatorship (1964–85), Meireles's work during this period is the link between the Neo-Concrete aesthetic and subsequent generations of artists.
2) Jesus Martín-Barbero, *Communication, Culture and Hegemony: From the Media to Mediations*, trans. Elizabeth Fox and Robert A. White (Newbury Park: SAGE Publications, 1993). The concept of *mestizaje* sheds light on the definition of *cultura popular*. According to Martín-Barbero, within the scope of Latin American tradition, *mestizaje* (the nonsymmetric coexistence of "the cultural histories of the Native American, the Afro-Americans, and the people of European descent") represents a defining category. It "does not refer to something that happened in the past, but what we are today. *Mestizaje* is not simply a racial fact, but the explanation of our existence, a web of temporalities, places, memories and imagination" (ibid., 151).
3) Gerardo Mosquera, "Good-Bye Identity, Welcome Difference," *Third Text* 56 (2001): 32.
4) According to Ticio Escobar, indigenous cosmology does not include the concept of an autonomous art. Art is separate from the realms of religion, society, economy, power, and sex. Beauty, in this context, is an argument to promote goals that are beyond aesthetics. Julio Ramos, "La contemporaneidad de Ticio Escobar," interview, *80grados*, August 31, 2012, online at www.80grados.net.

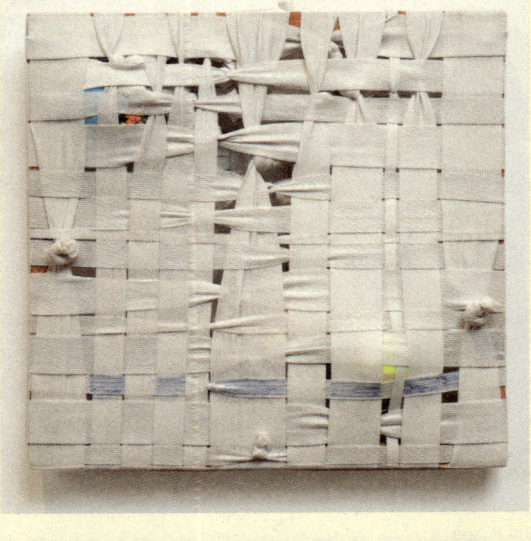

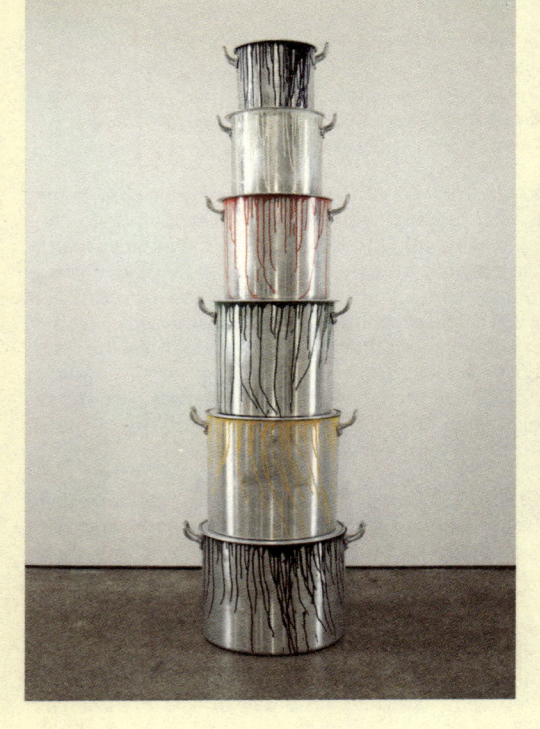

Fig. 4 Marepe Você tem fome de que?, 2008
Paint on aluminium,
102 x 30.75 x 24.75 in.
(259 x 78 x 62.8 cm)
Courtesy of Anton Kern Gallery, New York

Fig. 5 Jarbas Lopes
Untitled, 2013
Foam globe balls, tennis balls, ballpoint pen, and shells in woven elastic on wooden frames
13.7 x 11 in. (35 x 38 cm)
Courtesy of Tilton Gallery, New York

Fig. 6 Adriana Varejão
Azulejões (Curl & Sleeping Arabesque), diptych, 2004
Oil and plaster on canvas
43 5/16 x 43 5/16 in.
(110 x 110 cm) each
Photo: Vincente de Mello
Courtesy of Inhotim Collection, Minas Gerais, Brazil

5) Handmade weaving refers to the practice of indigenous Brazilian people and has been previously used by Lopes.
6) Regarding his *Sandcastles* series, Muniz has written: "While touring the chateaux of the Loire and other castles in Europe I took the opportunity to sketch the buildings with my camera lucida. After I met an engineer from Intel, who confirmed that with the use of nanotechnology a drawing could be made in a grain of sand, my castle drawings came to mind. It seemed to me that the technical approach involved in their making could be the start of an intertwining of scales and technologies. In 2003 we started some tests. It was however, only after a residency at MIT Media Lab I was able to fully develop the project. The castles are etched with

not directly represent Afro-Brazilian and the indigenous aesthetic, nor is it fully informed by "dissolved European culture in Brazil," as the designer puts it. *Africa Chair* (2009)—created by wrapping colorful bungee cords around a wood structure forming layers of yellow, blue, and green—has a rhythm and design that somewhat alludes to African culture in Brazil, although the designer did not select the materials to be obviously Afro-Brazilian. The materials bend, deform, and intertwine with the structure, creating a spontaneous movement. Almeida's practice centers on the concept of limbo, the place in between, a transitional space well-supplied with nuances of meaning. In this gray zone, the notions of deficiency, imperfection and foreign influence become part of the object's *raison d'être*. Dissolution, discontinuity, reconfiguration, and repurposing are fused into the artist's creative repertoire.

While in dialogue with the popular culture, Jarbas Lopes shapes his narrative by an experiential, sensory exercise written in the materials themselves. In 2013 he created paintings that combine woven elastics lightly dipped in ink along the edges with rattles inserted within the surfaces, and knots. These canvases can be seen, held, shaken and touched on both sides.[5] The large elegant works casually leaning against the wall blur the definition of art and object, radically breaking with pictorial formalism (Fig. 5). The concept of turning subject matter into an art object is also embraced by Fernanda Gomes, for whom pieces of fabric, thread, glass, stones, feathers, wood, burnt cigarette paper, and anything else she comes across while preparing an exhibition are incorporated into the artistic process. Some of these materials remain untouched, some are combined with others or painted white—the only color employed by the artist—and some become part of the architectural landscape.

The dialogue between high and low—between technology and materials—runs through much of Vik Muniz's prolific production. Although his subject matter is informed by the use of nontraditional materials, such as chocolate, sugar, wire, paper, garbage, and sand, Muniz has had a long relationship with cutting-edge technology, from high-resolution cameras to his work in MIT's research labs. He makes drawings that are later transformed into a photographic form, their final stage. In the series *Pictures of Garbage* (see page 150), each image is composed of piles of rubbish, such as empty bottles, toilet seats, dirty clothes, old tires, refrigerators, and car parts. These items were sorted and arranged by type in a vast hangar-like studio and photographed with an 8 x 10 view camera, twenty meters above the ground. Sheer scale requires each composition to be visually processed from a bird's-eye view.

In recent projects, Muniz contributes to the development of microscopic images onto miniscule grains of sand, which later become large, high-resolution prints of drawings of castles on a grain of sand.[6] He has also collaborated with MIT postdoctoral fellow Tal Danino on a technique that enables him to draw with live bacteria.[7] Muniz's pictures combine the complexity and variety of the technological tools with an aesthetic and intellectual approach that deliberates over the nature of visual perception and representation. However, while the scientific world focuses on the specific application of the material, Muniz concentrates on the Gesamtkunstwerk, a synthesis of art forms, the total creative process.

In the practices of contemporary Brazilian artists, one can find the history of the country, spanning from centuries of social and artistic traditions, from twenty-first century modernity back to the colonial period. Such is the case of Adriana Varejão's *Azulejões*[8] (Big Blue Tiles), an ongoing series that began in 2000 and was inspired by the formal design of traditional Portuguese tiles—a prosaic object assimilated by Brazilian culture and applied to local architecture, from its opulent churches to the common *botecos* (neighborhood bars) found throughout the country (Fig. 6). Varejão's interest lies less in the exuberance of forms and colors of the tiles than in the subversive political appeal that underlines its references from the Baroque aesthetic to Brazil's colonial past. *Azulejões* is a meditation on historical, cultural, and racial issues derived from the country's colonization and the dissimilarities of its heritage.

Impelled by the need to revisit Brazil's history, many other artists set off to freely absorb the rich vocabulary of the vernacular—navigating the realm of materials, simple and sophisticated, popular and erudite, new and old—attributing different dimensions and meanings to the entities they encounter in their day-to-day lives.[9]

---

a focus ion beam and 'photographed' with a scanning electron microscope. Although photography is a bit of a misnomer, since no photons were actually used. The focused ion beam (FIB) heats up a gallium filament, which emits ions. These ions are directed towards the grain and controlled by a computer to ablate the castle drawing. After the drawing is complete, the electron microscope uses a beam of electrons (similar to a television tube) to scan the grain and create the image." Vik Muniz, statement, in *Vik Muniz: Pictures of Anything*, exh. cat. (Tel Aviv: Tel Aviv Museum of Art, 2014).

7) On his *Colonies* series, Muniz has written: "During my residency at the MIT Media Lab, I was able to pursue and develop ideas that I have been storing for many years.... To make these images, a silicon stamp of the image was created using photolithography in a clean-room facility at MIT. This stamp was placed on a dish coated with collagen, a molecule known to stick to cells, and plasma was used to remove collagen except where the stamp is not present. Cells were then added to a culture dish and washed several times, resulting in an image with an approximate size of one centimeter and features on the order of the size of cells (10 micrometers) that are imaged on a microscope. Ibid.

8) Although Varejão began the Azulejões series in 2000, she has used Portuguese tile in her work since 1994.

9) The undervalued role of materials in Brazilian art has been a subject of numerous conversations between Nessia Pope and art historian Olivier Berggruen.

ESSAYS

Productive Conflicts of Interest

Interview with Jorge Pardo by Regine Basha

Looking back to the 1990s, a period in both art and design where boundaries were often blurred, Jorge Pardo stands out as having thrust forward a sustained and complex, sometimes even controversial, conversation with the tenets of architecture and design in his work. Born in Havana in 1963, Pardo moved to Chicago with his family in 1969 and then to Los Angeles in 1983 for graduate school at the Art Center College of Design, Pasadena. He believes that much of his experience and attitude regarding art was shaped by being an immigrant in Los Angeles and immersing himself in that city's unique architectural history. Throughout the 1990s, Pardo traveled back and forth to Mexico—Guadalajara and Oaxaca—to work with artisanal craft production, such as ceramic and textiles, which began to inform his overall work in nontraditional but significant ways. Projects such as *4166 Sea View Lane* (built as an artwork in 1997–98 for the Museum of Contemporary Art (MOCA), Los Angeles, and his home for more than a decade) and the design of Dia: Chelsea's bookstore in New York City not only boldly carved out space to conceive of architecture as expanded sculpture, but also pushed institutions beyond their usual comfort zones. Though Pardo may never really have been considered a Latin American artist, nor may he want to be, his particular history and position in both worlds has allowed new possibilities and productive conflicts that reflect how cultural stimulus flows. For the past several years, Pardo has lived and worked in Mérida, Mexico.

Regine Basha: Can I ask if you were exposed to design through the Art Center Pasadena?

Jorge Pardo: The school was basically an illustration school and a product design school that focused more on packaging. I arrived in 1983 and, by 1985, people like Mike Kelly, Stephen Prina, John Baldessari, and Jeremy Gilbert-Rolfe were a big presence in the art department. I started out in painting and moved into a quasi-conceptual photography. But I sensed that art school was a bubble, and I wondered if I was really interested in being an artist, if one could do it without it being this kind of social laboratory.

RB: Did you have a sense that you wanted to be more connected to, say, "everyday life" like more of a worker than an artist who only functions in a closed circuit?

JP: I didn't have any delusions about art being kind of a rarified system of knowledge and objects that get exchanged; I have no problem with that, in fact I embrace that. It was really more a question of how I want to live my life. So I just started to make work and taught myself how to be a carpenter, really . . . a pretty good one. I started making these things that kind of had problems—most of the problems are anecdotal. Like the piece you said you liked about my mom and Corbusier (Fig. 1). I started to look hard at architecture, as kind of the cultural anchor of a city like Los Angeles. Unlike New York, we don't really have an international gallery scene. I mean there are a lot of galleries and artists, but for the art world, LA is kind of the minor leagues.

RB: Yes, especially at the time.

JP: I started to look at architecture because there were things you could experience in a very quotidian way . . . as if you were going to a museum in New York to see some Jackson Pollock paintings—you couldn't do that here. What you could do was go to your friend's house, which was actually a shitty dilapidated Rudolf Schindler house.[1] And if you inquired about the history of that place as an object, really interesting things emerged. These were

---

1) Rudolf Schindler (1887–1953) was an Austrian-born American architect whose most important works were built in or near Los Angeles during the early to mid-twentieth century.

truly modernist places, high modernist architecture. And those examples weren't even derivative examples but were historically concurrent with anything happening in Europe with architecture at the time.

This was interesting because we are living in a city that probably has the most important domestic architecture in the world from the 1920s to the 1960s or 1970s. I just became interested in that. I thought, what can I do with this? I'm not an architect, I'm not trained as an architect, and I have no interest in becoming an architect, but there were places where interesting overlaps would happen. I started making exhibitions with things in them that were discreet, some of them big, some smaller, and the titles were anecdotal and, after a while, this was not interesting to me. I started to become less and less interested in the methodologies of conceptual art and more interested in how you can make works that require a kind of a real autonomy in terms of consumption; by that I mean that you had to be in them, you had to experience them. You know, architecture, if framed properly, can ask a lot of questions even about sculpture of the last forty or fifty years. What happens if an artist doesn't take for granted the nature of the space the work is being made in, and instead begins the work with that space? That's where it comes from.

RB: Would you say there is a kind of narrative that you are interested in? You mention the anecdotal, and I'm wondering if there is an implicit narrative.

JP: I'm more interested in the processional experience—like something you have to move through—like a procession of events that are the work. The ideas unfold as you walk through a room. What I try to continue to do is resist a narrative or totalization

Fig. 1 Jorge Pardo,
Me And My Mom, 1990
Copper, cloth
36 x 36 x 36 in. (91.4 x 91.4 x 91.4 cm) approx.
Courtesy of the artist and Petzel, New York

Fig. 2/3 Jorge Pardo,
4166 Sea View Lane, 1998
Museum of Contemporary Art, Los Angeles
Courtesy of the artist and Petzel, New York

of the work. I was just interested in where the work begins. And how you use your body, which is really a very traditional sculptural problem.

RB: In those early encounters with LA architecture, was there an interest in what could be seen as a collapse of cultures or a confluence of time-zones; for instance, you're in LA, you're looking at modernist houses, in the 1980s when Postmodernism prevailed, it seems to be both a cultural displacement and an aesthetic displacement.

JP: I started making things, then put them in my house, then at friend's houses, then sometimes at galleries, and I was learning, so I wasn't really thinking about progressive methodologies. It was a way to have a relationship with the city. How do you make interesting spatial work, how do you make a work that was actually a place?

In the early 1990s when I was asked to exhibit my work at MOCA, I thought, well, this is a larger, more ambitious place, so I thought of making a house [now called 4166 Sea View Lane] (Figs. 2-3); even though I'm not really qualified to make such things, I was more interested in what happens when you instrumentalize those disabilities? What would folk architecture look like? You could really only see it through the matrix of traditional sculpture at that time. Architects and others were definitely doing things like Watts Towers[2] at the time, but I wasn't really thinking about that. I was more interested in how you take that and have it communicate with contemporary sculptural issues—of site, place, etc.

RB: Issues based on the writings of Robert Smithson and Gordon Matta-Clark[3] for instance?

JP: Yeah and a bunch of other people too. Art Center was a very theoretical program, and it was a lot about how to set up a really interesting optical object and about what the problem of a painting was.

RB: So that set you up for a kind of double-vision?

JP: Yeah, if the work can operate in different fields simultaneously, something interesting has to happen because it's not something I can really predict. If it's really interesting, I can just observe . . . instead of making artwork, I could collect "behavior." Making these things actually affects the way you behave; I was always interested in that.

RB: What's also interesting about the MOCA house project is that it allowed people to go back into the landscape of LA and look at everything else as sculpture. There was a flip effect.

JP: Yes, certainly more so about sculpture, because at the time, the most progressive architecture was from the theses coming out of SCI-Arc (Southern California Institute of Architecture). Their take on how to "arti-fy" architecture seemed kind of simplistic to me, because instead of making drawings, they would go out and find a carburetor and make a house out of it, things like that. It seemed like a very exhausted model, like object making from the beginning of the century. The more interesting contemporary models for me were coming out of Europe with Rem Koolhaas rather than out of LA. I was more interested in that parallel history, living in a city where thousands of modernist houses hadn't been destroyed. And I would go to see them and was very interested in them. Rudolf Schindler designed about forty houses! He was an eccentric. Everything was used; it wasn't so much about making houses for clients. There are some weird ones where they used terracotta tiles in the wrong way. I was very interested in that. Those gestures were valuable to me, but not necessarily important to other people—especially those in the field.

RB: Have you ever had a situation where an architectural team or firm asked you to participate in an architectural project?

JP: Not really. Not yet.

RB: Did Dia: Chelsea's lobby and bookshop come closest to something like that? (Fig. 4)

JP: Yeah, but Dia was a very traditional invitation. . . . When I was invited to make a work there, I was asked to just do something on the first floor. It could have been anything.

RB: So it wasn't "Can you design our bookshop?"

JP: No, I took the initiative to do that. But it was very clear when Dia came forward that it was also to be an exhibition.

RB: I'm curious if, whether through your background or through working and living in Mexico, you've become more interested in working in a Latin American context?

JP: No, not really. No, I think everything that is happening with me in Latin America is about the First World. My perception of Latin America is pretty much what it has always been—that it's a beautiful place, with so many fucked-up conflicts of interest, with a brutal relationship between the poor and the rich, and it's impossible for anything other than the perverse to come out of it. I mean the best thing you can do in Latin American is just get lost.

RB: In a Jorge Luis Borges kind of way?

---

2) The Watts Towers are a series of seventeen interconnected towers built by Simon Rodia, a construction worker and Italian immigrant, over a period of thirty-three years from 1921 to 1954.

3) Smithson and Matta-Clark are conceptual artists of the 1970s whose investigations of architectural space and land usage have become an important resource for many contemporary artists.

4) José Noé Suro is the owner of a Tlaquepaque-based ceramics factory which has collaborated with numerous contemporary artists.

JP: I happen to love Borges, he's actually my favorite Latin American writer. He's so much fun to read. He really makes worlds that abide by very strange and odd psychological states. All the others are still tethered to a certain Latin American surrealism, but with Borges, it's all placeless.

RB: It reminds me of what you said about your work once: "It's hard to distinguish the difference between making it and consuming it," which is very much the experience of Borges, where you are a reader and a writer—it's constantly collapsing onto itself.

JP: Yeah, you don't need him once it starts to operate; you don't think of the writer. He is actually just making space, you get lost in it. It's so compelling, it becomes your space—you're dislodged from the notion of reading somehow.

RB: When you began working in Mexico—for instance, with Suro Ceramics[4] in Guadalajara—did it usher in a whole new way of working?

JP: I went to Mexico in the early to mid-1990s for the first time, and I was invited to do these tapestries. When I got there, I noticed the artisanal tradition of blown glass, ceramics, all kinds of crafty things, so I ended up working with a variety of other materials. It was interesting to tap into that; that is one of the reasons I'm moving to Mexico.

RB: Was there a particular craft that you were interested in when you got there?

JP: Well, in the 1960s and 1970s, Mexico had a pretty thriving textile industry, but by the 1990s, it had already been taken over by India or China, so it's not even like those things are really made there anymore. I became interested in the Yucatan, because Mérida has this colonial core, and it's weird and surrounded by these little villages that have been uninhabited for the last few thousand years. I just like it there. I like living there, going to the ocean. But yeah, making things work there requires a lot of effort.

RB: But you mentioned once that since there is broadband Internet service in Mérida, it's not really as remote as one would think. We struggle to articulate this phenomena with ridiculous words like "glocal."

JP: I'd like to make works that actually behave the way the world is moving. Not because I necessarily want to mirror it, but more to take seriously how things really happen.

RB: Tell me more about *Tecoh*, your new project in Mérida. You mention how you'd like to make Yucatan a lens through which you can see the rest of the world. I found that really interesting.

JP: *Tecoh* was commissioned by Mexican patrons, Roberto Hernández and Claudia Madrazo. They bought this hacienda—a colonial ruin . . . I like that it's got a very odd kind of plasticity and scale that you don't normally see.

Fig. 4 Jorge Pardo
Project, 2000
Three parts: lobby, bookshop, gallery
Overall dimensions: 108 x 108 ft. (33 x 33 m)
Courtesy of David Sundberg/Esto

The most important thing about it is what it is going to be—is it going to be a school? A house? A corporate library? That's really what mandates all the decisions. We just went to the jungle and found interesting ways to work with it, but we still need to know how it's going to behave.

RB: What would be the driving principle behind it?

JP: The immersion into the Yucatan and how to be in that place.

RB: Are you involved with envisioning the program there?

JP: Oh yeah, we've been doing a lot there so far, I brought my students and I did a workshop with David Adjaye, the architect. Mostly content based on the Yucatan. The Hernándezes have a deep interest in conservation, and so three or four times a year they have a study group come. But *Tecoh* really belongs to the Hernández family, so how it's read also affects them privately.

RB: Would you say it's more like a summit?

JP: It's like a very strange salon with many conflicts of interest.

ESSAYS

Toys for Adults:
Kawaii in South American Design

Magdalena Grüneisen

The phenomenon of adults collecting trendy toys made specifically for them started in the twentieth century and has since become well established. Toy design has expanded far beyond the realm of childhood, and in South America, there is a growing market for designer toys, or "art toys," aimed at the adult consumer.[1] These toys, mostly the work of young designers, range from dolls, figures, and robots, to eco-friendly objects and construction toys. Like children's toys, they are made in vinyl, plastic, wood, cloth, and metal. The resulting objects might look like pure toys, but most designer toys also serve a purpose, whether utilitarian or decorative. Their presence on an office desk might help stir the imagination and stimulate the senses, providing opportunities for a childlike enjoyment of everyday life.

The designers who engage in this field reference the work of theorists who divided and classified forms of play. Writing in 1938, Dutch cultural historian Johan Huizinga identified "higher forms of play" that are social, distinguishing them from primeval ones that are engaged in by children or animals.[2] According to his theories, the human species was characterized as much by its play as by its manner of thinking or tool using, behaviors then used as a yardstick to separate humans from other animals. Today's adult collectors of designer toys are simply drawn to something that provides amusement or enjoyment, allowing them to engage in childish things often as a way to relieve stress.

The present-day "designer toy movement" began in Japan during the mid-1990s, and gradually, Japanese popular culture developed an international audience. Japanese *manga* (comics and cartooning) and *anime* (action animations) became especially popular. Japanese characters, creatures, and games, which had originated earlier, such as Pokémon (video game), Doraemon (*manga* and *anime*), Astro Boy (known in Japan as Tetsuwan Atom, *manga* and *anime*), Hello Kitty (character), Dragon Ball (*manga* series), and even Godzilla, the old standby of science fiction movies, found new followers in the West.[3] In South America, many toy designers were influenced by *manga* and *anime* and began creating objects redolent of what the Japanese call *kawaii* (cute, adorable, childlike), a term used for all things "cute," from characters, toys, and games to food and fashion.

Kawaii figures are characterized by simple and stylized features, geometric and curvilinear shapes, vibrant colors, and an implied sense of humor. *Kawaii* objects are also strongly anthropomorphic. These aspects of Japanese pop culture and toys influenced designs for youth culture worldwide.[4] Younger generations of South American designers grew up not only knowing Mickey Mouse and Bugs Bunny, but also Japanese *anime* characters such as Astro Boy, Speed Racer, Robotech, and Sailor Moon (Fig. 2). Designers and artists exposed to Japanese toys and art in their childhoods then began to make reference to them in their adult work.[5]

---

1) Jorgelina Peciña, "Distrito de Diseño: Bs. As. piensa el diseño desde el Sur," *90mas10* (August 24, 2012), online at http://90mas10.com.
2) Johan Huizinga, *Homo Ludens: A Study of the Play-Element in Culture* (Reprint, Boston: Beacon Press, 1971), 36.
3) Graham Parkes, "The Role of Rock in the Japanese Dry Landscape Garden," in François Berthier, ed., *Reading Zen in the Rocks* (Chicago and London: University of Chicago Press, 2000), 136.
4) Brian Bremner, "In Japan, Cute Conquers All," *Bloomberg Businessweek* (June 25, 2002), online at www.businessweek.com.
5) Patricio Oliver, "Art Toys Transformers," *90mas10*, March 13, 2013, online at http://90mas10.com.

In Argentina, *kawaii* traits are evident in Fabián Bercic's brightly colored plastic sculptures, perhaps with some Buddhist influence as well (see page 158). With their familiar toylike features, these pieces look machine-made, like toys rather than sculptures. Their shiny brightness was created via polyester resin, plastic, and fiberglass that begs to be touched. Bercic's work both excites and seduces the viewer, and has a strong element of humor.

As designer toys found a place in an avant-garde playtime, they attracted critical attention, and new types of products initially developed for the young have been taken up by adults and designers.[6] *Robot Naturito* (see pages 166–167), for example, created by Satorilab (Luján Cambariere and Alejandro Sarmiento) is an eco-conscious design made from Natura Cosméticos packaging. At just 7.7 by 4.23 inches, it demonstrates how small proportions can emphasize the *kawaii* of the figure. As a designer toy, this innovative decorative object evokes fun and pleasure.

The Argentinian design group vacaValiente creates animal-shaped desk accessories from recycled leather. They have developed a range of leather finishes to create different visual effects, and, by embossing, they are able to imitate animal skin and geometric patterns.[7] Their horse-shaped desk organizer has a sophisticated yet playful design (see page 163), bringing an element of play and and even nostalgia to the workplace. Another Argentinian designer, Lola Goldstein, uses clay to create whimsical kitchenware such salt and pepper shakers (Fig. 1) or a teapot wearing a hat as a tea cozy.[8] Her style is childlike and delicate, and she works completely by hand in small numbers, with a great deal of attention to detail. Her smooth, stylized figures, with their cheerful features, appeal to a wide audience. Like vacaValiente's desk accessories, Goldstein's kitchen objects bring humor to everyday chores. These designers reference childhood and the notion that adults can simultaneously be serious and playful, curious and unconventional.

A popular form of designer toy is the paper model. Chilean designer/illustrator/artist Angello García Bassi created *Cubotoy* (see page 159), designing, sculpting, and producing each original figure. Once the form is established, it is printed on paper templates, which are then covered with a transparent adhesive for extra strength. The templates are cut into pieces and formed into the toy design. Garcia Bassi's work is influenced by urban cultural trends and by plush and vinyl toys, but there is an unmistakeable element of *kawaii* in the figures.

Understanding a toy as a design object brings a different type of awareness to toys as a creative field. The realm of play is no longer exclusive to children; that image of a child at play has been expanded to include a more flexible, age-resistant adult, one for whom the childlike qualities of curiosity and openness are important. Designer toys, whether made for home or office, for use or decoration, also may stir up memories of childhood or an intuitive emotion, while revealing—or concealing—their true nature as toys. These designer toys may carry subliminal messages and often challenge expectations, showing how aggressively South American designers have pushed the limits of convention.

Fig. 1 Lola Goldstein
Amigo Salt & Pepper Shakers, 2005
Painted ceramic, 1.5 x 2 in. (3.8 x 5 cm)
Photo: Lola Goldstein

Fig. 2 Mamegoma character, 2014
Illustration
Courtesy of San-X Co., Ltd, Japan

6) Amy F. Ogata, "Creative Playthings: Educational Toys and Postwar American Culture," *Winterthur Portfolio* 39 (Summer–Autumn 2004): 150–56.

7) Natalia Iscaro, "vacaValiente: La vaca domada," *90mas10*, August 16, 2012, online at http://90mas10.com.

8) Marco Fajardo, "Lanzan el primer libro de juguetes de papel en Chile," El Mostrador TV, January 24, 2014, online at http://www.elmostrador.cl/cultura/2013/09/06/lanzan-el-primer-libro-de-juguetes-de-papel-en-chile/.

ESSAYS

Notes on Design and Material Culture in Latin America at the Global Crossroads

Gabriela Rangel

From the Río de la Plata basin in South America to Central America, Mexico, and the Caribbean, the concept of material culture and the formal discipline of design have tended to create clashing yet intermingling force fields. Contemporary practices by postmodern designers, craft makers, and artists have resulted in encounters and divergences in the dominant perceptions of what is considered design and in the ongoing debate over the serial and/or artisanal production of objects in the region. *New Territories: Laboratories for Design, Craft and Art in Latin America* examines the world of "design" and its metonymic relationship to contemporary art and craft. The exhibition encourages an exploration of normative practices and institutional pedagogies and strategies of design that were begun in the postwar era as part of a utopian impulse of industrialization.

Historian Silvia Fernández declared that the design boom in Latin America, including the design schools that proliferated in the region between 1960 and 1970, coincided with the emergence of various public agendas regulating the politics of imports and the initiation of economic development projects representing different ideological tendencies.[1] During the Cold War, design in Latin America reached sufficient maturity to generate a regional theoretico-practical apparatus. Invaluable contributions came from, among others, Tomás Maldonado, a fascinating and controversial proponent of Argentinian Concretism, and his disciple and friend Gui Bonsiepe.[2]

By contrast, the field of material culture, which explores possible links between artifacts and social history, originated in Anglo-North American academia. As anthropologist Daniel Miller noted, material culture as a model of critical thought was revived in the 1990s and subsequently mutated "as a vanguard area liberating a range of disciplines, from museum studies to archaeology."[3] Its resurgence was part of the revisionist methodologies and the break up of meanings that shook the humanities and social sciences starting with an interrogation of the teleological certainties of modernity and its modernisms. Thus, the context for identifying objects that deserve the label of "design" often leads us into a "fluid space." This, however, becomes stultified against a background of rapid institutionalization of Latin American modernisms by museums of the United States and Europe. Design continues to be considered as an industrial discipline by modernist architects, critics, and artists. It may even be seen as existing on the periphery of aesthetic discourse. This view was at odds with the processes of industrialization that were meant to serve the material needs of vast sectors of the population: from the production of wooden toys and low-cost furniture to the construction of medical machinery. Given that industrialization was not a fully accomplished goal in Latin America, however, some objects branded and marketed as design bring together the contradictions of a field that often overlaps with aesthetics and vernacular traditions.

Paradoxically, within the flow of disciplinary interchanges between design and material culture, there may exist the space that could help us navigate the various approaches and emphases related to design in Latin America, where design has tended to be on the periphery of global discourse. We might find a model in the concept of "liquid modernity," characterized by a fluid proposition and lacking in fixed formulas and structure.

---

1) Silvia Fernández, "The Origins of Design Education in Latin America from HfG in Ulm to Globalization," *Design Issues* 22, no. 1 (Winter 2005): 3–19.
2) Tomás Maldonado founded the journals *Arturo* (1944) and *Nueva Visión* (1951) in Buenos Aires. In the 1950s, he moved to Europe and, after teaching at the Hochschule für Gestaltung (HfG), Ulm, Germany, was appointed its director, and became a major intellectual influence, not only in Europe but in Latin America as well. Gui Bonsiepe is an industrial designer, who trained at Ulm and whose work in Latin America has contributed to the expansion of industrial design in Latin America. See Silvia Fernández, ed., *Historia del diseño en América Latina y el Caribe* (Madrid: Editora Blucher, 2008).
3) Daniel Miller, ed., *Material Cultures: Why Some Things Matter* (Chicago and London: University of Chicago Press, 1998), 4.

Such a molecular concept implies rapid mobility effectively dissolving the canonical premises of modernity. As sociologist Zygmunt Bauman suggested:

> The "melting of solids," the permanent feature of modernity, has therefore acquired a new meaning, and above all has been redirected to a new target—one of the paramount effects of that redirection being the dissolution of forces which could keep the question of the political order and system on the political agenda. The solids whose turn has come to be thrown into the melting pot and which are in the process of being melted at the present time, the time of fluid modernity, are the bonds which interlock individual choices in collective projects and actions—the patterns of communication and coordination between individually conducted life policies on the one hand and political actions of human collectivities on the other.[4]

This model demonstrates the contribution of material culture to economic development and mass production. At the same time it does not shape or alter the diffuse limits and interdisciplinary competence of a broad analytical field. From its inception this field has resisted compliance with mechanical and reductive frameworks of enunciation. It has ignored the domestic sphere or an examination of the transnational identity of consumer goods according to notions of kinship, class, or gender.[5]

While mapping Latin American design and taking into account the pulsations and rhythms of regional creativity, it is appropriate to consider an observation made by design historian Victor Margolin. He posited that, if design originates and develops exclusively in serial and mass production (as maintained by Maldonado and his colleagues in the Ulm School of Design of the 1960s), this would exclude countries and nations that, never having achieved industrialization, had nonetheless produced objects through the efforts of craftspersons or small production factories in a quasi-mass fashion.[6] Such design production coincides with the dominant notion of what design is, while serving the needs of local communities. It also participates in the logic of fragmentary production in the distribution and commercialization processes of international markets.[7]

Indeed, Ulm's industrialist position when applied to the "periphery" became conditioned on, as well as challenged through, the emergence of new technologies and what might be described as de-territorialized forms of production. Globalization of production systems through outsourcing became a main characteristic of postindustrial capitalism.[8] Not incidentally, Bonsiepe shifted his research and intellectual focus to revising design as an interface and large-scale mode of interaction between users and tools. For Margolin, however, this new technological and production order has succeeded in making visible the design produced in the so-called peripheries:

There are good reasons to raise questions about a world history of design at this time, as design is spreading rapidly across the globe and practitioners from Beirut to Beijing seek national or regional precedents for their own work as well as a global context in which to locate their practices.[9]

By identifying a handful of designers and their production circuits—and also by summarily mapping a restricted and significant ensemble of design agents and initiatives—various practices and circuits in Latin America provide a postindustrial framework for design in the twenty-first century, based perhaps on an analysis of modes of production that are not necessarily anchored in regional limits. This involves considering production, consumption, and the movement of objects and artifacts as conceived according to a de-territorialized, contingent, hybrid model that is founded not on planning and serial production but on an allegorical interpretation of the pulse of genres, conventions, and symbolic constructions manifest in the mere fact of its manufacture.

However, this solution is not without risk, given the incidental form of production in countries with great social and economic disparities. Economic models are increasingly dependent on the ups and downs of both local and international markets, regardless of labor controls and regulations. Multiple vectors, including a semi-industrial system of production based on the use of artisanal techniques, traverse this force field. Then there are the symbolic strategies of twenty-first-century visual arts informed by technology vis-à-vis the crevices of modernization. To confront and contrast these colliding worlds, we propose considering the concept of tradition within the narrative framework of "liquid modernity" with the variants that might eventually undo its static, conservative, or romantic element. This would occur, without losing sight of the fact that traditional design models involve an "essential and pragmatic characteristic of the formation of a nation, indicating the dual (or multiple) register of its persuasive nationalist discourse."[10] If we also link the idea of tradition to the creative processes of design, this operation, however abstract and complicated it may seem, might well facilitate our endeavor to take the pulse of several different and relevant movements in the present-day production of objects.[11]

Tradition was a central concern for influential Latin American ideologists of the first half of the twentieth century. Political philosopher José Carlos Mariátegui, poet and folklorist Juan Liscano, anthropologist Fernando Ortiz, and realist painter David Alfaro Siqueiros, among others, represented forces that if not oppositional, were at least culturally resistant to the processes of modernization and their traumas. They attempted to rescue and made use of referents derived from the pre-Hispanic world, from folklore and from popular culture—whether vernacular or mass-produced by techniques of mechanical reproduction. These ideologists viewed tradition and versions of tradition in general terms,

---

4) Zygmunt Bauman, *Liquid Modernity* (London: Polity, 2008), 6.
5) Daniel Miller, *Material Cultures*, 4.
6) The Hochschule für Gestaltung (HfG), Ulm, Germany, was an experimental school dedicated to design. It was founded in 1955 by Max Bill and closed in 1968 for economic reasons.
7) Victor Margolin, "A World History of Design and the History of the World," *Journal of Design History* 18, no. 3 (Autumn 2005): 235–43.
8) See James Fathers, "Peripheral Vision: An Interview with Gui Bonsiepe: Charting a Lifetime Commitment to Design Empowerment," *Design Issues* 19, no. 4 (Autumn 2003): 44–56.

Fig. 1 Abraham Cruzvillegas *Autoconstrucción: Maqueta subdesarrollada*, 2007 Wood, plastic boxes, wooden box, steel grid, screws, glass, and towel 51.18 x 31.5 x 27.56 in (130 x 80 x 70 cm); photo: Michel Zabé; courtesy of the artist and Kurimanzutto, Mexico City

using them to affirm patrimonial pride and conviction of the excluded sectors of the nation. Thus at the beginning of modernization, tradition functioned as an authoritarian, morally superior entity that sought to counteract the potentially destructive power of the new. Today, however, it places us globally within a paradoxical situation of emancipation and slavery that grounds to a locality in a similar manner to the apocryphal anecdote from the *Odyssey*, in which Odysseus fails in his attempt to break the spell that has transformed his crew into a herd of swine running wild through a meadow.[12] When Odysseus tries to free them, the sailors-turned-swine flee, except for one who, once trapped and anointed with the herb that undoes the spell, returns to human form to decry the meager and awful benefits of his "freedom." On the basis of this vexed, conflictive, and polemical sense of desire for and resistance to emancipation, art historian Geeta Kapur advises that tradition be considered as a problematic code applied to iconographic forms with a view to achieving emancipation, or at least self-determination. Thus we can confront the difficulties entailed in the promotion of tradition in the Third World, a category which, despite its antihistorical formulation, takes on importance when used as a wedge between the First World and Second World.[13]

We may juxtapose variable tradition with the analysis of an ensemble of ancient and new knowledge and practices that are linked to creative propositions approximating the idea of the national. This idea contains ingrained exclusions of racial and ethnic minorities and of class and gender. Such a juxtaposition would help clear the field for the above-mentioned critical mapping of design in light of the failure, and eventual dismantling, of the various utopian modernist models that signal identity and project apparently stable local cultural norms. The framework provided by material culture as a problematic yet useful approach is the very foundation of what artist Abraham Cruzvillegas has defiantly designated as *Autoconstrucción* (self-construction) (Fig. 1). Furthermore, modernity, with its different modernisms and those few emancipatory socialist-inspired experiments in Latin America, could not sustain themselves over time as universal constructs based solely on autonomous production and the democratized consumption of objects. The term *tradition*, frequently counterposed to *contemporary* in the visual arts, "is not what is given and received as an impartial legacy of civilization."[14]

Today, this liquid reading of tradition in its local and global variations and appropriations appears to challenge us to examine and reevaluate its meaning as an ambivalent or unstable sign of a living creative source that goes hand in hand with "the cultural vanguard of society in the course of a struggle."[15] While this volatile character has been focused on fashioning an ideological canon that would accompany different modernizing impulses, the radical changes in the patterns of production, distribution, and consumption brought by technology now enable us to track points and lines of flight that are constantly displaced, helping us map a discipline as fluid and elusive as design. In this sense, material culture offers the means to decipher the various cultural and political shields (and camouflages) that local traditions possess or appropriate, by identifying objects and artifacts that contain creative and symbolic codes still to be manifested in the field of design in Latin America.

9) Margolin, "A World History of Design," 237.
10) Geeta Kapur, "Tradición y Contemporaneidad en las Bellas Artes del Tercer Mundo," in *La Bienal de La Habana para leer: Compilación de Textos* (Valencia: Editorial Universitat de Valencia, 2009), 124.
11) Ibid., 124.
12) Bauman, *Liquid Modernity*, 18. Bauman is paraphrasing an idea of the German writer Lion Feuchtwanger.
13) In Geeta Kapur's analysis of the relationship of India's metropolitan elites to thinkers of different ideological "signs" such as Gandhi, Ananda K. Coomaraswamy, and Rabindranath Tagore, as well as the poetic re-elaboration of tradition in that country's cinema.
14) Geeta Kapur, "Tradición y Contemporaneidad," 129.
15) Ibid., 124.

ESSAYS

The Nerve Center: Identity and Production in Contemporary Latin American Design

Jorge Rivas Pérez

In every society, there is a crucial point in which the process of material production and reproduction takes place, that is to say, the point in which the correspondences between the "state of need" and "the object of need," i.e., between needs and wants, are sanctioned over time according to the demands of the production dynamics.[1]

Tomás Maldonado

The definition of design and the issues surrounding it have always figured among the major subjects addressed by scholars in the field. The Argentinian Tomás Maldonado, one of the most influential design theorists of the twentieth century, has written widely on these topics since his earliest days. Over the years, he has repeatedly revised and adjusted his definition of design, adapting it to the dizzying changes demanded by the times. In various editions of his now-classic work *Disegno industriale: un riesame* (Industrial Design: A Review), he presents updates to his original vision, declaring that in every society, the production and reproduction of material goods emerge as a correspondence between the "state of need" and the "object of need," and both design and its production are located at a "nerve center" between need and demand. In the same text, Maldonado also points out that design and production belong to a category of phenomena that cannot be examined in isolation, but must be seen in relation to other phenomena, with which they form a "single connective web." These two declarations, the product of a theoretical vision of design grounded in the basic principles of historical materialism, offer keys to a possible reading of the intricate, multicolored panorama of design, art, and craft in Latin America today.

In order to examine contemporary production and identify the "nerve center" of design, it is essential, as Maldonado declares, to accept that it forms part of a "single connective web,"[2] which, among other things, is conferred by identity. It is because of this that design is indissolubly linked to the modes of production of consumer goods. The analysis of the phenomenon must inevitably be framed within a broad panorama that contemplates the economic, social, historical, and cultural aspects of the societies where it is generated.

Latin American Design?

Latin America today forms part of the complex postindustrial, globalized network of contemporary design. However, to lump the entire production of a continent under the single label of "Latin American design" might result in a plethora of contradictions, especially taking into account that the so-called region of Latin America is an artificial construct imposed from outside and profoundly linked to topics of postcolonial identity. In the specific case of design production, this single label has little to do with the productive realities of the different countries in the region. Reexamining the historical settings of design production reveals that they have been quite heterogeneous and have generally been linked more to cultural specificities and the unique artisanal or industrial traditions of each country than to the general history of the region.

Another important factor to consider in this brief analysis is the training of designers. Although there are some points of convergence between the different programs of Latin American schools of design—many of them influenced by the teachings of the Ulm School of Design, where design is a scientific-based discipline and aesthetic considerations are not central to projects—there has never been any uniformity in design education.[3] Is it even possible for such a dissimilar set of manifestations to merge under any single label? Can "Latin American design" encompass the products of different expressions and adaptations of highly varied national temperaments? Yet if the design production of this community of nations is studied in detail, certain common parameters make it possible to group them together and differentiate them from products of other latitudes. This can be done despite current tendencies toward homogenization and the adaptation of design production to the uniform tastes and standards demanded by international markets in a globalized world. Even if a "scientific" definition of Latin American design does not exist, the phenomenon is real and continues to exist, to paraphrase British political historian Hugh Seton-Watson's conclusion on nationalism.[4]

Latin America is not a homogeneous region with a single society, but a complex entity whose definition—if it is possible to find a satisfactory one—must be framed within the phenomena of cultural perception. To locate Maldonado's design "nerve center," one must refer to a conglomeration of heterogeneous societies that share, along with a geographical dimension, a set of cultural denominators, including moments in history and certain models of production. Today, when the world is being reconfigured as a global, virtual, and intangible entity, rather than areas with precise geographical dimensions, the Latin American ethos must be considered as associated with a region defined in the collective imagination, meaning a virtual territory exceeding the conventional geographical limits assigned to it. Following political theorist Benedict Anderson's approach in *Imagined Communities*,[5] we could even speak of Latin America as an imaginary community, an entity of imprecise contours and permeable edges whose borders are set by the intersecting lines of shared cultural values linked to the Latin American *genius loci*. The identity of a design production in this imaginary territory cannot be exclusively attributable to its place of production. Rather, it is linked to a set of cultural values that define the virtual "Latin American" identity of production and the "single connective web" where, according to Maldonado, design must be studied.

Proposing Latin America as an imaginary community enables us to question traditional criteria of attribution of identity for a design production exclusively on the basis of where it was produced. Today, in fact, Latin American design might be produced anywhere. Taking this approach, we may group under the category of "Latin American" a range of geographically and temporally dispersed work. These would include textiles made in the 1930s in Paris by Peruvian designer Elena Izcue (Fig. 1); recent porcelain by ceramicist Daniel Reynolds, made in London, referring to urban Venezuelan material culture (Fig. 2); and artifacts by Sebastián Errázuriz, who works in Brooklyn but is frequently inspired by moments of recent Chilean history.[6]

The contemporary globalized material world mirrors a reality in which the locality of the production of a design bears little or no relation to the product's identity. It is the trademark associated with an item that generates such an identity, making it imperative to define the elements or strategies most often employed by designers and artists who ascribe to the "Latin American" trademark. This identifies the design's "nerve center."

The foundations of contemporary design production trace to the beginning of the sixteenth century in the Caribbean, during that historic first moment of contact between Europeans and the people of the Americas, and the assimilation, or *mestizaje* (mixture), of various cultures, often through force, resulting in *mestizos*, people of mixed racial heritage. A hybrid material world developed, with new modes of production linked to what is now known as Latin America. Postconquest material production had a decisively mestizo character—a mix of different sensibilities and ways of doing things that represented a cultural transcendence beyond the mere merging of elements from different cultures and places. From this early mestizo production, a distant ancestor of contemporary design, came, for example, *zemís*, religious sculptures of the Taino people, made during the first decades of the sixteenth century and in a range of traditional materials such as wood, stone, bone, and ceramic. In some of these small pieces, however, Taino artisans incorporated exotic elements such as glass beads and mirrors from Europe and rhinoceros horn from Africa. Inclusion of foreign materials was superficial, however, compared to the introduction of iron tools by the Europeans. This completely changed the panorama of the production of consumer goods by indigenous artisans in the Americas. Hybridization thus encompasses technologies and productive processes.

Beginning with the Europeans' arrival, design started to follow other premises of production and new manufacturing processes developed. The *mestizaje* of the material world of the early postconquest period established a pattern of incorporation, adaptation, and recontextualization of elements and processes of production that has continued to the present day. More than five centuries later, *mestizaje* remains one of the essential components of Latin American design, a fundamental part of the "single connective web" inscribed within the Maldonado's "nerve center."

Design, Production, and Strategies of Hybridization

The role of hybridization as a primary component of Latin American cultural identity has been discussed in Latin American intellectual circles since the early twentieth century. In the mid-1920s, the prevalent concept was of local identities associated with the existence of an archetypal mestizo Latin American individual, resulting from the mixing not only of races but of cultural values associated with them.[7] Over time, this discourse faded, and by the end of the century, the idea of *mestizaje* would be reconsidered—this time unburdened by the emphasis on racial elements and viewed from a broad perspective that understood *mestizaje* above all as a cultural phenomenon.[8] Through this latter vision, it becomes possible to locate hybridization as a strategy of identity in contemporary design.

Looking over representative examples of contemporary Latin American design production reveals several of the most commonly employed regional strategies of identity through hybridization. Preeminent among them is the use of local materials and traditional manufacturing techniques. This approach is not innovative,

---

1) Tomás Maldonado. *Disegno industriale: un riesame* (Milan: Feltrinelli, 1991), 15.
2) Ibid.
3) See Silvia Fernández, "The Origins of Design Education in Latin America: From the HfG in Ulm to Globalization," *Design Issues* 22, no. 1 (2006): 3–19.
4) "I am driven to the conclusion that no 'scientific' definition of a nation can be devised; yet the phenomenon has existed and exists." Hugh Seton-Watson, *Nations and States: An Enquiry into the Origins of Nations and the Politics of Nationalism* (Boulder: Westview Press, 1977), 5.
5) Benedict Anderson, *Imagined Communities: Reflections on the Origin and Spread of Nationalism* (London and New York: Verso, 1991).
6) On Elena Izcue, see Natalia Majluf and Luis Eduardo Wuffarden, *Elena Izcue: el arte precolombino en la vida moderna* (Lima: Museo de Arte de Lima and Fundación Telefónica, 1999); and Natalia Majluf, *Elena Izcue: Lima-Paris, années 30* (Paris: Musée du Quai Branly and Flammarion, 2008).

however, but has been a distinctive feature of Latin American design throughout its history. Many mid-twentieth-century designers employed it successfully to connect their designs with a regional identity. In 1940, for example, Latin American artists who submitted work to the design competition and exhibition *Organic Design in Home Furnishings*, organized by the Museum of Modern Art (MoMA), New York, used natural local materials and artisanal workmanship.[9] However, today's designers are much more subtle in their use of materials connected to themes of national identity. For example, the Brazilian Zanini de Zanine in his easy chair *Moeda* (see page 149) uses perforated metal sheets left over from the production of coins in Brazil, a modern material that is at the same time inextricably linked to his country's identity. Another example is the *Gudpaka* lamp (Fig. 3) by the Chilean collective gt2P (Great things to People). Made with Chilean alpaca wool and wood combined with thermoformed plastic, this design represents recent developments of digital crafting, juxtaposing traditional textures, materials, and craft with modern plastics and high-technology production using Computer Numerical Control (CNC).

Fig. 1 Elena Izcue
Handkerchief with pre-Columbian-inspired designs, c. 1930
Private collection

When traditional manufacturing techniques are used, the process often involves cooperation with communities of artisans. The present tendency is toward a symbiotic production whereby the designers collaborate with master craftsmen until they reach a conclusion agreeable to both parties. Additionally, part of the earnings usually goes directly to the communities involved in the production. There are many examples of this type of cooperation. The chair *Miss Delta Amacuro* (see page 115) was designed by MáximaDuda (Anabella Georgi and María Antonia Godigna) and realized by women of the Warao people in Venezuela. The project is of interest not only for the complexity of its production but also because women designed and produced it—according to Warao ancestral tradition, only women of the community are allowed to weave Moriche palm fiber.

Another strategy of *mestizaje* consists of what is now called appropriation and reelaboration of traditional types, forms, and even visual repertories associated with artistic legacies of more recent periods. This strategy is, in a way, an updating of design projects and research by mid-twentieth-century creators such as Cuban-Mexican designer Clara Porset, who was frequently inspired by *butaques* (small easy chairs) based on Colonial-Mexican forms and even earlier prototypes, and Brazilian architect Lina Bo Bardi, who rescued the structural wisdom of Brazilian vernacular design in some of her most famous projects of the 1960s, such as the *Beira de Estrada* (roadside) chair from 1967.[10]

Today, this approach is taken in very direct ways. Forms from the traditional repertory are reinterpreted, as in Bernardo Mazzei's *Anauco Aalto* chair (see page 126), which refers to the Venezuelan *ture*—a seating form with preconquest origins. In other examples, iconic pieces of modern design are revisited, reelaborated, or deconstructed, as in the work of Mexican Edgar Orlaineta and Brazilian Leo Capote (see pages 134–135 and 129–130). Venezuelan Rodolfo Agrella takes yet another approach, reinterpreting the visual vocabulary associated with national artistic legacies. Among some designers, this kind of exercise is posed as a more elaborate operation, and instead of making direct reference to visual repertoires, the redesign reinterprets typologies of traditional objects. Such is the case with the *8 Lamp* (2012) by Puerto Rican designer Eddie Figueroa Feliciano (see page 174), which applies an industrial style to the concept of lighting used in rural dwellings of the Caribbean.

The production of objects can be as hybrid as the design. Often one encounters the combination of craft processes with roots in preconquest cultures or colonial traditions, combined with new materials or new technologies. Such is the case with some of the textiles of Taller Morera (María Eugenia Dávila and Eduardo Portillo) in Mérida, Venezuela, in which silk produced in the studio is blended with other natural fibers and industrial metallic filaments (see pages 108–109). Recycling, especially of discarded materials like plastic or metal, or by reusing objects, has a prominent role in contemporary design. Mana Bernardes in Brazil and Thierry Jeannot in Mexico, among many others, use recycled material from the large municipal garbage dumps (see pages 153–154). In São Paulo, Studio MK27 (Marcio Kogan) proposes new uses for discarded furniture (see page 143).

Following the path of modernist Latin American designers, such as Sergio Rodrigues in Brazil and Bauhaus-trained Michael Van Beuren, an American who worked in Mexico, designers often have no option other than to produce their own maste pieces. As Maldonado explained, this has to do as much with demand—generally reduced for this kind of design production—as with the channels of commercialization found in the region. A significant part of contemporary Latin American design production is therefore the result of designers also being producers. In general, they are found in individual ateliers, independent artisanal workshops, and family businesses. Some designers produce designs in their own studios, usually in limited editions, but they may also outsource designs to manufacturers who work either with the designers' direct guidance or under their license. The Campana Brothers, Humberto and Fernando Campana, in Brazil, for example, produce individual pieces as well as products for mass-market consumption.

Fig. 2 Daniel Reynolds
Hot Water Bottle Vase, 2008; *ACE Bottle Vase*, 2002; *Stacking Picnic Plates*, 2002-13; *Cup Tower Vases* (large amd small), 2002; slip cast porcelain, unglazed exterior, glazed interior; dimensions variable
Photo: Daniel Reynolds

Fig. 3 gt2P
Gudpaka Lamp, 2011; interior in coigue plywood over a thermoformed ABS structure; exterior in woven alpaca hair on alpaca felt strips
39.3 x 17.7 x 17.7 in. (100 x 45 x 45 cm)
Courtesy of the artists

Such growth has led some designers into collaboration and promotion. Although still not common, the role of agent, a commercial step beyond traditional mentoring, is gradually being established. Ariel Rojo in Mexico has attracted an important group of younger designers to his studio and has built bridges to international manufacturers such as Kikkerland Design. Another example, Dennis Schmeichler, worked at Casa Curuba in Caracas, which served from 1988 to 2011 as an incubator of design and top-level craftsmanship in Venezuela. Schmeichler commissioned designers, both emerging and established, to develop products that could find a mass market. In recent years, design agencies have emerged to represent artists and tap into the international design world and its markets. One of these small entrepreneurial companies, ARRé Design, in Rotterdam, Holland, was founded by Venezuelan Antonio Paiva. It manages, produces, and promotes designs by Latin American designers, among others.

In the twenty-first century, international design fairs have become essential stages for the promotion of design. Contemporary Latin American products and designers are frequent participants in premier annual events such as Salone Satellite during the Salone del Mobile, Milan. This alone has guaranteed the presence of Latin American talent in the global design market.

Artisanal design—handcrafting—is very active throughout Latin America, with many traditional methods of production being pursued. Artisans are frequently supported by handicraft organizations, both governmental and nongovernmental, or by individuals or commercial entities. Some associations are linked to specific communities, such as the Centro de las Artes de San Agustín de Etla, Oaxaca, Mexico, which has become one of Latin America's most important centers of artisanal design. It was founded in 2006 by artist Alejandro Toledo who designs or supervises a large part of the production. Another modality used by artisanal Latin American designers to reach the wider design world has been through specific collaborative projects rather than an organization, almost always with an intermediary who functions as an agent, matching designers and their projects to appropriate craftspeople, and usually arranging the financing and marketing as well. SURevolution, founded by Marcella Echavarría, for example, has been especially successful in providing indigenous craftspeople from Colombia, Bolivia, and elsewhere with a platform in the global market.

As tempting as it is to view "Latin America" as an imaginary, diffusely outlined geography of the mind, existing almost as a contradiction unto itself, this "nerve center" where *mestizo* design is produced in fact reflects the new terrain of contemporary design in which the borders between reality and potential are dynamic. Identity has been progressively redefined as it has adapted to the global scene. This design production, generally limited, and often combining ancient traditions with new materials and technologies, is ideologically opposed to a contemporary culture of unbridled consumerism. It seeks to open new avenues for environmentally sound, socially sustainable manufacturing, as it builds new bridges between designers, manufacturers, and consumers. It is a design that opposes the generic homogenization of the global product and presents an alternative production as an instrument of continental identity and an expression of the peoples and cultures we know collectively as *Latinoamérica*.

7) Perhaps the most famous exponent of these theories in the 1920s was José Vasconcelos. See José Vasconcelos, *La Raza Cósmica: Misión de la raza iberoamericana y notas de viajes a la América del Sur* (Barcelona: Agencia de Librería, 1925).

8) Authors such as Serge Gruzinski and Néstor García Canclini have written extensively on *mestizaje* and modern culture in Latin America. See Serge Gruzinski, *El pensamiento mestizo* (Barcelona: Paidós, 2000); and Néstor García Canclini, *Culturas híbridas: estrategias para entrar y salir de la modernidad* (México: Grijalbo, 1990).

9) See Eliot F. Noyes. *Organic Design in Home Furnishings* (New York: Museum of Modern Art, 1941).

10) On Clara Porset, see Jorge R. Bermúdez, *Clara Porset: diseño y cultura* (Havana: Editorial Letras Cubanas, 2005); Oscar Salinas Flores, *Clara Porset: una vida inquieta, una obra sin igual* (Mexico City: Universidad Nacional Autónoma de México, Facultad de Arquitectura, 2001); and Museo Franz Mayer, *El diseño de Clara Porset: inventando un México moderno* (Mexico City: Museo Franz Mayer, Difusión Cultural UNAM, 2006). On Lina Bo Bardi, see Zeuler Lima, *Lina Bo Bardi* (New Haven: Yale University Press, 2013).

ESSAYS

The Circulation of New Design: Trends in Latin America

Ana Elena Mallet

In the twenty-first century, Latin America has shown a new face: stable economic models, hence growth; an expanding middle class, hence greater purchasing power; and large and promising markets, hence opportunities for new investments. Design has been a part of these emerging economies, and designers have found paths that extend their practices, establishing an industry and, most importantly, creating a design culture. Taking as a point of departure the distribution of design objects in three countries—Brazil, Mexico, and Venezuela—elucidates the way in which designers in Latin America circulate their work and ideas. Through the networks they establish, they gradually buildmarkets in which their products are not only useful, but also generate meaning.

The prime movers in this development were the first generation of formally educated designers, who sought to open a path beginning in the 1960s and 1970s.[1] These individuals have had to understand the profession of design and familiarize themselves with the particulars of the field to be able to communicate to new clients and businesses both what design means and what its primary function is. Almost forty years after this beginning, designers have staked out their field of action. Some have entered industry, others are educators, and a good number are professionals who have opted for an independent path. These designers have become entrepreneurs, who have their own studios or manufacture limited-edition products with artisans. Some have founded their own brands and own shops or sell their products directly. Nevertheless, one characteristic that Latin America shares with many other places in the world is that recognition in one's own country comes only after becoming international.

Brazil: National Identity in Design

As the Brazilian curator Adélia Borges has perceptively observed, contemporary Brazilian design is distinguished by its diversity and plurality.[2] Today, there is a clearly recognizable industrial vein, but craft has not been sidelined. Brazil clearly understood that it had to generate an internal market to succeed later in exporting talent along with furniture and objects. Brazilian design strategically entered the world market, and designers have known how to find their market niches, just as entrepreneurs have understood that they can lend a hand to local design initiatives in order to generate fruitful businesses. Brazil is an emblematic case. In addition to developing its own market and raising design awareness from within, it has gained international attention. Attentive entrepreneurs have wagered on the sale and promotion of national design. Shops such as Dpot and Tok & Stok follow the model of offering furnishings associated with luxury and comfort, while focusing on Brazilian design and the promotion of local designers. Others such as Etna offer various products for daily life at more competitive prices, while also emphasizing local designs.

The Campana Brothers first internationalized contemporary Brazilian design, putting it on the map after being invited by Paola Antonelli, now senior curator of architecture and design at the Museum of Modern Art, New York (MoMA), to participate in a 1998 exhibition entitled *Projects 66*, sharing credit with the lighting designer Ingo Maurer. Beginning with this event, the Campanas' career gained recognition, and they began to receive invitations to lecture and give workshops all over the world. They gained such fame in Brazil that the director of the prestigious jewelry store H. Stern commissioned a series of pieces from them. This suggests that the circulation of Brazilian design is highly successful in this type of retail operation. Designers and collectives such as OVO, Hugo França, Sergio Fahrer, Marcenaria Baraúna, Paulo Alves–São Paulo, Carlos Motta, Juliana Liussá, Jacqueline Terpins, and Estúdio Bola have opened their own shops in São Paulo, while

---

1) CFR. Silvia Fernández, "The Origins of Design Education in Latin America: From the HfG in Ulm to Globalization," *Design Issues* 22, no. 1 (Winter 2006): 6–19.

2) Adélia Borges, "Brazilian Contemporary Furniture: Polyphony," AT THE BOOK, *Contemporary Brazilian Furniture* (Rio de Janeiro: FGV Projetos e Aeroplano Editora, 2013), 9–41. Adélia Borges, e-mail interview with Ana Elena Mallet, January 10, 2014.

Fig. 3 Showroom of the Metropolitan at the Abierto Mexicano de Diseño (Mexican Design Open), 2013
Photo: Ana Elena Mallet

Fig. 4 Showroom of the Metropolitan at the Abierto Mexicano de Diseño (Mexican Design Open), 2013
Photo: Ana Elena Mallet

Rodrigo Calixto has done the same in Rio de Janeiro and Jader Almeida in Florianópolis.

While São Paulo has been the country's design center par excellence, Rio de Janeiro has recently begun to stake out a position, welcoming designers, shops, and projects that have gradually been generating a design identity for the city, such as Lattoog (see page 132). Bento Gonçalves in the south of the country is a highly industrialized region, which has also recently begun showing interest in design. In the absence of galleries promoting contemporary work,[3] Brazil has initiated design fairs and biennials as a means not only to disseminate commercial products, but also to position design as a cultural production. The first biennial, organized by the industrial design department of the Museu de Arte Moderna do Rio de Janeiro, took place in 1968 and was held three times. After an absence of more than thirty years, they resumed in 2006 as the Bienal Brasileira de Design, circulating as a large traveling exhibition that helps to diffuse and conceive a design culture in Brazil.

In addition, Mercado Arte Design (MADE) is a recent annual fair that takes place in São Paulo in August. Its main objective is to position design in the art milieu by including other artistic media such as painting, photography, and graphic art. Galleries and collectives of designers also participate in this event, which aims to reach other Brazilian cities by promoting both historical and contemporary designs, as well as cultivating a circuit of collectors who value design from an artistic, cultural, and economic standpoint. Paralela Gift and Feira de Design e Decoração is another platform that has been in existence for more than a decade and takes place semiannually in São Paulo. Its primary goal is to promote artistic design and high-end decoration as well as contemporary craft design. In this fair, the Brazilian craft tradition intermingles with new industrial products, generating an interesting vision of a Brazil that possesses diverse and multifaceted design.

Prizes for local designers have also been a determining factor to promote the circulation of design in Brazil. A prestigious prize bestowed by the Museu da Casa Brasileira since 1986 generates a great deal of publicity. The museum is unique in specializing in design and has a large collection of local objects. Additionally, the Premio Movelso, a prize given by Sindmóveis–Sindicato das Indústrias do Mobiliario de Bento Gonçalves since 1988, is another point of reference as it includes all countries in Latin America. Brazil's high level of production has resulted in the emergence of media outlets specializing in design. In addition to blogs and websites devoted to design, a large number of print journals that once focused on decoration now passionately disseminate information about developments in Brazilian design: *Arc Design*, *Casa Vogue*, *Projeto Design*, *Casa e Jardim*, and *Bamboo*, to name a few. Brazilian publishers of design books have been fundamental to the circulation of local design, both within the country and beyond its borders. Publishing houses such as Edgard Blucher, Rosari, and Viana & Mosley specialize in books on Brazilian design production in various languages.

---

3) Gallery culture in Brazil has focused on modern design, as is the case with Mercado Moderno in Rio de Janeiro. At the same time the sale and collection of modern Brazilian furniture has greatly expanded in New York, with galleries such as Espasso, and R & Company (formerly R 20th Century Gallery), which not only offer period furniture but also new editions of modern Brazilian classics along with the work of several contemporary designers.

4) I would like to thank Jorge Rivas Férez for his support and assistance in providing a panoramic view of the design scene in Venezuela. Jorge Rivas Pérez, interview with Ana Elena Mallet, January 12, 2014.

5) See *Diseño en Venezuela y en Latinamérico* at http://disenoenvenezuela.blogspot.com/.

Fig. 3 Showroom of the Metropolitan at the Abierto Mexicano de Diseño (Mexican Design Open), 2013
Photo: Ana Elena Mallet

Fig. 4 Showroom of the Metropolitan at the Abierto Mexicano de Diseño (Mexican Design Open), 2013
Photo: Ana Elena Mallet

Venezuela: Individual Initiative in Design

Venezuela's great craft tradition, as well as its established design scene, has succeeded in maintaining itself at the forefront of design excellence despite the difficult social, economic, and political situation that the country has been experiencing since the early 2000s. While Caracas continues to be the most important center of design in Venezuela, other points of development have strong craft traditions, notably Mérida, home of the design school associated with the Universidad de Los Andes, and Quibor, a small but important center for the production of wood objects. Several noteworthy studios, such as that of designer Mark Fiallo, are located there.

However, design fairs in Venezuela are virtually nonexistent, nor is there a defined market for national design, yet designers continue to produce and move forward, forging a genuine design culture.[4] The majority of Venezuelan designers aim to sell directly to the public through their studios or via the Internet and other media. National newspapers regularly publish the work of local designers, enabling interested readers to form direct relationships with the creators and carry out transactions without middlemen. Such is the case with *Todo en Domingo*, a weekly supplement to *El Nacional* or *Estampas* devoted to style and folded into the newspaper *El Universal*. Other lifestyle publications such as *Complot Magazine* and *Estilo* also disseminate the work of Venezuelan designers. On the Internet, design historian Elina Pérez Urbaneja's blog has also become a point of reference for Venezuelan design and an important publicity tool.[5] Pérez Urbaneja has also had a vigorous presence in the local design scene. In addition to giving lectures and organizing seminars, she has curated exhibitions in the Museo de la Estampa y del Diseño Carlos Cruz-Diez, Caracas.

Without a doubt, an essential space for understanding design in Venezuela and its dissemination was the Casa Curuba, a shop that opened in the 1980s in Caracas and was run by the collector of Venezuelan crafts Dennis Schmeichler. A lover of fine Venezuelan wood, Schmeichler organized workshops for artisan communities with the goal of improving their creative and productive processes. At the same time, he invited distinguished local designers and architects to create designs that were then commercialized under the aegis of Casa Curuba. Of these, for example, Emile Vestuti's *Palette Chair* and Jorge Rivas's *Zig Zag Table* have become classic designs. Casa Curuba's specialty was wood, and it offered high-end design and high-quality craftsmanship. Schmeichler also encouraged emerging designers who worked with other materials, such as ceramicist Daniel Reynolds.

Casa Curuba closed in 2011, marking the end of an era. Other spaces devoted to fine craftsmanship, furniture, and objects of an international type as well as pieces by local designers include Möbel, Greenella, Objetos Dac, Tierra Azul, and Quincalla Zoco. Also notable was the Serrucho shop that sold only the designs of the engineer Tomás von Wachter. The artists' collective Krearte markets pieces by contemporary Venezuelan designers on the Internet and in two small outlets in Caracas. Under the rubric "Made in Venezuela," they promote young designers and make their works visible and accessible. Another outlet is the shop in the exhibition space Trasnocho Arte Contacto, a nonprofit organization of singular importance in Caracas. Its inventory usually includes small pieces by Venezuelan designers and fabric by Taller Morera. A section of the gallery features design exhibitions, both historical (such as Cornelis Zilman and Miguel Arroyo) and contemporary (including Jorge Rivas). The store in the Sala Mendoza, the oldest foundation and private gallery devoted to art in Venezuela, also sells design objects, primarily ceramics, and works are occasionally exhibited and sold in the Centro de Arte Los Galpones, in which Caracas's major galleries of contemporary art share space with local design shops.

Mexico: Constructing a Design Culture

If we can associate the decades of the twentieth century with efforts to promote national design in Latin America, the last ten years have been important for defining Mexican design, developing a local market, and especially creating a design culture.

In December 2003, Carolina Kopeloff and Manuel Sekkel, Argentinian designers residing in Mexico City, organized the first Bazar Fusión, a traveling fair in which each version changed location and presented the work of new local designers who sold their products directly to the customer. The project, presented in the living room of a local resident, began with just five designers, and 130 designers participated in its peak version in 2007. The bazaar became widely known throughout the country, and in 2012, the organizers chose to integrate Fusión into the permanent marketplace and opened what is now known as Casa Fusión in Colonia Juárez: a sort of concept store with small spaces that sell work by independent designers, many of whom developed their businesses through Bazar Fusión.

La Lonja Mercantil, which opened in 2009, also in the format of a traveling bazaar, was organized every three months by Joanna Ruiz Galindo, Mariana Aguilar, Regina Barrios, and Carmen Casanova. It was distinguished by the quality of its products and its rigorous selection of designers, and like Fusión, it sold directly to the public. For the first three years, La Lonja Mercantil promoted a barter system, which was unsuccessful. This changed in 2012, when the organizers advertised the sale, not exchange, of various Mexican design products: furniture, shoes, clothes, jewelry, objects, and even small quantities of foodstuffs. Oaxaca and San Miguel Allende were among the venues, and since its inception, La Lonja Mercantil has grown considerably, bringing together more than 150 designers with a turnover of nearly $200,000. Widespread attention in lifestyle magazines and local media has enabled it to position itself favorably in both the local and world market.

As a precursor, the Galería Mexicana de Diseño, has been the most enduring promoter of Mexican design. Opened in Mexico City by Carmen Cordera in 1991, it has been a meeting place for the design community, a venue of exhibitions, a sales space for international design, and a point of reference for local talent.[6] In the twenty-first century, designers have changed their modus operandi, however, choosing mobility and more dynamic spaces without intermediaries to promote their work. Bureaucratic obstacles and measures imposed by the Mexican government on small-scale entrepreneurs, combined with complicated fiscal measures, have persuaded many designers to opt for informal arrangements to reach a buying public.

The early years of the twenty-first century have been crucial for the dissemination of Mexican design and the birth of a market, but above all, for the development of a design culture. It is no longer unusual to find design increasingly embedded in the realm of contemporary art. Seeking to increase markets, contemporary art fairs like Art Basel Miami have coincided with design fairs such as Design Miami. In Mexico City, Zona Maco Arte Contemporáneo has included a design section since 2011, and as of 2012, participating curators were invited to refine this idea. Although it is relatively costly to reserve booths in the design section of this fair, known as Zona Maco Diseño, this venue has become an important platform for local designers, allowing them to publicize their products to a wide market and to reach high-end customers (Figs. 1–2).

Following the model of other world cities noted for their promotion of design, in 2008 a group of architects inaugurated Design Week México. The project, centered on interior design, has launched many local architects and interior designers onto major trajectories. Design House is the culminating event of the fair: architects and interior designers are invited to decorate a living space in accordance with their specific style. Design stores in the exclusive neighborhoods of Polanco and Lomas coordinate the presentation of new lines or products with Design Week México, and local museums schedule concurrent design exhibitions and lectures.

Another celebration of Mexican design is El Abierto Mexicano de Diseño (Mexican Design Open), which was founded in 2013 in response to the lack of design exhibition space and design promotion in the country. Initiated by a group of designers, promoters, and curators, this festival takes place in the center of Mexico City and showcases young national talent alongside established designers, including invited guest artists from around the world. In its first year, it succeeded in presenting nearly two hundred events over four days. Workshops, lectures, exhibitions, presentations, and installations reflected the face of local design (Figs. 3–4).

Despite this lively design scene in Mexico, however, more government involvement is needed to promote design as a potential economic resource, a creative industry capable of generating not only jobs and wealth but also international prestige. Yet as of 2014, design has not been included in government programs of support and stimulus for the arts. For example, design continues to be considered outside the purview of grants given by the Fondo Nacional para la Cultúra y las Artes (FONCA) and is not eligible for the scientific or technological support provided by the Consejo Nacional de Ciencia y Tecnología (CONACYT).

Beyond the Local

Emerging Latin American designers have found various ways to ensure a livelihood within their countries of origin, although there is still a need for international promotion to gain access to other markets. Since about 2004, design in Latin America has grown and there has been much cross-fertilization, but there remains more to accomplish. A design for all, as conceived by the Bauhaus in the 1920s, which improves social and human conditions even in marginal areas, remains a quest. Designers have not connected as strongly with industry as they might, and industry itself has not embraced design.

Projects such as MoMA's *Destination* series, which spotlights a different country in its prestigious Design Store in New York, have given space to Latin American designers and serve as a point of entry into the North American market. Since 2009, the store at MoMA has organized these semiannual events with the help of institutions in various cities and countries around the globe, presenting the work of designers from those places. Argentina, Brazil, and Mexico have each been represented. Of the nearly fifty designers participating in each occasion, up to 10 percent have later become permanent suppliers to MoMA, and under its guidance have entered other stores and markets. Such is the case with Argentinian designer Pedro Reissig, with his brand of leather goods, vacaValiente, which after being presented at MoMA, has found multiple outlets within the United States. Mexican designer Mauricio Lara's *Erizo* pencil holder has sold more than six thousand pieces annually at MoMA. Another important stop for emerging Latin American designers is Milan, Italy, especially the Salone Satellite, which is part of the annual Salone Internazionale di Mobile, the design fair that brings buyers, curators, producers, and designers to Milan every April. Founded in 1998, Salone Satellite welcomes students and young designers from around the world. It is an international observatory of nascent design, which has caught the attention of many Latin American designers.

Both the efforts discussed here and other initiatives throughout Latin America reveal a design field populated by individuals who demonstrate a great deal of drive while facing many difficulties, some of which are unnecessary. There remains a need for a design culture in which government, industry, and designers establish a common front to find solutions for daily problems and reach a complete understanding of "design" as a tool to bring about improvements in society as a whole. Although progress has been made, only when all the players truly come together will the region's design take on meaning across physical, economic, geographic, and symbolic borders.

ESSAYS

Designers and Artisans in Latin America: A Fruitful Collaboration

Adélia Borges

Today's Latin American design scene is marked by an alliance between designers and artisans.[1] It is a virtual collective—large-scale and widespread—of fairly recent origin. Around the mid-twentieth century, a deliberate desire to replace handmade with machine-made objects followed a view in which handicraft was seen as part of a backward past, associated with underdevelopment and poverty. Prosperity was attainable through machines. In the name of progress and Latin America's wish to join the world's developed nations, old empirical practices would be jettisoned in favor of purely rational principles—meaning science, technology, and mechanization.

Industrialization seemed to threaten the survival of craft, and it was feared that preindustrial production would disappear altogether. To "defend" craft in this scenario was viewed as counter to the flow of history and demonstrated a hostility to humanity's development. Craft was a nostalgic backward view that would be buried by world progress. Adopting a functional language of design became the new norm in the teaching and practice of Latin American design. New design schools prepared students for a serial production market, typical of large manufacturers in developed countries. Yet industrialization in the region was still in its infancy, which meant that designs could not be implemented and new graduates of design schools found an abysmal job market waiting for them.

In Brazil, the founding of the Escola Superior de Desenho Industrial (ESDI) in 1963 served as a seminal moment. Its curriculum was based on that of the Ulm School of Design (Hochschule für Gestaltung Ulm), in Germany, a promulgator of universal "good form" or "good design" expressed in an international language.

The Ulm School promoted the idea that "form follows function," which downplayed the diverse aesthetics of local cultures. Once an "adequate" form is reached, this becomes the universally accepted form, independent of time and place, the only valid aesthetic for rational serial production. Emerging Brazilian designers were expected to desire and demand this kind of mass-market production.

At the same time, the Latin American craft tradition, which was largely spread over rural areas of poor regions, was in a serious decline. Craft in the Latin American context is different from the craft techniques learned in schools and universities in North American and Europe, where handcrafting is largely viewed as a form of self-expression, closer to art than to design. In Latin America, craft has been an essential activity in rural areas, as well as in the *favelas* (slums) and fringe areas of cities. Artisans in these places make objects collectively as a way of coping with adverse conditions. The objects, however, can be reproduced in series and are conceived within the parameters usually attributed to design, such as fulfilling a functional requirement (pottery made for cooking, for example) or using specific materials (bamboo woven into baskets, another example). The production techniques have been transmitted through generations by elder members of a community, rather than learned at school.

Yet by the 1960s, craft was losing its cultural significance and craftspeople were turning to other livelihoods. The rich heritage of local hand-production could not compete with industrial products, such as those imported from China. In many places, foreign "motifs," however out of sync with Latin America they might be, were applied to local wares: such as scenes of fluffy polar bears

---

1) For further discussion of designer–artisan collaboration, especially in Brazil, see Adélia Borges, *Design and Craft: The Brazilian Path* (São Paulo: Terceiro Nome, 2011).

2) In Brazil, some surveys made by the Mundareu NGO found that participation in the Entrepreneurs Qualification Programs increased average income by 50–300 percent.

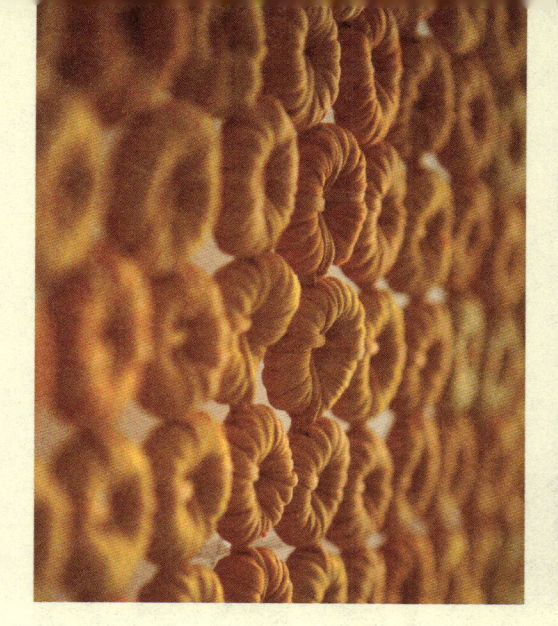

Fig.1 Broinha rug by Claudia Araújo and Associação das Tecelãs de Caldas, Minas Gerais, Brazil
Photo: Roberto Setton

Fig.2 Caroá fiber baskets dyed with cashew and umbu peels in Valente, Bahia, Brazil
Photo: Lena Trindade

or plants native to the northern hemisphere. Latin American craft traditions, in all their diversity, were becoming endangered species.

Different Paths Coming Together: Sustainable Development

In the 1980s, in many countries—Colombia, Mexico, Argentina, Uruguay, Chile, Brazil—designers began to recognize the value of work made by local craftspeople and to seek ways to revitalize craft practices. They followed various paths throughout the process, such as improving the working conditions of artisans and solving technical production issue to assure standards of quality. Identifying and using local materials that could be adapted for craft production was another approach. Marketing was also pursued—ranging from advertising to package design for artisanal products. Most of these different paths converge in the direction of sustainable development, which embraces concepts of environmental responsibility, economic inclusion, social justice, and cultural diversity.

Historically, local artisans fulfill many of the conditions of environmental responsibility. Most craft production is closely connected to the use of local materials, relying on what is available nearby. Craftspeople rarely waste fossil fuels by requiring supplies and raw materials to be transported over long distances, and their finished products are often sold locally, although this is changing as Latin American crafts extend to global markets. In Brazil, artisans are constantly innovating new uses for natural materials, from golden grass (*Syngonanthus nitens*) found in the savannahs and woven into baskets to rubber from the Amazon that is fashioned into body adornments or bags, among other objects, and dry leaves from various species of trees are used to make wall panels. Fish skin or leather, which was once discarded, has been utilized over the past decade to make various objects, and natural tanning technologies are currently in development. Another aspect of environmental responsibility has long been entrenched in Latin American life: recycling or repurposing. Well before environmental concerns were of interest to governments and businesses, recycling was a way of life in poor communities throughout the region. There are abundant examples of objects made from plastic bottles, cardboard, rubber tires, fabric scraps from textile factories, and more. Some are made for personal use, but most are for sale. Craft production thus offers a viable way to earn income in economically depressed areas—not just for the artisans but also those involved in producing or collecting raw materials, making necessary craft equipment, transporting wares, and finding markets.[2] It is hardly news that economic improvement and self-sufficiency enhance a person's well-being and self-esteem. In communities that have developed a craft industry, craft associations have sprung up, often taking on issues that benefit the entire community: dealing with aspects of health and hygiene such drilling a freshwater well for clean drinking water.

Programs of regional craft development and designers who have partnered with local artisans have helped to interrupt the migratory flow of people from the countryside into overcrowded cities. Through the revitalization of craft, local cultural identities can be maintained, meaning the survival of cultural diversity. Craft—and cuisine—are powerful expressions of local singularity, even within different villages of the same region. Projects that incorporate and work with local cultural identities encourage each artisan's pride in his or her origins and their day-to-day lives, which in turn enhances a sense of belonging. Brazilian designer Ronaldo Fraga calls this the "mechanism of a cultural appropriation" of the place in which they live. Increases in self-esteem affect families, husbands, children, social groups, and neighborhoods.

Designers and artisans develop standards of quality for production and finishing together. For example, they identify paint that will fade and poorly baked pottery that easily breaks, and experiment with untreated organic materials, such as seeds, on which mold can grow. These technical enhancements improve the artisanal practice overall. When designer TT Leal chose to work with

Fig. 3 Rubber necklace from Manicoré, Brazil
Photo: Lena Trindade

Fig. 4 Bowls made of fish skin by Amor-Peixe Women's Association, Mato Grosso do Sul, Brazil
Photo: Lena Trindade

Fig. 5 Flowers made from recycled cardboard pulp and banana tree fiber by the Gente de Fibra Cooperative, Minas Gerais, Brazil; color photograph
19.7 x 23.6 in. (50 x 60 cm)
Courtesy of the collection of Saul Dennison, New York
Photo: Domingos Tótora

Fig. 6 Pottery with rock painting motifs, Piauí, Brazil
Photo: Mariana Chama

Fig. 7 Mandala table, designed by Claudia Moreira Salles for Casa 21
Plaited straw from Piauí, Brazil
Photo: Mariana Chama

Fig. 8 Crochet work at Distrito Federal, in collaboration with Renato Imbroisi
Photo: Mariana Chama

Fig. 9 Capello lamp, designed and produced by Tina Moura and Lui Lo PumoStraw, produced by artisans from Rio Grande do Sul, Brazil
Photo: Lucas Moura

Fig. 10 The long journey from raw materials to finished objects
Photo: Lena Trindade

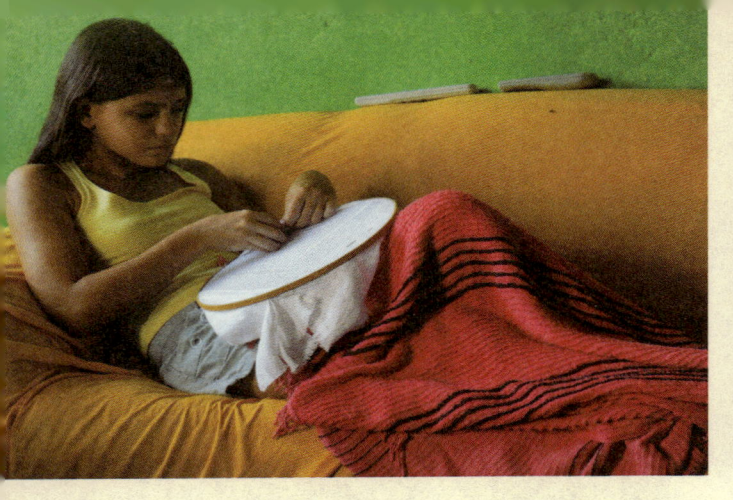

Fig. 11 Teenager Mariana Lima follows in her mother's steps and embroiders in Alagoas, Brazil
Photo: Celso Brandão

Fig 12 Rejânia Rodrigues and her nephew at home in Pão de Açúcar, Alagoas, Brazil
Photo: Celso Brandão

the *nozinho* (little knots) technique to make rugs at Cooperativa da Rocinha, she sought to set their work apart from most of what was being sold in roadside stalls in Rio de Janeiro at extremely low prices. This was attained through a high degree of dedication, which is evident from the reverse side of the fabric.

Delicate Relationships

The alliance between designers and artisans is, undoubtedly, a crucial phenomenon owing to its social and economic impact as well as its cultural implications. While the reach of artisanal objects from the Southern Hemisphere has widened, there have also been many unequal exchanges that lack continuity and respect for local cultures.

At times, design teams visit communities with ready-made projects or prototypes for artisans to complete. This scenario does not allow for a meaningful dialogue, as the designers are seen as providing the talent and the artisans the supplier of hands. In such situations, when a designer or company is seeking nothing more than labor, the parameters should be clearly defined with fair compensation, rather than representing the projects as "social design."

German designer and theoretician Gui Bonsiepe, who is based in Brazil, is wary of the "productivity approach" toward craft and design that defines "artisans as qualified and cheap labor, utilizing their ability to produce objects developed and signed by designers and artists." This reflects the long-standing conflict between those who invest in or set up incentive programs and the designers and artisans who are involved in these projects. Administrators usually have high expectations for demonstrable results within the shortest time possible. Designers and artisans, however, often label such administrators as well-meaning but insensitive to the nuances of place, and more concerned with figures and reports rather than qualitative changes. According to Bonsiepe, "a great deal of naïveté is necessary to accept this approach, presented as an 'aid' for artisans in remote areas. They use humanitarian interests as excuses to produce designs 'inspired' by the local folk culture or designs brought directly from the center in order to take advantage of cheap labor in those communities. This practice in design tends to continue dependency relationships instead of contributing to their eradication."[3]

American journalist Bruce Nussbaum, who teaches design strategies at Parsons The New School for Design, New York, echoes this last concern when he asks "should we take a moment, now that the movement is gathering speed to ask whether or not American and European designers are collaborating with the right partners, learning from the best local people, and being as sensitive as they might be to the colonial legacies of the countries where they want to do good?" He turns the equation around when he also asks, "might Indian, Brazilian and African designers have important design lessons to teach Western designers?"[4]

Lessons are sometimes learned through error, and mistakes have certainly been made in the name of improvement. During the nineties, the Inter-American Development Bank (IDB), an international financial organization based in Washington, launched a program to improve Guarani pottery production in Paraguay. The Guarani potters traditionally fired their work in an open fire, much like the Pueblo Indians of the American Southwest. Consultants hired by the bank introduced kilns, which were sold to the artisans through loans. The kilns, however, changed the colors of the pots. It became a different process and their work was no longer distinctively Guarani. The changes did not open new markets, and the potters had a difficult time repaying the loans. Mistakes, such as that made by the well-meaning bank, have the power to teach lessons. The lesson here is: "Before introducing resources, it is necessary to research cultural and historic meanings of a given production."[5] The more traditional a craft technique is, like the Guarani pottery, the less the designer should interfere with its production.

What kind of relationship must be established between designers, communities, and program managers for a program to have a long-lasting success? What kinds of beneficial interventions will resonate in the community? What kind of work draws from local experience and aesthetics? Such questions revolve around an essential give-and-take between different factions. Responses require the involvement of the community, as well as designers and program managers. As John Thackara, founder of Doors of Perception, an organization focusing on sustainable collaborations between grassroots innovators and designers, notes, "The most powerful lesson for me, after twenty years working as a visitor on projects in India and South Asia, is that we have more to learn from smart poor people regarding things like ecology, connectivity, devices and infrastructures, than they have to learn from us."[6]

A Promising Future

Apart from identifiable problems, the revival of crafts in Latin America is promising. In Brazil, for example, there has been a significant increase in young artisans taking up traditional craftwork. Until a few years ago, the older generation of artisans thought their children would do better in other areas and many age-old craft traditions were in danger of extinction. Today, in Latin America and around the globe, young people—both men and women—are being trained anew in craft.

In Latin America, craft has proven to be a crucial change maker. As a revitalized activity with an international outreach through alliances with designers and incentive programs, craft can help to preserve the environment, express cultural identities, and lead to an improved quality of live for craftspeople and their customers. Handmade objects are also weighted with a symbolic dimension beyond their functional contributions to daily life. They bring values that have only been recently rediscovered and acknowledged, making a connection to the wider human community while recognizing the individuality of producers and consumers alike. Things handmade are never identical. They possess the beauty of imperfection. They age with dignity, reflecting their makers and the place where they were made. They convey culture and memory. Because of all these things, they can touch—a verb used not by chance—our hearts, our souls.

---

3) Gui Bonsiepe, *Design, Cultura e Sociedade* (São Paulo: Blucher, 2011), 63. Bonsiepe identifies various slants taken in the study of craft and design: conservatively focused; with a view to nationalization, productivity, or cultural integrity; paternalistic; or focused on promoting innovation.

4) Bruce Nussbaum, "Is Humanitarian Design the New Imperialism? Does Our Desire to Help Do More Harm Than Good?" *Fast Company*, July 7, 2010, www.fastcodesign.com/1661859/is-humanitarian-design-the-new-imperialism.

5) Oswaldo Salerno, Museo Del Barro, Assuncion, Paraguay. Interviewed by the author, February 24, 2008.

6) "We Are All Emerging Economies Now" *Design Observer*, June 5, 2008, http://observatory.designobserver.com/entry.html?entry=6947. See also Thackara, "Humanitarian Design vs. Design Imperialism: Debate Summary" *Change Observer*, July 16, 2010, http://changeobserver.designobserver.com/entry.html?entry=14498.

ESSAYS

The Ethical Dimensions of Design: A Cautionary Note from Latin America

Adriana Kertzer

Latin American designers and artists often reference social, political, and economic issues in their work and the descriptions that accompany their projects. Among the most obvious visual manifestations of socioeconomic inequality in the region are the squatter settlements that spring up along the hillsides and lowlands of many Latin American cities. *Favelas* and *ranchos* (slums) have become an increasingly common theme in design and art from Latin America and, not surprisingly, they are the focus of several works in the *New Territories* exhibition.

This trend echoes a global phenomenon: changes in attitudes toward subcultures. The rise of rap culture and "ghetto fabulous" style during the 1980s and 1990s in the United States, the growing recognition of graffiti as art, and the popularity of "*cholo*" culture in Brazil are just a few examples of how "sub" is now cool.[1] However, mainstream market-based focus on certain populations, social matters, and urban spaces can stylize and fetishize very real issues to the point of pure commodification. In other cases, these references reflect earnest engagement by makers with their subjects. While nuances are important, trends such as ghetto fabulous, *cholo,* and favelization[2] require a careful consideration of how poverty, disadvantage, and discrimination can be reconfigured as commercialized signifiers.

Allusions to Latin American slums in creative projects demand consideration of the ethics of design. Design often has political nuances since it reflects and influences power relations and human relationships. As such, projects that relate to slums reflect and influence existing hierarchies of power as well as interactions between individuals of different socioeconomic status. Objects are, by nature political, and can become even more politicized because of how and by whom they are produced, used, presented, branded, marketed, and consumed. Whether or not a designer intends an object to be political, their design may become politically activated in ways that deviate from the designer's original intention.

Several objects in *New Territories* allude to Latin American slums, such as the chairs by Carolina Tinoco and Deborah Castillo, which make an explicit connection with the *ranchos* in Caracas, Venezuela.

In the case of *Panton Catuche* (2014), Tinoco manually and mechanically carved out a maquette of the *rancho* Catuche along the center of the chair (Fig. 1). Tinoco is an architect, designer, and artist who worked in different *ranchos* in Venezuela for more than ten years. Her chair was part of the Re(d) project, a collaboration with Deborah Castillo, which used design objects to reflect on certain social and cultural issues in Venezuelan society where, as the designers point out in their statement about the project, a majority of the population lives in areas affected by violence and poverty.

Another example is Eddie Figueroa Feliciano's modular storage system *Zanco* (Fig. 2) Although the object does not visually reflect an obvious connection to the slums of Puerto Rico or elsewhere in Latin America, in his project description the designer states that his *Zanco* collection draws from the basic building system practiced in Puerto Rican and other Caribbean slums before mid-twentieth-century industrialization took hold in the region. Another project in *New Territories* bears a closer connection to its source: two videos by Projeto Morrinho were filmed in the diorama created by a group of young residents-turned-artists in Pereira da Silva, a *favela* in Rio de Janeiro. They depict the role-playing games and storytelling the miniature *favela* was designed to stimulate (see page 216).

Designers, artists, and filmmakers have long engaged with primitivism and stereotypes to make their goods more desirable. I explored the different issues related to the use of references to *favelas* in *Favelization*, my book that discusses the ways in which specific producers of contemporary Brazilian culture capitalized on misappropriations of the *favela* in order to brand luxury items as "Brazilian."[3] I used three case studies—the films *Waste Land* (2010) directed by Lucy Walker, Karen Harley and João Jardim, and *City of God* (2002) directed by Fernando Meirelles; shirts designed by Fernando and Humberto Campana for Lacoste; and furniture by Bruno Jahara and David Elia—to demonstrate that the processes of interpretation, aestheticization, transcendence, and domination are part of the favelization phenomena.

Fig. 1 Carolina Tinoco
Panton Catuche, 2013-2014
(detail), From the RED
(Redesign, Reinvent, Redeem)
initiative; polypropylene
Panton chair, manual and
mechanical carving
18.5 x 20.5 x 33 in.
(47 x 52 x 84 cm)
Courtesy of a private collection
Photo: Carolina Tinoco/Pancho Quilici

Fig. 2 Eddie Figueroa Feliciano
Zanco, 2011 (detail)
Oak, nylon mesh; 36 x 15 x 15 in.
(91.4 x 38.1 x 38.1 cm)
Courtesy of the artist

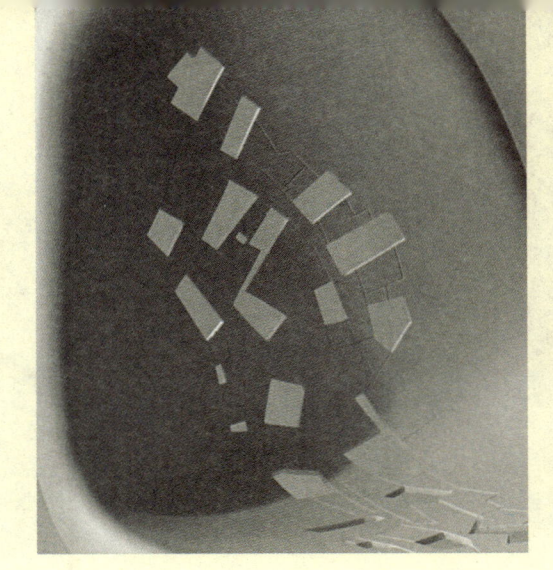

New Territories focuses on some of the same works, artists, designers, artisans, and themes that formed part of my study. The Cooperativa de Trabalho Artesanal e de Costura da Rocinha (Coopa-Roca), for example, a women's cooperative in Rocinha (a *favela* in Rio de Janeiro), made some of the shirts that were part of the 2009 Campanas + Lacoste project. The *favelas* were mentioned extensively in this project's marketing materials.[4] *New Territories* includes the chandelier *Come Rain, Come Shine* (2004), which was designed by Studio Tord Boontje, commissioned by Artecnica as part of its Design with Conscience Campaign, and handmade by Coopa-Roca. It is an example of the kinds of transnational partnerships the cooperative has engaged in over the years (see page 106).

Design da Gema's *Stray Bullet* chair (Fig. 3) was also discussed at length in *Favelization* and is included in the exhibition alongside a table from the same series (Fig. 4). David Elia, Design da Gema's founder and main designer, is a Monaco-based Brazilian designer who employs the tropes associated with favelization in descriptions of his furniture. In my book, I argued that Elia replicates a tactic deemed successful: blending strategic allusions to Brazil's poverty and violence with fantasy and desire in the service of commerce. In *New Territories*, the chair and table are among other works that address the theme of violence in Latin America.

In my earlier writing, I focused on the particulars of favelization and Brazilian contemporary culture, and I drew on postmodern theory and historical examples to deepen my analysis, raising questions about the ethical conundrums associated with using the "other" and "primitive" in film, fashion, and design. I made no suggestions for avoiding the problematic aspects of favelization. However, *New Territories* includes numerous projects, from different Latin American countries, that refer to social issues or collaborations with artisans in a manner that begins to illuminate what some best practices or strategies may be.[5] For example, certain projects identify each maker involved by name. The Oax-i-fornia lamp project gives equal credit to each collaborator, whether an artisan from Oaxaca, or a student from the California College of the Arts, or the project director/designer Raul Cabra. All are individually named (see pages 84–86).

Sometimes measured specificity is preferred as a sign of respect. In the credit line for *Robot Naturito* (2007), Alejandro Sarmiento and Luján Cambariere are given top billing followed by a statement: "in collaboration with an individual of the Instituto Correcional de Mujeres Nr. 3 de Ezeiza." While it would not be appropriate to name the woman prisoner who worked on the object, the designers give as much information as they can about their Argentinian collaborator, in an appropriate show of respect (see pages 166–167).

Many projects engage with development issues without portraying them as charity. Liliana Ovalle's and Colectivo 1050°'s collaboration on the black ceramic vessels in wooden frames in the *Sinkhole* series (2013) reflects a commitment by young designers to partner with craftspeople (see pages 94–95). During the project, they catalogued traditional practices and then created pieces that resonate with contemporary audiences. This is also the case with DFC and Glimpt, who engage craftspeople in Mexico and Peru, respectively, acknowledging their participation in terms of value, not altruism (see pages 87–90 and 113).[6] Marcella Echavarría, a branding, marketing, and sustainability consultant showcased in the video *Los ojos lo tocaran* in this exhibition, describes her objective in clear economic terms, stating that she aims to "build sustainable bridges between artisans in developing communities and developed markets who buy their products

---

1) See Lyneise E. Williams, "Heavy Metal: Decoding Hip Hop Jewelry," *Metalsmith* 27, no. 1 (2007). See *South American Cho-low* (2014), a short documentary that examines São Paulo's *cultura chicana*, www.southamericancholow.com.

2) Other authors identify this phenomenon using different terminology such as "*favela* factor," "slum chic" and "*favela* chic." The word "favelization" has also been used in other contexts to describe, for example, the increased number of *favelas* in a given region of the world and by the music group Afroreggae as the name for one of its international tours. I use the term *favelization* not in relation to the general fascination with *favelas* among social scientists.

Fig. 3 Design Da Gema (David Elia)
Stray Bullet Chair, 2011 (detail)
Polypropylene chair, stainless steel eyelets
31.9 x 23.6 x 47.3 in.
(81 x 60 x 120 cm)
Courtesy of the artist
Photo: Robson Curvello

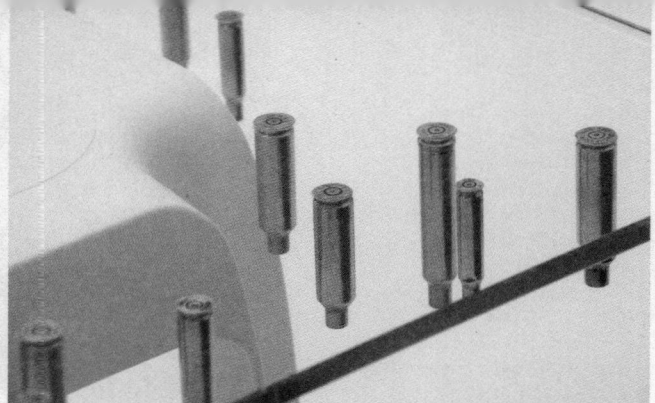

Fig. 4 Design Da Gema (David Elia)
Bulletproof Side Table, 2013 (detail)
Polypropylene monobloc side table, used bullet shells, glass
27.6 x 27.6 x 16.1 in.
(70 x 70 x 41 cm)
Courtesy of the artist
Photo: J.J. l'Heritier

for fair prices, creating what [she] hope[s] is a healthy symbiotic relationship which benefits all parties involved." Echavarría's language choice reflects an awareness that development, sustainability, and fair trade are not charity (see pages 182–183), and that these terms should not be used interchangeably.

The particular challenges as well as the successes seen in examples in *New Territories* clearly illustrates how artists, designers, market agents, and academics continue defining best practices that are useful to all participants. This can be a thorny undertaking and suggests a number of considerations that these agents might consider when presenting a project in a commercial or museum setting: What kind of attached value am I trying to create? What does a reference to *ranchos* or *favelas* add to my marketing and branding strategy? Have I accurately represented my professional and/or personal relationship with the individual artisans or the organization from a specific slum? Will this project affect the relative distribution of power, authority, and privilege in a community? The answers might not be simple. Yet in many cases, had different production, branding, and marketing choices been made, the answers to these questions would be different. For example, a chair in and of itself may not affect the power relations between different sectors of a country's society, but the stories behind that chair—for examples, who produced it and where?—may serve to politicize the object and its design.

Discussions about references to Latin American slums in the context of design, craft, and art force us to question the representation and the creation of identity, value and storytelling—issues that are relevant when speaking about Latin American design in general. While many Latin American artists are celebrated in international museums and designated—perhaps to their chagrin—as an investment category in the art world, designers from Latin America still struggle to gain recognition in their countries of origin and abroad, in museums, and among collectors. The ways in which they distinguish themselves in the field and market their work reflect this struggle. At times the "benefit" of existing stereotypes can be usefully deployed, and simplistic references can be appealing and practical toward these ends. However, many designers and artisans are finding ways of citing specific communities and spaces when providing information about their work in a manner that is sensitive and nuanced. Marketing and branding often require stressing differences through the processes of dichotomizing, essentializing, and "other"-izing. The challenge is how to create design projects that receive international recognition and use storytelling about certain socioeconomic issues in a way that does not exacerbate stereotypes and unequal power relations. The debate about the ethical dimensions of design continues.

3) Adriana Kertzer, *Favelization: The Imaginary Brazil in Contemporary Film, Fashion and Design*, Design-File e-book 4 (New York: Cooper-Hewitt, National Design Museum, 2014).
4) See ibid. For further discussion of theories of commodification, fetishization, and the use/creation of a primitive "other" in the process of defining national identity, as these issues relate to the collaboration with Coopa-Roca. See also "Campanas + LACOSTE," Lacoste website, accessed on July 13, 2013, http://shop.lacoste.com/Campanas/b/6199301011.
5) The scope of this essay is limited to exploring examples from *New Territories*. An in-depth discussion of best practices in the field of public-interest design should consider literature about socially responsible design, the methodologies used to qualify and quantify how design addresses issues faced by communities, and existing guidelines for engaging in community-based design such as the Social Economic Environmental Design (SEED) metric.
6) *Mis Ojos Lo Tocarán* (My Eyes Will Touch It), a digital audio slideshow on the work of Marcella Echavarría produced by Dia Felix Media, commissioned by MAD for *New Territories* in 2014, with musical score by Ava Mendoza.

ESSAYS

Rediscovering and Reinventing Latin American Food

Marcella Echavarría

Latin American cuisine has changed a great deal in the last twenty years, as well as in the fields of design and craft (see Adélia Borges's essay on page 68). Inspiration no longer derives from the use of foreign ingredients and recipes by cooks who lived isolated lives and largely ignored local ingredients, along with their cultivators and the nature that embraced them. Today, inspiration is right at home with new discoveries being made daily. Food is an engine for development and a real source of collective national identity. Latin American cooks are part of an unprecedented revolution in which the palate is the epicenter for social, cultural, and environmental change. As expressed by Peruvian chef and restauranteur Gaston Acurio, "Such opportunities will benefit society in fields as intimately linked to it as culture, social solidarity, the environment, education, nutrition or innovation. Today, the cook is finally playing a new role: that of someone who is able to tell stories through his kitchen that not only stir the senses but also the soul, the mind and the heart."[1]

Since Acurio's return to Peru after studying at the Cordon Bleu in the 1990s, he has been a catalytic agent in promoting this new way to embrace food as a venue for social change and national identity. He defines himself first as Peruvian and second as a cook, spreading his influence from Peru to the far reaches of Latin America. His starting point is a conceptual journey through Peruvian history—pre-Inca cultures, Incas, Spaniards, Africans, Italians, Japanese, Chinese, and finally Peruvians who return home and discover flavors and culinary opportunities unimaginable until recently. He has a deep respect for all the links in the chain, giving credit to farmers, fishermen, regions, markets, dinning tables, families, and cooks, voicing and valuing the invisible. He notes that "Peru has an immense biodiversity expressed in thousands of products that have been preserved by small producers as authentic treasures."

Acurio's work inspired the Spanish chef Ferran Adria to proclaim, "Food is the new rock 'n' roll, and the place to see this phenomenon is Peru." Since Adria's first visit to Peru in 2011, he has become an advocate of its food, recognizing its importance as a role model. The Peruvian model, now extended to the rest of Latin America, is a mix of biodiversity, cultural diversity, and commitment to social equality, environmental sustainability, harmony, and beauty.

Acurio has built his concept into a diverse portfolio of restaurants through which his empire has expanded to London, Madrid, Mexico City, Caracas, Bogotá, Santiago de Chile, Chicago, and San Francisco. Among others they include: La Mar in New York City, where his distinct take on a typical *cevicheria*, or Peruvian fast food place, is featured; Madame Tusan in Lima, where one finds a celebration of the Chinese influence in Peru; Tanta in Chicago, a café with all the childhood flavors ready to go; and Astrid y Gaston in Bogotá, the acclaimed jewel of the Acurio crown, now ranked fourteen in the *San Pellegrino List of Best Restaurants*. Instead of taking a cut-and-paste approach, Acurio has embraced each new territory with his signature approach: humble questioning, subtle seduction, rigorous tasting, sensual discovering, and above all, a profound belief in each region's potential for discovering its own brand of paradise.

At the Astrid y Gaston franchises, local ingredients are used in new ways. At the restaurant in Bogotá, *guasca*, a local herb that is an ingredient in the famous *ajiaco* chicken soup, now dominates the bread basket, while coconut rice from the coast becomes the base for a new Colombian risotto. In Mexico, the *causa limeña*, a pre-Columbian recipe made with mashed yellow potato, includes chile chipotle as its main spice. In Madrid, as in every country where an Astrid y Gaston restuarant is present, there are two menus: the "Classic Peruvian Menu," where there will always be an abundance of potatoes (Peru has more than three thousand known varieties of potatoes), corn, herbs, and spices, and a regional menu that expresses Acurio's style and pays homage to the local cuisine as he explores it.

Fig. 1 Women at Chichcastenango market, Guatemala
Photo: Marcella Echavarría

Fig. 2 Painted characters at San Martin Tilcajete's Devil Carnival, Oaxaca
Photo: Marcella Echavarría

Fig. 3 Colorful gelatin in the streets of Oaxaca
Photo: Marcella Echavarría

Fig. 4 Woman in Tlacolula, Oaxaca
Photo: Marcella Echavarría

Fig. 5 Woman making tortillas in Antigua
Photo: Marcella Echavarría

Fig. 6 Market in Antigua
Photo: Marcella Echavarría

Fig. 7 Dying with bark in Peru's Sacred Valley
Photo: Marcella Echavarría

Fig. 8 Tomatoes from Chiapas
Photo: Marcella Echavarría

Farther south, in Brazil, Alex Atala has "discovered" and created a contemporary interpretation of Amazonian food that has put Brazilian food on the map, distinct from the kind of imported food that was long repeated, like the mantra, in restaurants throughout the country. Helena Rizzo of Maní in São Paulo tells local stories with traditional Brazilian ingredients that are transformed with a mix of culinary techniques—mostly learned at El Celler de Can Rocca in Spain—and served as works of art. She makes a highly sophisticated version of *feijoada*, the typical Brazilian bean stew, and *maniocas* (a root vegetable) baked and served with *tucupi* froth (also made from *manioc*), coconut milk, and white truffle oil. As Rizzo explains, "We work with what we take from our lives here, and from our childhood tastes. We are always searching for authenticity."

In Mexico, the food scene is vibrant and artistic. Mexican cuisine, a fusion of Mesoamerican and Spanish with African and mestizo accents, was added by UNESCO to its Intangible Cultural Heritage list. The Spaniards could not colonize or convert the tables of this conquered land, replete with such native staples as corn, avocado, beans, and hundreds of chilis and spices. In colonial times, Mexico's convents instead became melting pots of regional flavors and techniques, where local cuisines emerged. Culinary customs have been passed down through generations and ensure community cohesion. This immense cultural heritage comes to life in the work of chef and restauranteur Enrique Olvera, owner of of Pujol in Mexico City, ranked thirty-six in the *Sar Pellegrino List of Best Restaurants*. "It's a good time to be cooking Mexican," says Olvera. "For one thing, the possibility of a cooking career in Mexico is something new. Before, you weren't a cook by choice—it was your destiny. In order to evolve, we need to start thinking beyond our own traditions. We need to make Mexican food a little bit lighter, more in tune with modern tastes. It's already so flavorful. It's like a bomb in your mouth." One of Olvera's innovations has been making everyday food that is modern and artistic, and connected to modern lifestyles, not just dishes for special occasions. "At Pujol," Olvera continues, "we do a taco with *hoja santa* (an aromatic herb) in the tortilla, which isn't necessarily new—you'll find it in Oaxaca—but we pair it with ceviche and black beans. We're using peppers and spices to enhance, not to cover. This approach to cooking is new for Mexicans."

As geography defines food, so too does the new Latin America and its view of itself: a more open society where expressions of authenticity are valued, where there is a return to indigenous voices that were silenced in the past. It is a place of progress and development. In present-day Latin American, many cuisines serve a world hungry to hear echoes of the past, to glimpse hints of the future, and to taste what's new.

1) All quotes derive from interviews that I have conducted over the years and from Gaston Acurio's Facebook page, https://www.facebook.com/gastonacurio.

Focus:
MEXICO CITY & OAXACA

Raul Cabra, Emily Jan, Rie Hirai Dion, Michele Marti, Zak Timan, Maria Magdalena Angeles Vasquez, Timoteo de Jesus Bernardino Cruz, Timoteo Bernardino Angeles
Double Barrel Lamp, 2009
Carrizo, copper wire, electrical materials
Lamp: 13 x 28 in. (33 x 71.1 cm) each;
Metal rod: 4.9 ft. (1.5 m)
Courtesy of the artists
Photo: Romina Hierro

Raul Cabra, Emily Jan, Rie Hirai Dion, Michele Marti, Zak Timan, Maria Magdalena Angeles Vasquez, Timoteo de Jesus Bernardino Cruz, Timoteo Bernardino Angeles
A Lamp for Ruth Asawa, 2009
Carrizo, copper, wire, electrical materials
50 x 12 in. (127 x 30.5 cm)
Courtesy of the artists
Photo: Romina Hierro

**Raul Cabra, Lander Cruz, Serena Franklin,
Lydia Davis, Emily Jan, Sarahi Garcia**
Blowfish Lamp, 2008
Carrizo, wire, electrical materials
22 in. (55.88 cm) diameter
Courtesy of the artists
Photo: Frederick Jimenez

DFC
Casual dinnerware, 2013
Hand-cast, hand-glazed stoneware featuring famous
(and infamous) Mexican icons
Dimensions variable
Courtesy of the artists
Photo: David Franco

DFC
Orange Crush fiberglass wall console, 2013
Fiberglass, hand airbrushed
55 in. (139.7 cm) diameter
Courtesy of the artists

DFC
Rosario mirror, 2013
Gold-tinted mirror (14 kt gold glaze), ceramic butterflies
39.4 in. (100 cm) diameter
Courtesy of the artists

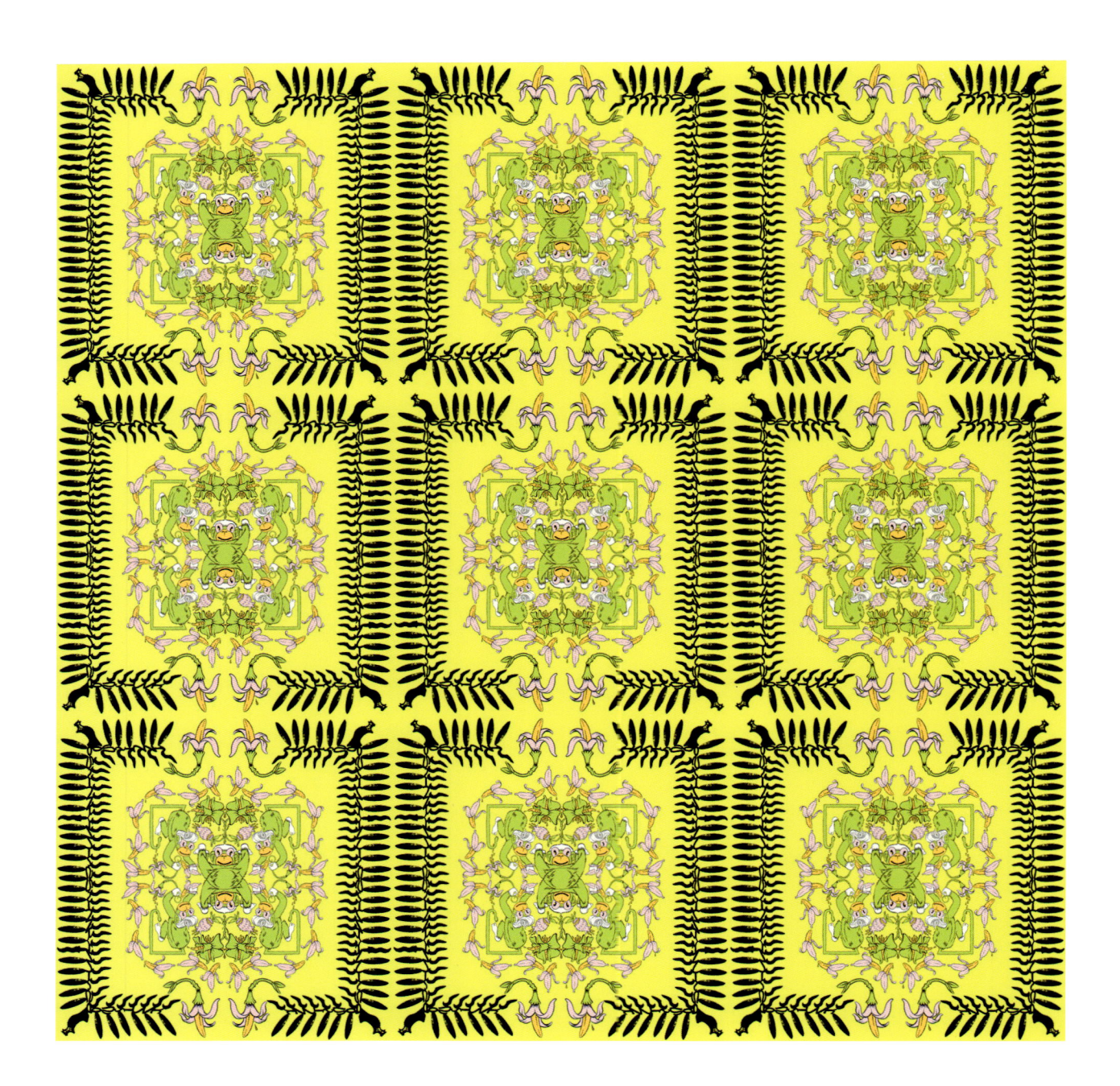

**DFC in collaboration
with David Franco and Flavor Paper**
Lemon Zest Wallpaper, from the series *Love Monkey,* 2012
Digitally printed paper
6 x 9 ft. (1.8 x 2.7 m)

**Carla Fernández in collaboration
with Taller Flora and Pascuala Sánchez**
Square Chamula Coat from the *Estridentistas* collection, 2014
Wool handwoven in a waist loom, dyed with mud
23.6 x 23.6 in. (60 x 60 cm)
Courtesy of the artist
Photo: Ramiro Chavez

**Carla Fernández in collaboration
with Taller Flora and Pascuala Sánchez**
Square Chamula Coat, from the *Casa Barragan* collection, 2008
Wool handwoven in a waist loom, dyed with mud
63 x 63 in. (160 x 160 cm)
Courtesy of the artist
Photo: Diego Pérez

**Carla Fernández in collaboration
with Taller Flora and Pascuala Sánchez**
Barragan, from the *Casa Barragan* collection, 2008
Wool handwoven in a waist loom
Top: 39.3 x 23.6 in. (100 x 60 cm)
Skirt: 23.6 x 23.6 in. (60 x 60 cm)
Courtesy of the artist
Photo: Diego Pérez

Liliana Ovalle in collaboration with Colectivo 1050°
Sinkhole No. 1 Bola, 2013
Red clay, oak
13.4 x 13 x 11.8 in. (34 x 33 x 30 cm)
Courtesy of the artist

Sinkhole No. 2 Olludo, 2013
Red clay, oak
12.6 x 10.2 x 15.7 in. (32 x 26 x 40 cm)
Courtesy of the artist

Sinkhole No. 4 Bule, 2013
Red clay, oak
10.6 x 10.2 x 11.8 in. (27 x 26 x 30 cm)
Courtesy of the artist

Sinkhole No. 3 Botita, 2013
Red clay, oak
11.8 x 9 x 13 in. (30 x 23 x 33 cm)
Courtesy of the artist

Sinkhole No. 5 Chaparrito, 2013
Red clay, oak
14.2 x 11 x 9 in. (36 x 28 x 23 cm)
Courtesy of the artist

Rodrigo Almeida
Hammock, 2013
Handmade cotton fabric, perforated leather (bovine)
7.5 x 4.9 ft. (2.2 m x 1.5 m) diameter
Courtesy of the artist

**Angelica Coyopol in collaboration
with Angelica Moreno**
Original Talavera Jar, digitized as part
of the the series *Losing My America*, 2009
Talavera ceramics, paint, vitrified glaze
10.8 x 6.3 x 5.5 in. (27.5 x 16 x 14 cm)
Courtesy of Coletivo Amor de Madre

Ariel Rojo
Talavera Jar from the series
Losing My America, 2014
Talavera ceramics, paint, vitrified glaze
10.8 x 6.3 x 5.5 in. (27.5 x 16 x 14 cm)
Courtesy of Coletivo Amor de Madre

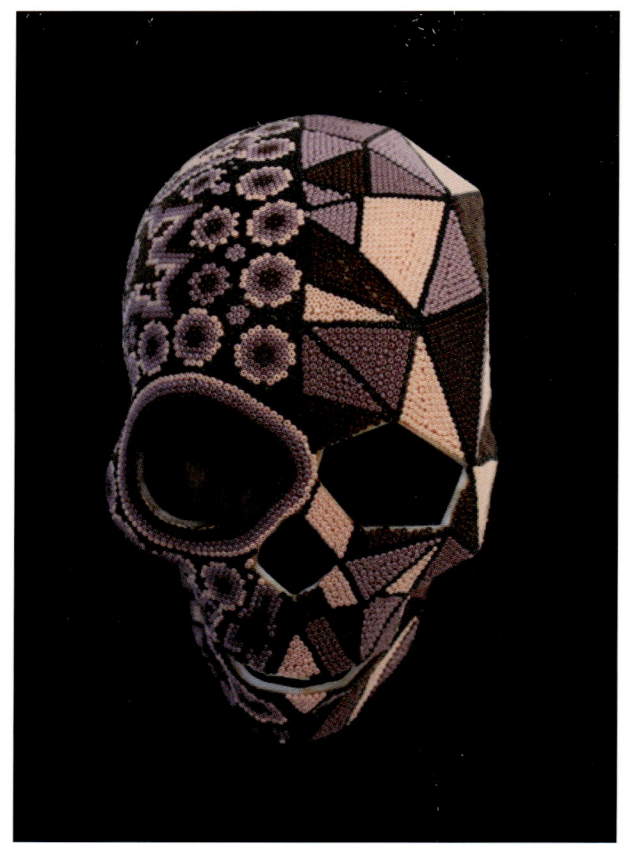

**Florentino López in collaboration
with Makoto Nancarrow Sugiura**
Original Huichol Skull, digitized as part
of the the series *Losing My America*, 2012
Ceramics, wax, glass beads
7.5 x 3.9 x 4.7 in. (19 x 10 x 12 cm)
Courtesy of Coletivo Amor de Madre

Ariel Rojo
Huichol Skull, from the series
Losing My America, 2012
Ceramics, wax, glass beads
7.5 x 3.9 x 4.7 in. (19 x 10 x 12 cm)
Courtesy of Coletivo Amor de Madre

Vanderlino Miguel de Souza
Nossa Senhora Aparecida, digitized as part of the the series *Losing My America*, 2013
Wood
5.9 x 13.4 x 5.9 in. (15 x 34 x 15 cm)
Courtesy of Coletivo Amor de Madre
Photo: Vitor Reis

Estúdio Guto Requena
Nossa Senhora DESAparecida, virtualized from the series *Losing My America*, 2014
Wood, bronze
5.9 x 13.4 x 5.9 in. (15 x 34 x 15 cm)
Courtesy of Coletivo Amor de Madre
Photo: Vitor Reis

Inés Carter
Dama en Crin, digitized as part of the series
Losing My America, 2014
Horsehair
15 x 5.9 x 5.9 in. (38 x 15 x 15 cm)
Courtesy of Coletivo Amor de Madre

gt2P
Krina, from the series *Losing My America*,
2014
Horsehair
13.4 x 7.9 x 8.3 in. (34 x 20 x 21 cm)
Courtesy of Coletivo Amor de Madre

Victorina Gallegos
Jarro Unesco, digitized as part of the series
Losing My America, 2014
Clay, cow dung
8.3 x 7.9 x 7.5 in. (21.5 x 20 x 19 cm)
Courtesy of Coletivo Amor de Madre

gt2P
Jarro Unesco, from the series *Losing My America,* 2014
Clay
7.3 x 6.7 x 7.9 in. (18.5 x 17 x 20 cm)
Courtesy of Coletivo Amor de Madre

Néstor Miranda
Trio de Pocillo (large), digitized as part of the series
Losing My America, 2011
Wood, 4.7 x 4.1 x 3.9 in. (12 x 10.5 x 10 cm)
Courtesy of Coletivo Amor de Madre

Trio de Pocillo (medium), digitized as part of the series
Losing My America, 2011
Wood, 4.1 x 4.1 x 3.9 in. (10.5 x 10.5 x 10 cm)
Courtesy of Coletivo Amor de Madre

Trio de Pocillo (small), digitized as part of the series
Losing My America, 2011
Wood, 3.5 x 7.9 x 5.3 in. (9 x 20 x 13.5 cm)
Courtesy of Coletivo Amor de Madre

gt2P
Trio pocillo (large), from the series
Losing My America, 2014
Wood, 8.1 x 4.9 x 8.1 in. (20.5 x 12.5 x 20.5 cm)
Courtesy of Coletivo Amor de Madre

Trio pocillo (medium), from the series
Losing My America, 2014
Wood, 2 x 4.3 x 7.3 in. (5 x 11 x 18.5 cm)
Courtesy of Coletivo Amor de Madre

Trio pocillo (small), from the series
Losing My America, 2014
Wood, 1.4 x 3.5 x 6.1 in. (3.5 x 9 x 15.5 cm)
Courtesy of Coletivo Amor de Madre

Teresa Olmedo
Baker, digitized as part of the series
Losing My America, 2014
Clay, paint
5.3 x 4.3 x 3.1 in. (13.5 x 11 x 8 cm)
Courtesy of Coletivo Amor de Madre

Oven, digitized as part of the series
Losing My America, 2014
Clay, paint
4.5 x 3 x 3 in. (11.5 x 7.5 x 7.5 cm)
Courtesy of Coletivo Amor de Madre

Tree, digitized as part of the series
Losing My America, 2014
Clay, paint
7.9 x 6 x 6.3 in. (20 x 15.5 x 16 cm)
Courtesy of Coletivo Amor de Madre

Table, digitized as part of the series
Losing My America, 2014
Clay, paint
3 x 3.3 x 2.6 in. (7.5 x 8.5 x 6.5 cm)
Courtesy of Coletivo Amor de Madre

gt2P
Ovenera Oven, from the series
Losing My America, 2014
Clay, paint
8.3 x 7.9 x 7.5 in. (21.5 x 20 x 19 cm)
Courtesy of Coletivo Amor de Madre

Ovenera, from the series
Losing My America, 2014
Clay, paint
3 x 3.3 x 2.6 in. (7.5 x 8.5 x 6.5 cm)
Courtesy of Coletivo Amor de Madre

Ovenera Table, from the series
Losing My America, 2014
Clay, paint
3.5 x 2.6 x 3.5 in. (9 x 6.5 x 9 cm)
Courtesy of Coletivo Amor de Madre

Tree, from the series
Losing My America, 2014
Clay, paint
9.1 x 8.3 x 8.3 in. (23 x 21 x 21 cm)
Courtesy of Coletivo Amor de Madre

Victor San Martin
Milk Jar, digitized as part of the series
Losing My America, 2005
Clay, glaze
4.5 x 6.3 x 4.5 in. (11.5 x 16 x 11.5 cm)
Courtesy of Coletivo Amor de Madre

Palmeta (large), digitized as part of the series
Losing My America, 2005
Clay, glaze
3.5 x 7.9 x 5.3 in. (9 x 20 x 13.5 cm)
Courtesy of Coletivo Amor de Madre

Palmeta (small), digitized as part of the series
Losing My America, 2005
Clay, glaze
1.2 x 2.7 x 3.5 in. (3 x 7 x 9 cm)
Courtesy of Coletivo Amor de Madre

gt2P
Milk Jar, from the series
Losing My America, 2014
Clay, glaze
4.1 x 6.1 x 4.5 in. (10.5 x 15.5 x 11.5 cm)
Courtesy of Coletivo Amor de Madre

Palmeta (large), from the series
Losing My America, 2014
Clay, glaze
2 x 4.9 x 3.5 in. (5 x 12.5 x 9 cm)
Courtesy of Coletivo Amor de Madre

Palmeta (small), from the series
Losing My America, 2014
Clay, glaze
1.4 x 3.3 x 2.8 in. (3.5 x 8.5 x 7 cm)
Courtesy of Coletivo Amor de Madre

Pedro Barrail
El Castor tattoo stool, 2008
Cedar, pyrogravure
32 x 14 x 14 in. (81.5 x 35.5 x 35.5 cm)
Courtesy of Cristina Grajales Gallery

Shoot tattoo breakfast table, 2010
Cedar, pyrogravure
32 x 32 x 32 in. (81.2 x 81.2 x 81.2 cm)
Courtesy of Cristina Grajales Gallery

Designed by Studio Tord Boontje and comissioned by Artecnica as part of Artecnica's Design with Conscience campaign. Handmade by Cooperativa de Trabalho Artesanal e de Costura da Rocinha Ltda. (Coopa-Roca)
Come Rain, Come Shine Chandelier, 2004
Metal rods, ribbons, organza, cotton silk
53.1 x 23.6 in. (135 x 60 cm)
Courtesy of Artecnica

Guillermo Bert (woven by Anita Paillamil)
Redemption, 2012
Wool, natural dyes
7 x 4 ft. (2.1 x 1.2 m)
Courtesy of Michael and Frances Weber
Photo: Ronald Dunlap

Guillermo Bert
Redemption, 2012
Video
8 mins.
Courtesy of Michael and Frances Weber

María Eugenia Dávila and Eduardo Portillo
Sol de la tarde, 2013
Triple weave, silk, moriche palm fiber (Mauritia flexuosa)
from the Orinoco River delta, copper
74.8 x 37.4 in. (190 x 95 cm)
Courtesy of the artists
Photo: Rafael Lacau

Guardian Indigo, 2007
Triple weave, Mérida silk, moriche palm fiber
(Mauritia flexuosa) from the Orinoco River delta, wool,
natural dyes (indigo, cochineal, eucalyptus, onion)
36.2 x 80.7 in. (92 x 205 cm)
Courtesy of the collection of Jack Lenor Larsen
Photo: Rafael Lacau

María Eugenia Dávila and Eduardo Portillo
Textil Fundido, 2013
Bronze
8.3 x 8.7 in. (21 x 22 cm)
Courtesy of the artists
Photo: Rafael Lacau

Chiachio & Giannone
La ciudad frondosa, 2011-2012
Hand embroidery: cotton, rayon, wool
9.2 x 14.8 ft. (2.8 x 4.5 m)
Museum of Arts and Design; museum purchase with funds
provided by Nanette L. Laitman, 2014

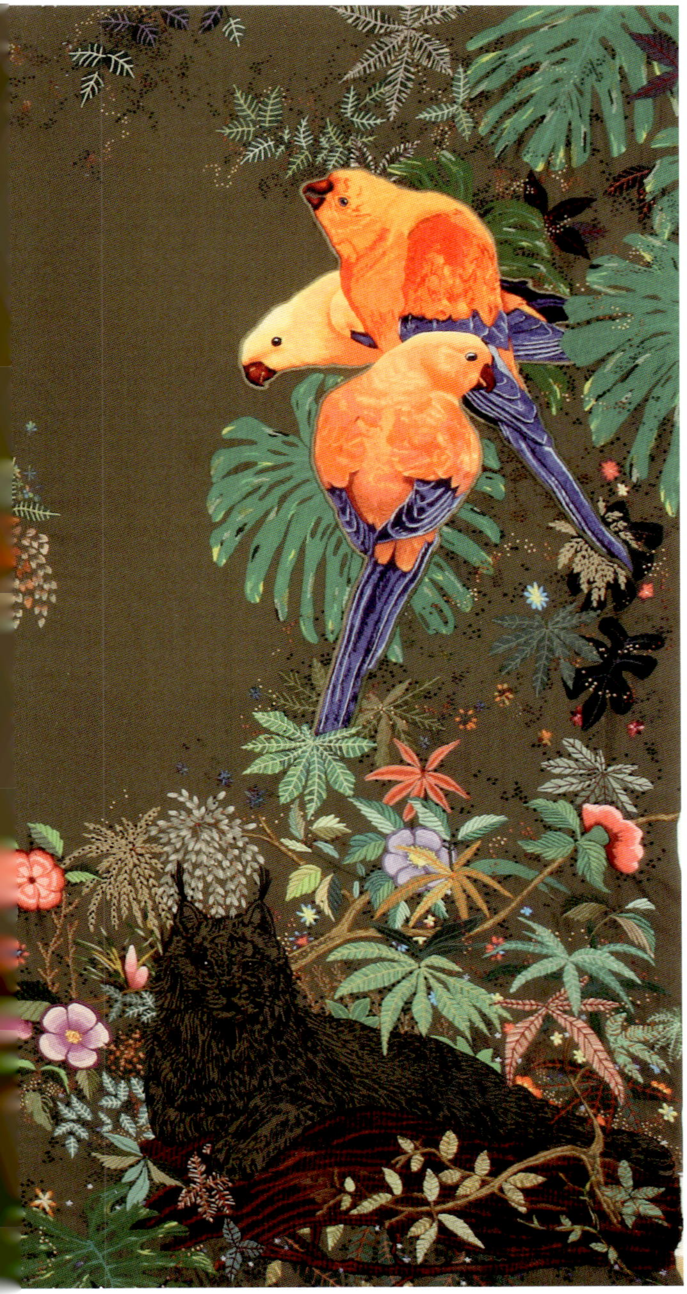

Chiachio & Giannone
Ekeko Triptico, 2010-2012
Porcelain, handmade crochet, Cordonet Spécial Crochet
DMC thread
13.3 x 10.6 in. (34 x 27 cm) each
Courtesy of Ruth Benzacar Galería de Arte

Glimpt
The Robot, 2012
Wood (lengha and cedar), glass
11.8 x 15.7 in. (30 x 40 cm) diameter
Courtesy of the artists
Photo: Daniel Thrue/Trueproductions

The Spaceship, 2012
Wood (lengha and cedar), glass
23.6 x 13.8 in. (60 x 35 cm) diameter
Courtesy of the artists
Photo: Daniel Thrue/Trueproductions

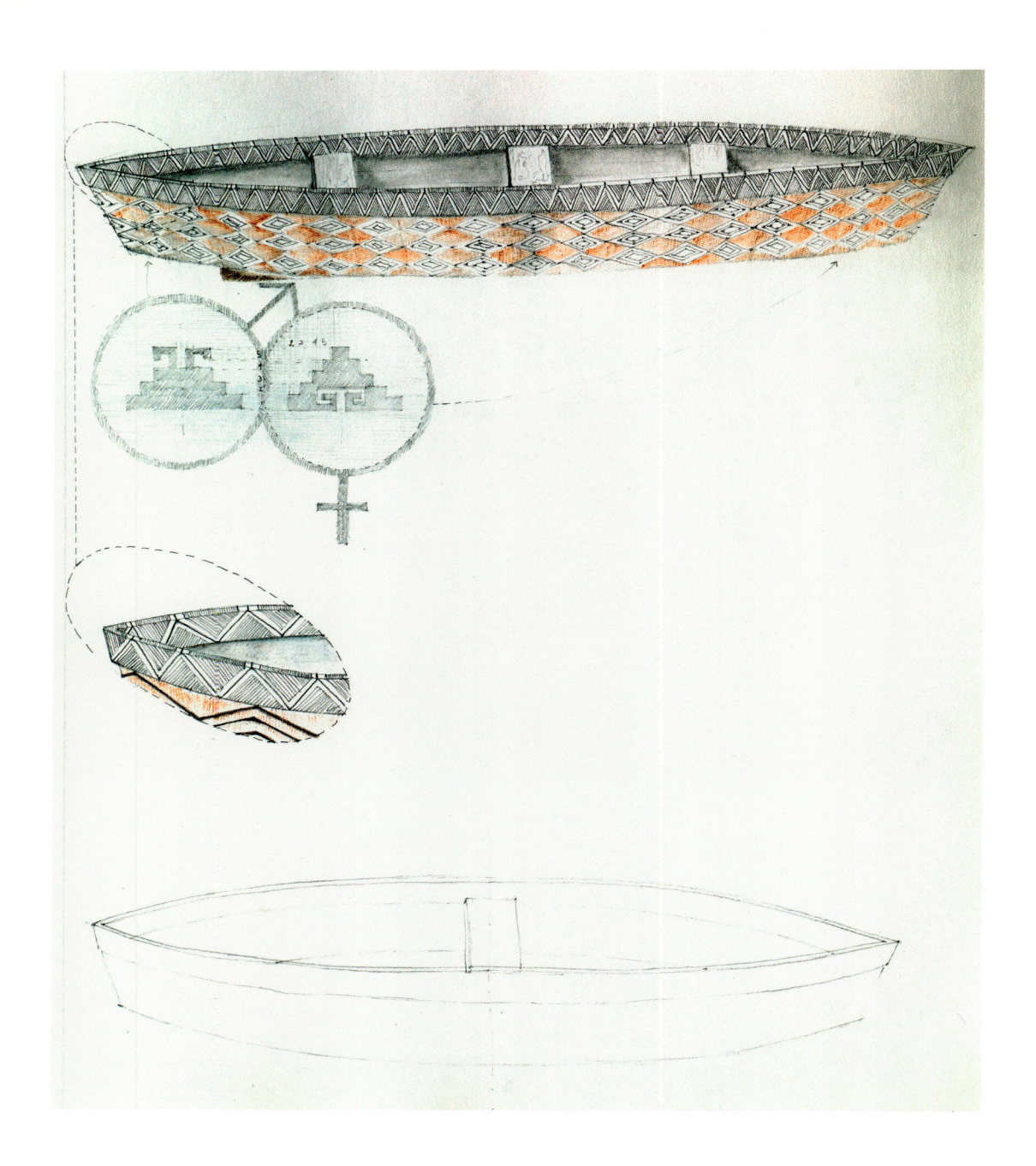

Hechizoo & Jorge Lizarazo
Canoe (rendering), 2014
Wood, wheat, copper
11 x 158 x 29.5 in. (27.9 x 401.3 x 74.9 cm)
Courtesy of Cristina Grajales Gallery

MáximaDuda (Mária Antonia Godigna and Anabella Georgi)
Miss Delta Amacuro chair, 2006
Morich palm fiber, metal, leather (bovine), plastic
35.5 x 31.5 x 31.5 in. (90.6 x 80 x 80 cm)
Courtesy of the artists
Photo: Valentina Gamero

Nada Se Leva in collaboration with Cultura em Foco, IPTI
Fuxico Design, 2011
Tricoline, cotton thread
51 x 71 in. (130 x 180 cm)
Courtesy of Fellicia

Maria Nepomuceno
Untitled, 2010
Synthetic plastic rope; sisal rope; colored plastic beads;
terracota beads and containers; glass fiber and resin
pieces; braided, dyed, and natural *palha de carnauba*
(carnauba hay)
35.4 x 98.4 x 51.2 in. (90 x 250 x 130 cm)
Courtesy of the Tiroche DeLeon Collection and Art Vantage
PCC Limited

Focus:
CARACAS

Alessandro Balteo Yazbeck in collaboration with Media Farzin
Eames-Derivative (small version from the series *Cultural Diplomacy: An Art We Neglect*), 2006-2013
1,242 custom-made slotted cards, silk thread, five framed vintage magazine ads, narrative wall labels, vinyl wall lettering, glass and wood platform, metal fixtures

Platform: 19.5 ft. (5.94 m) long; house of cards: 59 in. (150 cm) approx. high; framed ads: 21 x 17 in. (54 x 43 cm) approx. each; vinyl wall lettering: minimum size 30 x 206.5 in. (75 x 520 cm)
Courtesy of Henrique Faria Fine Art, New York
Photo: Arturo Sanchez

1970 Charles and Ray Eames design *Computer House of Cards* as a souvenir of the IBM Pavilion at the Osaka World's Fair.

IBM introduces the first magnetic stripe plastic cards, which will be standardized for international use in credit cards within two years.

1971 President Richard Nixon ends the convertibility of the dollar to gold — under the pressures of U.S. war expenses and persistent budget deficits — thus ending the Bretton Woods system.

From this point onward, the value of the U.S. dollar will be based on its global demand, and dependent upon the military, technological and ideological power of the United States.

Deborah Castillo
Panton Vias, from the RED (Redesign, Reinvent, Redeem) initiative, 2013
Polypropylene Panton chair, Dupont Chromas Surfacer KK paint
18.5 x 20.5 x 33 in. (47 x 52 x 84 cm)
Courtesy of a private collection

Carolina Tinoco
Panton Catuche, from the RED (Redesign, Reinvent, Redeem) initiative, 2013-2014
Polypropylene Panton chair, manual and mechanical carving
18.5 x 20.5 x 33 in. (47 x 52 x 84 cm)
Courtesy of a private collection
Photo: Carolina Tinoco/Pancho Quilici

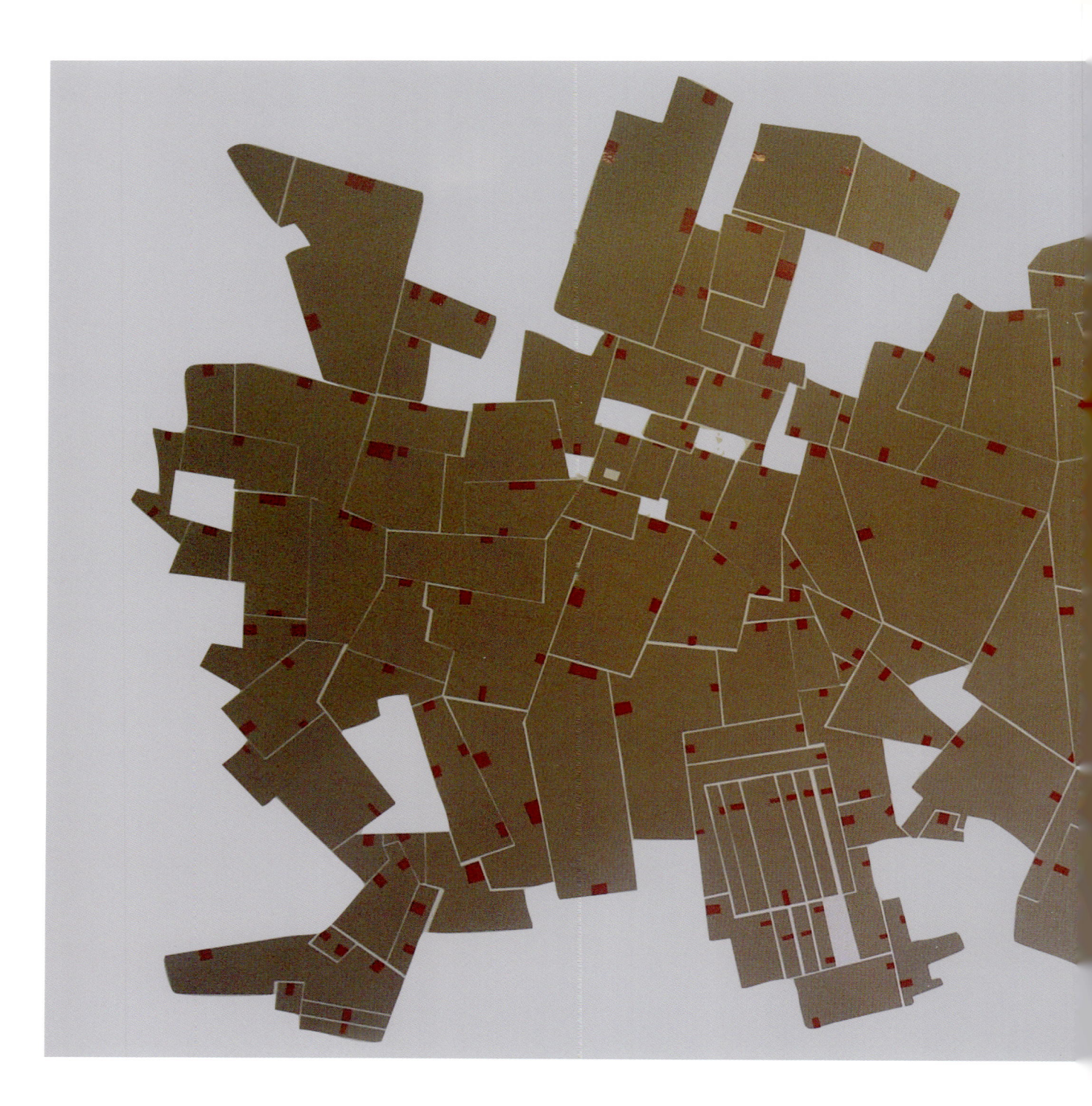

Pepe López
Geometrias marginales (maquette), 2014
Iron
Dimensions variable
Courtesy of the artist
Photo: Paloma Lopez

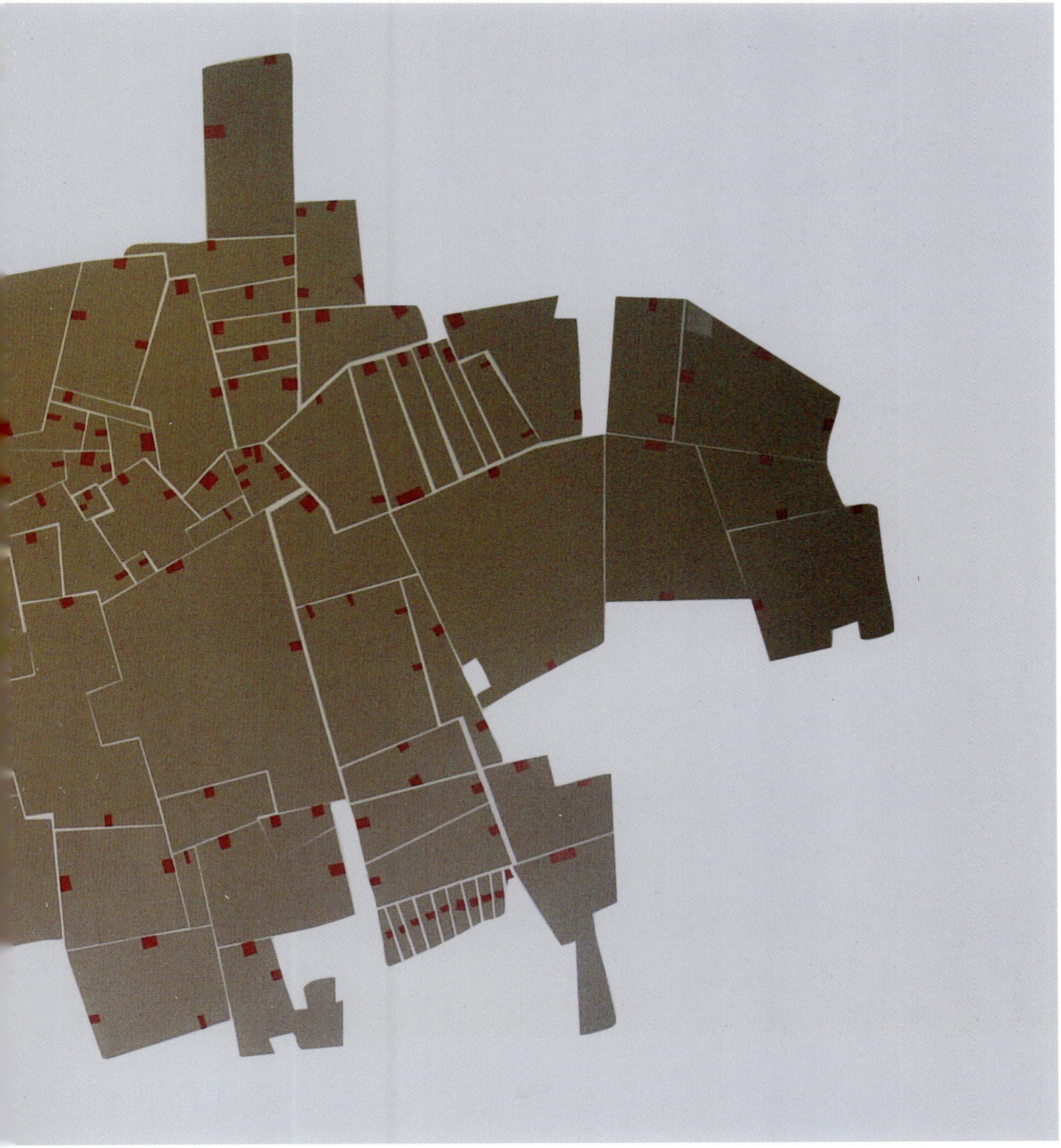

Bernardo Mazzei
Anauco Aalto, 2011
Aluminium bars, steel allen screws, cow leather
35.4 x 26 x 34.3 in. (90 x 66 x 87 cm)
Courtesy of the artist
Photo: Francisco Mazzei Boulton

Pepe López
Geometria blanda, from the series
Geometrics Desechables, 2010
300 polyethelene shopping bags
15 x 15 x 2 in. (38.1 x 38.1 x 5 cm)
Courtesy of Beatriz Gil Galeria
Photo: Valentina Atencio

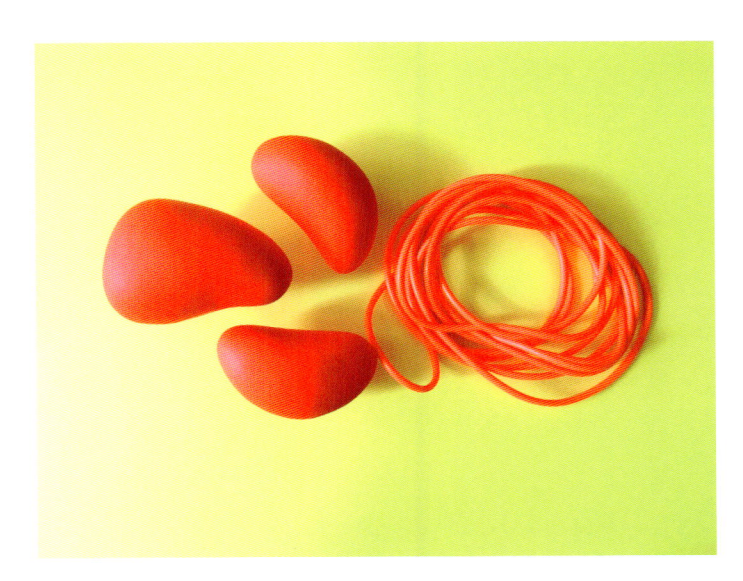

Rodolfo Agrella
Isidora, 2013
Glazed concrete, stainless steel bracket, rubber bands
Dimensions variable
Courtesy of the artist

Anabella Georgi
Silla Fuga Kids Policromatica, 2009
Iron, chrome, grupon leather, MDF wood
27.6 x 23.6 x 13.8 in. (70 x 60 x 35 cm)
Courtesy of the artist
Photo: Fernando Román

Jorge Rivas
Banco, 2003
Pardillo wood
11.8 x 22.8 x 11.8 in. (30 x 58 x 30 cm)
Courtesy of the artist
Photo: LSMP Fotografía

Leo Capote
Tulip Bolts Chair, 2013
Carbon steel bolts, electroless nickel plating
27.6 x 24.4 x 32.7 in. (70 x 62 x 83 cm)
Courtesy of Firma Casa Gallery
Photo: Marcelo Stefanovicz

Leo Capote
Panton Chair Bolts, 2013
Carbon steel bolts, electrostatic painting
22 x 23.6 x 33.9 in. (56 x 60 x 86 cm)
Courtesy of Firma Casa Gallery
Photo: Marcelo Stefanovicz

Hechizoo & Jorge Lizarazo
Homage to Cruz Diaz, 2010
Red copper; blue, violet, fuchsia, and green anodized
copper; gold and silver plated wire
101.5 x 51 in. (257.8 x 129.5 cm)
Museum of Arts and Design, gift of Cristina Grajales
Gallery and Jorge Lizarazo, 2011

Lattoog
Pantosh Easy Chair, from the series *Fusions*, 2008
Plywood
26.8 x 25.6 x 25.6 in. (68 x 65 x 65 cm)
Courtesy of the artists

Nada Se Leva
Ligero Mirror model 01, 1996
Laser-cut acrylic
29.5 x 48 x 1 in. (75 x 122 x 2.5 cm)
Courtesy of the artists

Ligero Side Table, 1996
Laser-cut acrylic
21.5 x 19.5 x 21.5 in. (55 x 50 x 55 cm)
Courtesy of the artists

Edgar Orlaineta
Mask II (DCW) After Charles Eames, 2013
Steel, brass, bent walnut plywood, turned wood,
wood veneer, river rocks, rubber, cambaya fabric,
natural wax, acrylic paint, lacquer, hardware
63.5 x 19.8 x 23.2 in. (160.7 x 49.5 x 58.9 cm)
Courtesy of the artist and Steve Turner Contemporary, Los Angeles

Edgar Orlaineta
Totem after Ettore Sottsas, 2013
Steel, mirror, glass, turned wood
75.3 x 76.8 x 15.8 in. (191.1 x 194.9 x 40 cm)
Courtesy of the artist and Steve Turner Contemporary, Los Angeles

Estudio Guto Requena
Nóize St. Ifigénia, from the Nóize Collection, 2012
3-D printed in ABS
15.7 x 17.3 x 31.1 in. (40 x 44 x 79 cm)
Courtesy of Coletivo Amor de Madre
Photo: Tomek Sadurski

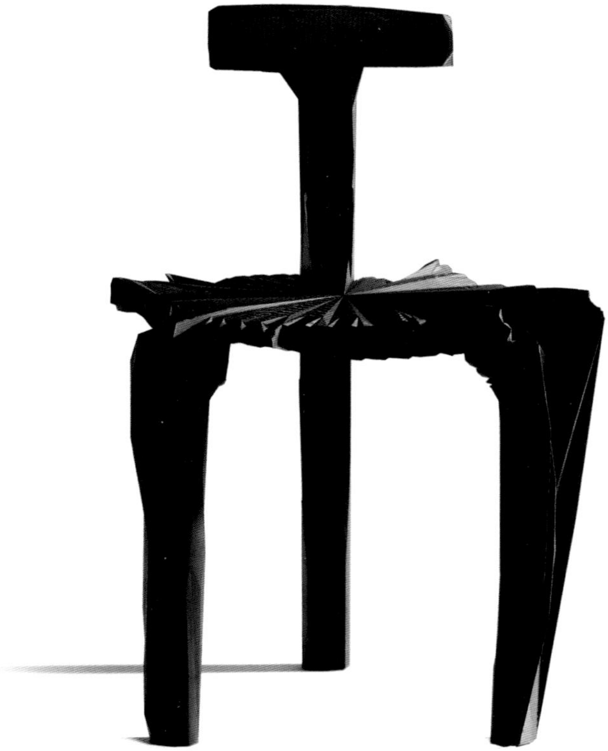

Focus:
SÃO PAULO
& RIO DE JANEIRO

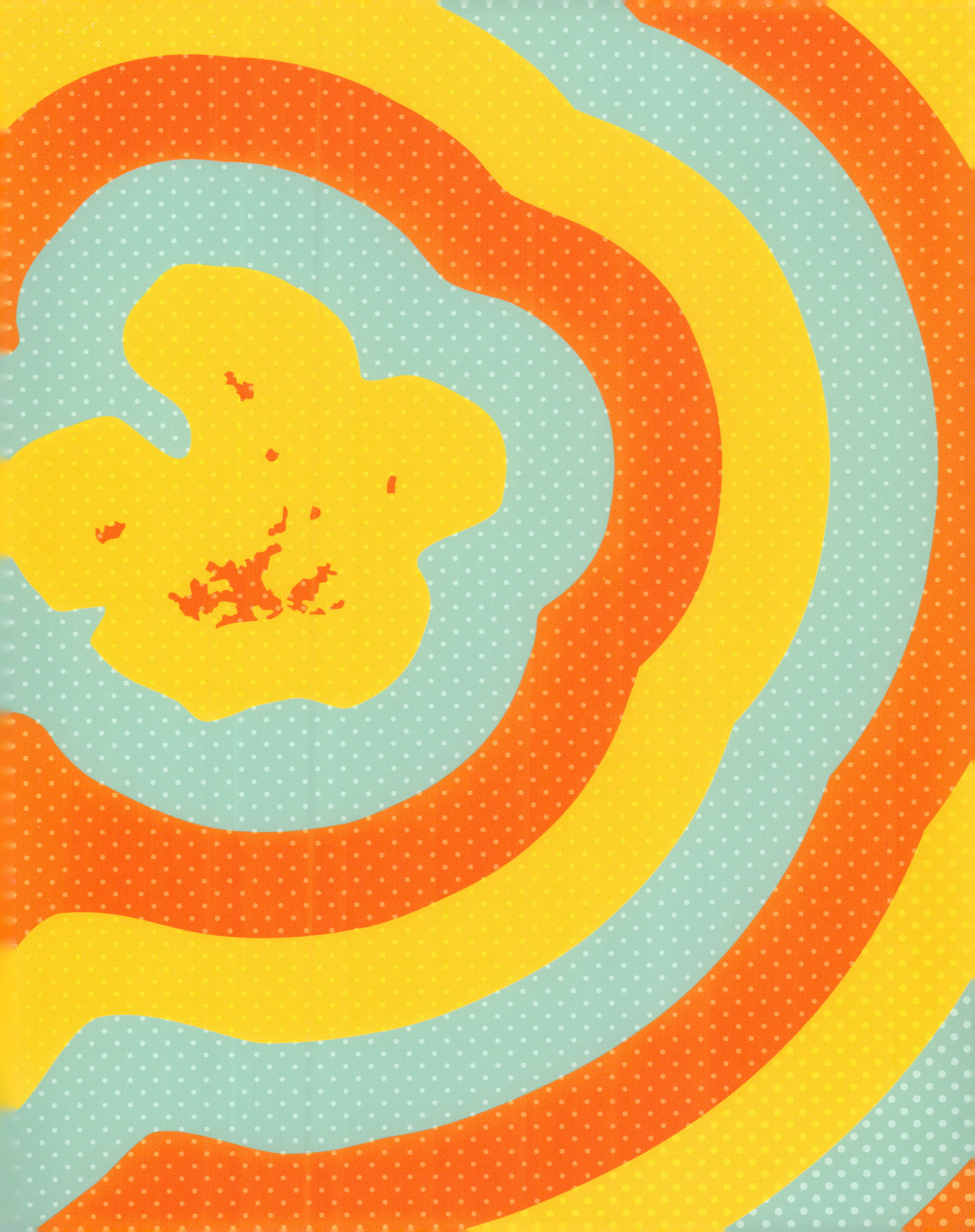

Rodrigo Almeida
Servant Lamp, from the *Slaves Series*, 2013
Steel, wood (pine), plastic
3.9 x 1.5 ft. (1.2 x 45 cm)
Courtesy of the artist

**Mana Bernardes in collaboration
with Zeca Cury and Aírton Pimenta**
Môbiluz, 2011
Leftover sequins material, freijo wood veneers,
LED lights, nylon thread, magnets, metal
3 ft. (91.4 cm) diameter
Courtesy of the artist
Photo: Mauro Kury

**Davi Deusdará, Érica Martins, Rafael Studart,
Alcenar Falcão and Tais Costa**
U Rock Chair, 2012-2014
Prototype: aluminum and eletrostatic paint
Final chair: recycled PET bottles and long-fiber polymers
30.3 x 29.9 x 26.8 in. (77 x 76 x 68 cm)
Courtesy of The Battery Conservancy
Photo: Steves Pierre

Studio MK27, Marcio Kogan, Manuela Verga, and Paolo Boatti
Murano, from the series *Prostheses Innesti*, 2012
Reclaimed wood (fir), Murano blown glass, gold
47.2 x 40.2 x 17.3 in. (120 x 102 x 44 cm)
Courtesy of the artists
Photo: Petr Krejci

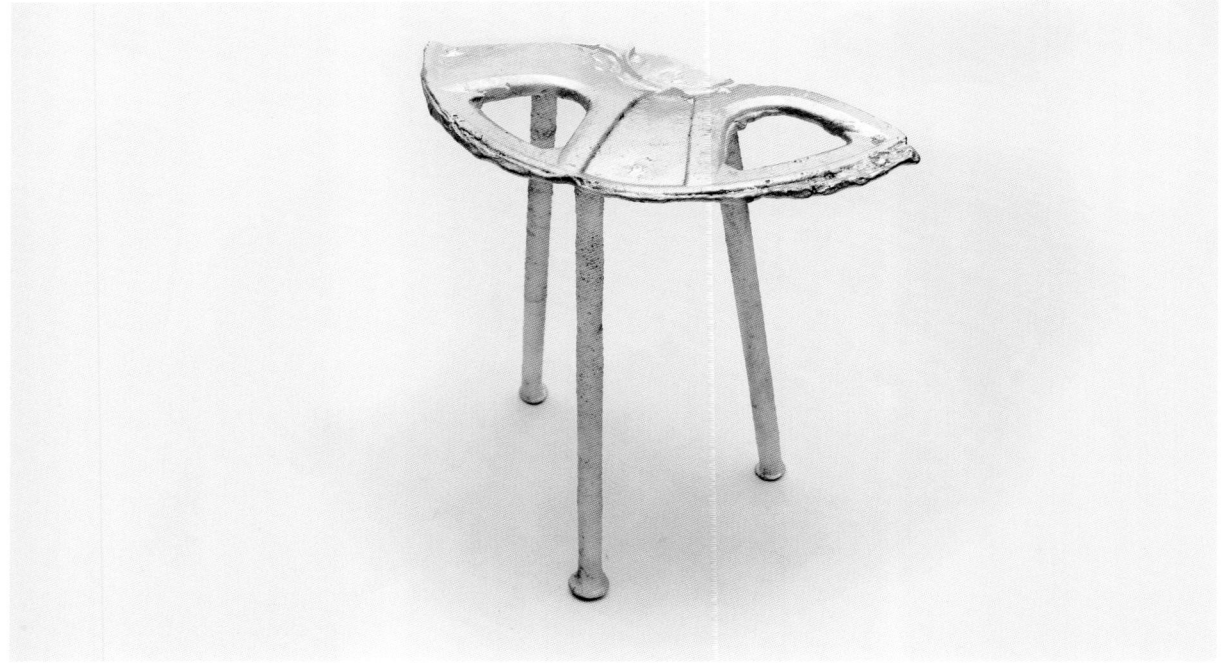

Studio Swine
Cesta Stool, 2012
Aluminum from cans
11.8 x 9.8 x 17.3 in. (30 x 25 x 44 cm)
Courtesy of the artists

Roda Stool, 2012
Aluminum from cans
13.8 x 9.8 x 17.7 in. (35 x 25 x 45 cm)
Courtesy of the artists

Studio Swine
Mangueira Stool, 2012
Aluminum from cans
13 x 10.2 x 18 in. (35 x 26 x 46 cm)
Courtesy of the artists

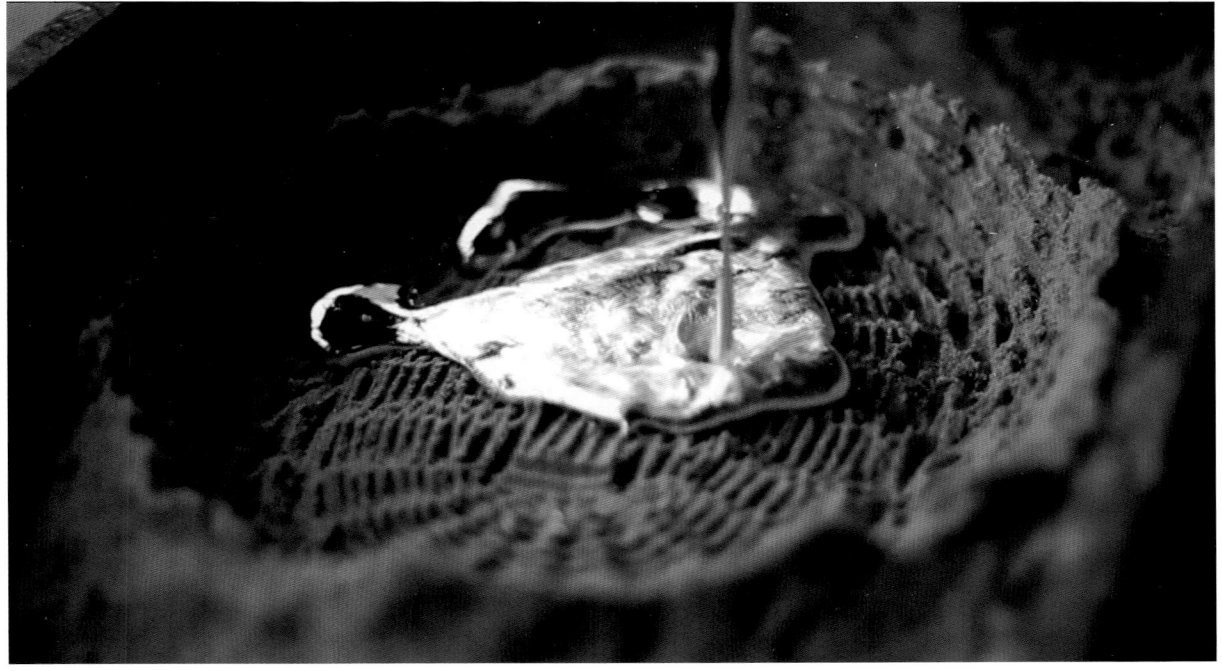

Can City, 2012
Video
4:40 mins.
Director: Juriaan Booij
Courtesy of Coletivo Amor de Madre

Cecilia León de la Barra
Jumbo, from the series *Plástico Fino*, 2011
Glazed ceramics
7.2 x 9 in. (18.5 x 23 cm) diameter
Courtesy of the artist

Grande, from the series *Plástico Fino*, 2011
Glazed ceramics
6.1 x 8.9 in. (15.5 x 22.5 cm) diameter
Courtesy of the artist

Chico, from the series *Plástico Fino*, 2011
Glazed ceramics
3.5 x 5.5 in. (9 x 14 cm) diameter
Courtesy of the artist

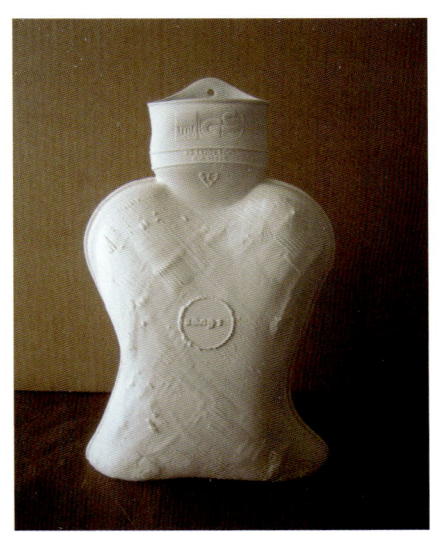

Daniel Reynolds
Hot Water Bottle, 2008
Slip-cast porcelain, unglazed exterior, glazed interior
10.2 x 5.9 x 3.5 in. (26 x 15 x 9 cm)
Courtesy of the artist

Milk Carton Vase, 2004
Slip-cast porcelain
7.5 x 3.3 x 3.3 in. (19 x 8.5 x 8.5 cm)
Courtesy of the artist

Stacking Pic-Nic Plates, 2002-2013
Slip-cast porcelain, unglazed exterior, glazed interior
Seven pieces: 1.75 x 5.9 in. (4.5 x 15 cm)
One piece: 1 x 5.9 in. (2.5 x 15 cm)
Courtesy of the artist

Studio Swine
Cactus Light, 2012
Pine offcuts, bottle bulbs, LED light, brass fittings, fabric cable
59 x 27.6 x 27.6 in. (150 x 70 x 70 cm)
Courtesy of Coletivo Amor de Madre

Zanini de Zanine
Moeda Chair, 2010
Stainless steel
33 x 25 x 37 in. (83 x 63.5 x 94 cm)
Courtesy of Espasso

Vik Muniz
Marat (Sebastião), from *Pictures of Garbage*, 2008
Digital C-print
30.2 x 23.5 in. (76.8 x 59.7 cm)
Courtesy of the Tiroche DeLeon Collection and Art Vantage PCC Limited

Alvaro Catalán de Ocón
PET Lamp, 2012
PET bottles, paja tetera
Dimensions variable
Courtesy of the artist

Abraham Cruzvillegas
Autoconstrucción: Low Budget Rider, 2009
Found wood (pine), bicycle frames and parts, mirrors, rubber
wheels, stainless steel, copper, towel, tin, solder
33.5 x 11.2 x 62.2 in. (85 x 28.5 x 158 cm)
Courtesy of the artist and Kurimanzutto, Mexico City

Thierry Jeannot
Green Transmutation Chandelier, 2010
Reclaimed PET plastic bottles, green dye, aluminum,
lightbulbs (24 watt, E14)
39.5 x 39.5 in. (100 x 100 cm)
Courtesy of Marion Friedmann Gallery
Photo: Felix Friedmann Photography

Thierry Jeannot
Coffee Table, 2014
Stainless steel, metal screws, burned wood, gold leaf, silver leaf, reclaimed plastics, acrylic, Perspex mirror, burned metals, resin, bronze, lost-wax casting process, glass
Base: 15.8 x 37.4 in. (40 cm x 95 cm) diameter
Glass top: 0.5 x 45.3 in. (1.2 x 115 cm) diameter
Courtesy of Marion Friedmann Gallery
Photo: Ypandri Hernández Pérez

Rolando Peña
Double Seat Barrel, 2013-14
Steel drum, leather (bovine), metal screws, foam
35.4 x 23.6 in. (90 x 60 cm) diameter
Courtesy of the artist
Photo: Nelson Garrido

Focus:
SANTIAGO & BUENOS AIRES

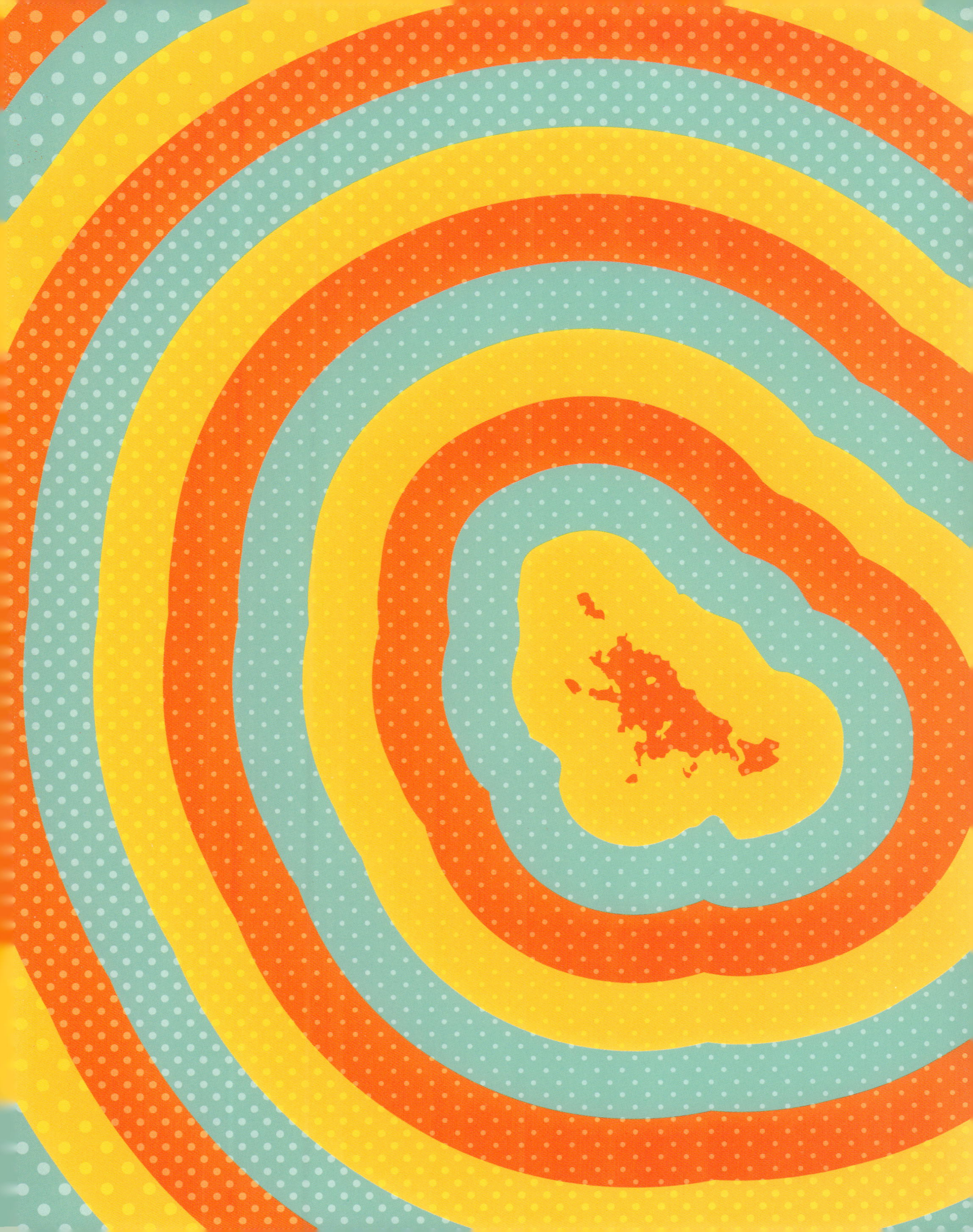

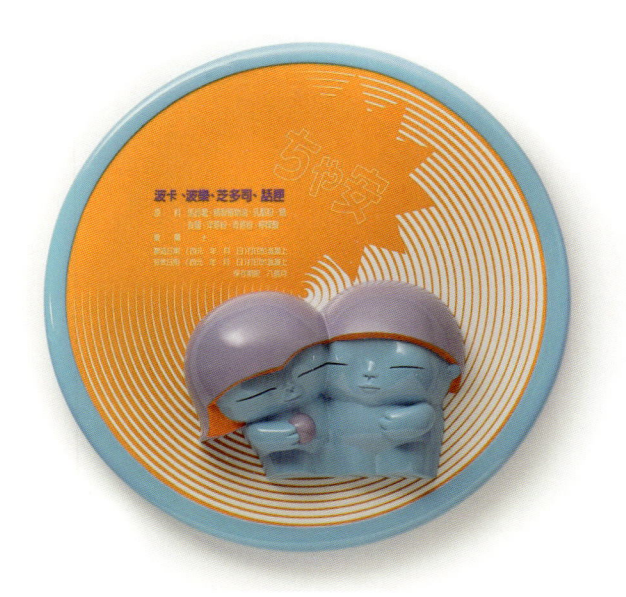

Fabián Bercic
Eva, 2013, diptych
Polyester resin, digital printing
13.4 x 3.1 in. (34 x 8 cm) each
Courtesy of the artist
Photo: Gustavo Lowry

Conviértenos Dios, el nacimiento de Eva, 2013
Polyester resin, digital printing
24.4 x 23.2 x 4.3 in. (62 x 59 x 11 cm)
Courtesy of the artist
Photo: Gustavo Lowry

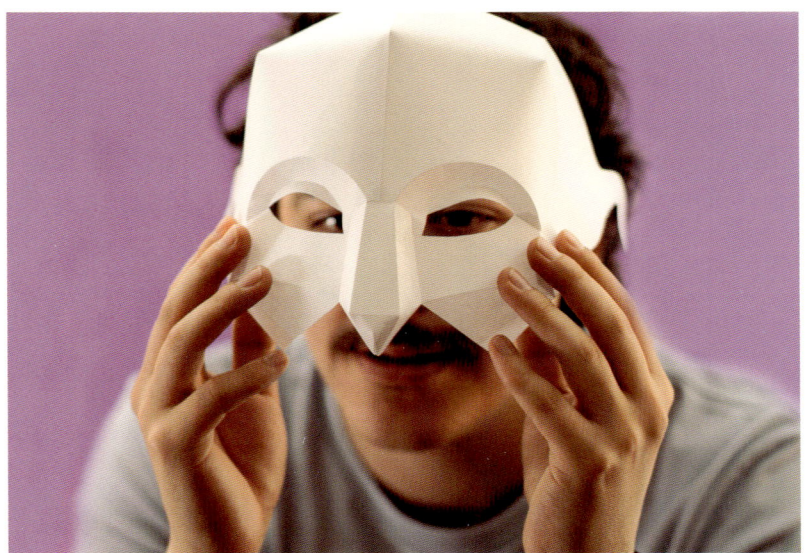

Angello García Bassi
Cubotoy: Un Mundo de Papel, 2013
Book
8.7 x 10.7 in. (22 x 27.1 cm)
Courtesy of the artist

Cubotoy, 2013
Paper (bond, 90 grams)
Dimensions variable
Courtesy of the artist

Prisma Perfiles, 2013
Video
5:05 mins.
Director: Carburadores Design and Animation Studio
Courtesy of the artist

gt2P
Chandelier, from the series *Less CPP N2*
Porcelain vs Lava Lights, 2014
Porcelain, lava, LED lights, electrical wires
12 lights measuring 5.9 x 5.9 x 3.9 in. (15 x 15 x 10 cm)
Courtesy of the artists

gt2P
Wall-mounted lights, from the series *Less CPP N2 Porcelain vs Lava Lights*, 2014
Porcelain, lava, LED lights, electrical wires
Six lights: 2 x 9.8 in. (5 x 25 cm) diameter
Courtesy of the artists

gt2P
Machine in wood, from the series *Less N1 Catenary Pottery Printer*, 2014
Wood; 59 x 31.5 x 11.8 in. (150 x 80 x 30 cm)
Courtesy of the artists

Video, from the series *Less N1 Catenary Pottery Printer*, 2014
Digital video; 2:03 mins.
Courtesy of the artists

Bowls in porcelain, from the series *Less N1 Catenary Pottery Printer*, 2014
Porcelain
5.9 x 5.9 x 3.9 in. (15 x 15 x 10 cm)
Courtesy of the artists

vacaValiente
Dog, 2005
Recycled and bonded leather (bovine)
8.7 x 9 x 10.2 in. (22 x 23 x 26 cm)
Courtesy of the artists

Lady Bug, 2008
Recycled and bonded leather (bovine)
2.4 x 5.5 x 3.9 in. (6 x 14 x 10 cm)
Courtesy of the artists

vacaValiente
Kangaroo, 2005
Recycled and bonded leather (bovine)
10.2 x 10.6 x 4.2 in. (26 x 27 x 11 cm)
Courtesy of the artists

Horse, 2009
Recycled and bonded leather (bovine)
9.9 x 11.8 x 4.7 in. (25 x 30 x 12 cm)
Courtesy of the artists

Alejandro Sarmiento
Banco de Carton, designed 1992, produced 2000
Cardboard
17.3 x 16.5 in. (44 x 42 cm)
Courtesy of the artist

166

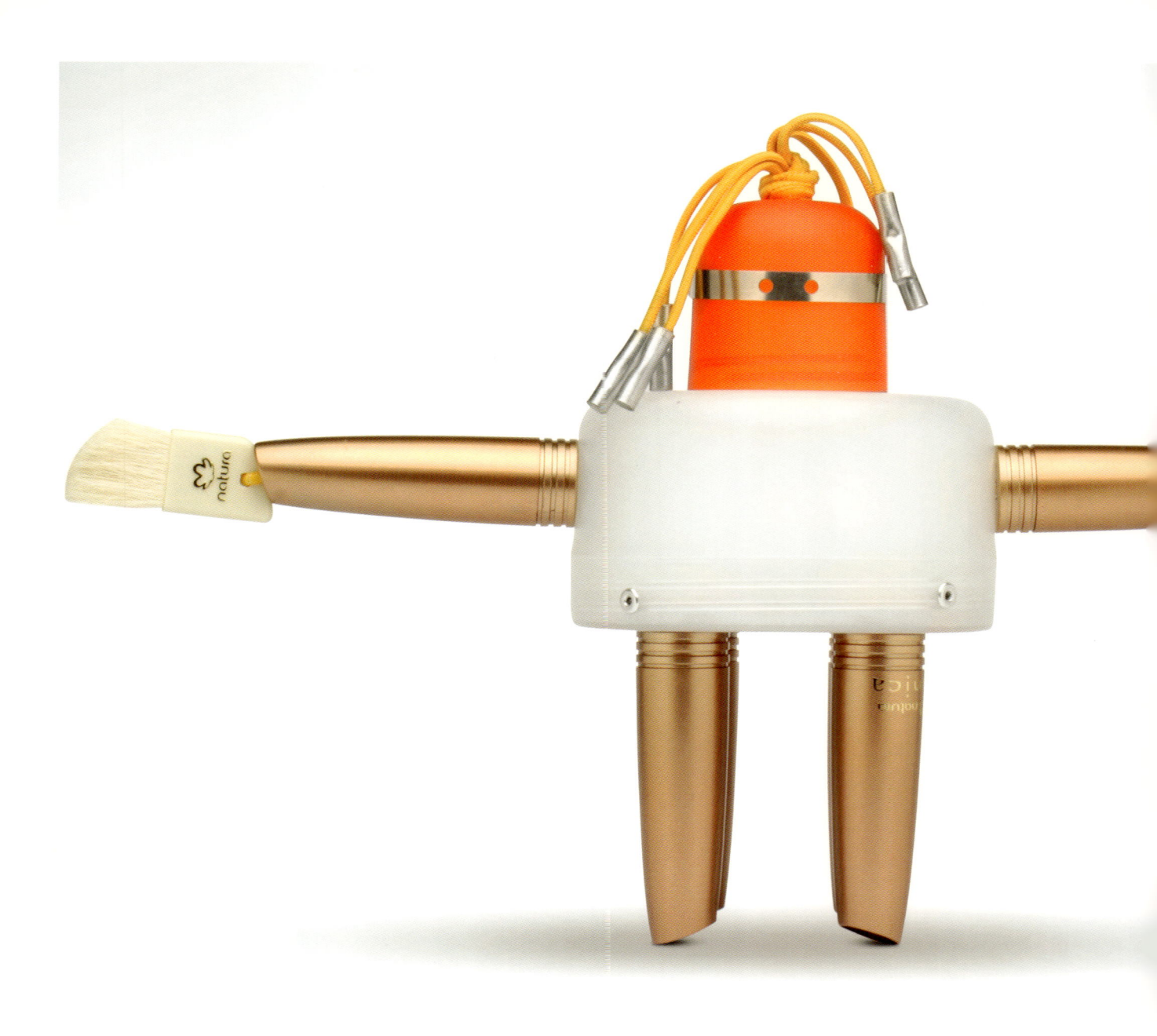

Satorilab in collaboration with an individual of the Instituto Correcional de Mujeres Nr. 3 de Ezeiza
Robot Naturito, from the series *Collection La Niñez en Juego,* 2007
Discarded products from Natura (cosmetics company), packaging, bottles, bottle caps, cream containers, paperboard, boxes
7.7 x 4.23 in. (20 x 12 cm)
Courtesy of the artists

Sebastian Errazuriz
From the series *12 Shoes for 12 Lovers*
Honey, Natasha, 2013
3-D printed ABS plastic, resin and acrylic paint
8.5 x 3.5 x 6.7 in. (21.6 x 8.9 x 17 cm)
All images courtesy of the artist,
Cristina Grajales Gallery, and Salon 94

Crybaby, Alexandra, 2013
3-D printed ABS plastic, resin and acrylic paint
10.2 x 3.2 x 11 in. (26 x 8.2 x 27.9 cm)

The Golddigger, Alison, 2013
3-D printed ABS plastic, resin and acrylic paint
6.5 x 3.2 x 10 in. (16.5 x 8.1 x 25.4 cm)

Heartbreaker, Laura, 2013
3-D printed ABS plastic, resin and acrylic paint
9.7 x 3.2 x 7.7 in. (24.6 x 8.1 x 19.5 cm)

Ice Queen, Sophie, 2013
3-D printed ABS plastic, resin and acrylic paint
7.4 x 3.4 x 9.5 in. (18.8 x 8.6 x 24.1 cm)

Hot Bitch, Carolina, 2013
3-D printed ABS plastic, resin and acrylic paint
7.9 x 2.7 x 7.9 in. (20 x 6.8 x 20 cm)

The Virgin, Anna, 2013
3-D printed ABS plastic, resin and acrylic paint
6.2 x 3.2 x 8.2 in. (15.7 x 8.1 x 20.8 cm)

The Jet-Setter, Josepha, 2013
3-D printed ABS plastic, resin and acrylic paint
6.5 x 3.2 x 9.5 in. (16.5 x 8.1 x 24.1 cm)

The Boss, Rachel, 2013
3-D printed ABS plastic, resin and acrylic paint
7.6 x 3.5 x 7.2 in. (19.3 x 8.9 x 18.3 cm)

GI Jane, Barbara, 2013
3-D printed ABS plastic, resin and acrylic paint
6.5 x 3.2 x 7.7 in. (16.5 x 8.1 x 19.5 cm)

The Ghost, Valentina (rendering), 2013
3-D printed ABS plastic, resin and acrylic paint

The Rock, Alice, 2013
3-D printed ABS plastic, resin and acrylic paint
7.1 x 4.2 x 9.5 in. (18 x 10.7 x 24.1 cm)

Focus:
SAN SALVADOR & SAN JUAN

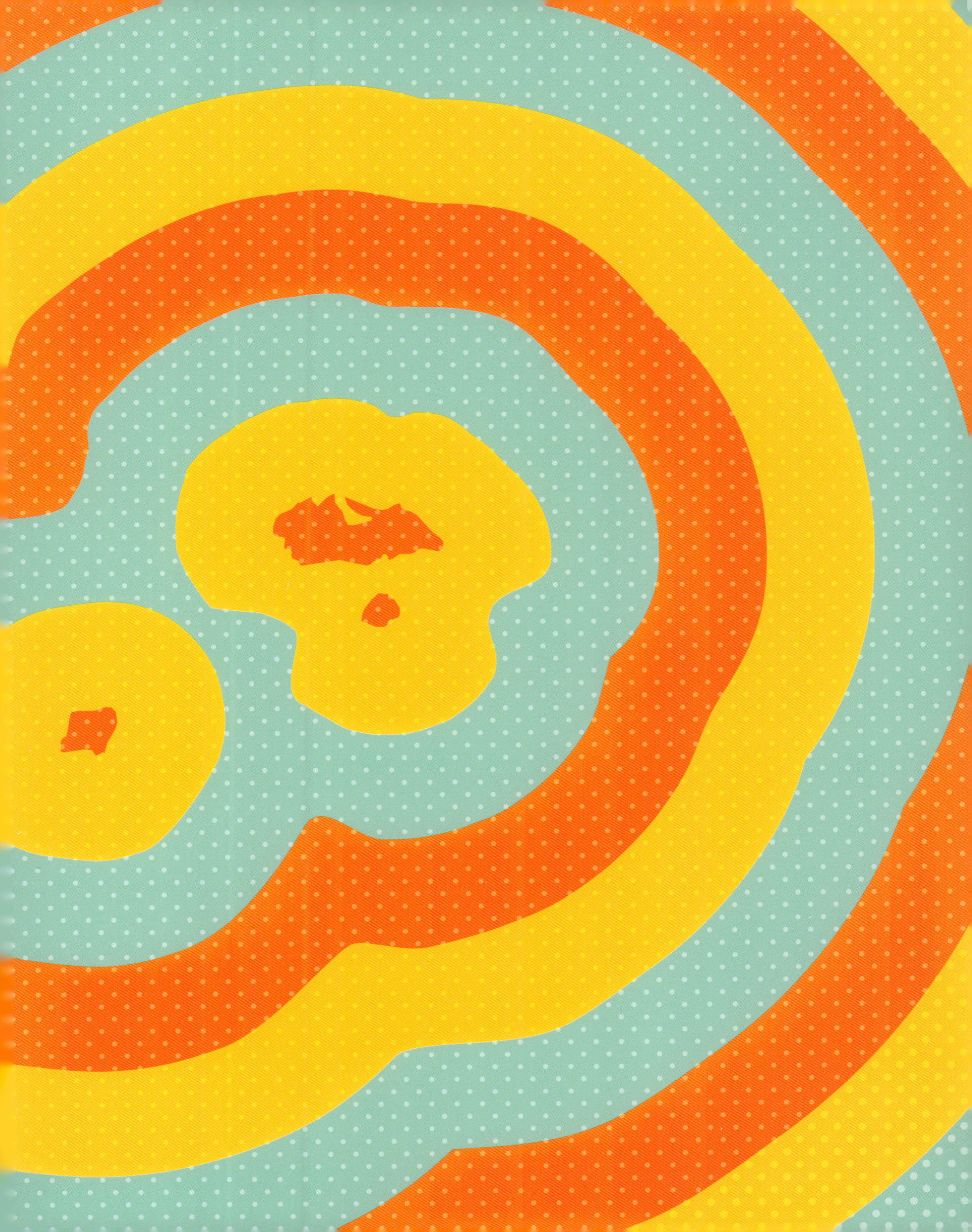

Vladimir García Bonilla
Meteoro (hanging), 2013
Powder-coated aluminum, fire-finished ceramic, stainless steel and aluminum fasteners, vinyl-coated wire rope
9.25 x 9.25 x 28 in. (23.5 x 23.5 x 71 cm)
Courtesy of the artist
Photo: Raquel Pérez-Puig

Meteoro (plant stand), 2013
Powder-coated aluminum, fire-finished ceramic, stainless steel and aluminum fasteners, vinyl-coated wire rope
13 x 13 x 60 in. (33 x 33 x 152.4 cm)
Courtesy of the artist
Photo: Raquel Pérez-Puig

Carlos Bobonis
Joint Coat Rack, 2012
Pine wood, ash wood, steel, brass plated steel, ABS plastic
23.6 x 23.6 x 53.4 in. (60 x 60 x 137 cm)
Courtesy of the artist
Photo: Raquel Pérez-Puig

Eddie Figueroa Feliciano
8 Lamp, 2012
Nylon, metal clamps, electrical components, LED
Dimensions variable
Courtesy of the artist

José Roberto Paredes
Canasto Lamp, 2013
Steel-wire frame, powder-coat finish, laurel wood handle
12 x 17.5 in. (30 x 44.5 cm)
Courtesy of The Carrot Concept

Roberto Javier Dumont
Fold Chair, 2009
Fiberglass, gelcoat finish
12 x 17.5 in. (30 x 44.5 cm)
Courtesy of The Carrot Concept

Eddie Figueroa Feliciano
Zanco, 2011
Oak, nylon mesh
36 x 15 x 15 in. (91.4 x 38.1 x 38.1 cm)
Courtesy of the artist

**Eddie Figueroa Feliciano in collaboration
with the Industrial Design Program
of the Escuela Internacional de Diseño
and manufactured by V'Soske**
La Alfombra, 2013
Dyed wool, silk pile
33 x 39.4 x 1.6 in. (84 x 100 x 4 cm)
Courtesy of the Escuela Internacional de Diseño,
Universidad del Turabo, Caguas, Puerto Rico
Photo: Jesús Gómez

Cecilia León de la Barra
Macetero 1, 2005
Painted or chromed iron, plastic polyvinyl
19.7 x 11.8 in. (50 x 30 cm) diameter
Courtesy of the artist

Macetero 2, 2005
Painted or chromed iron, plastic polyvinyl
19.7 x 11.8 in. (50 x 30 cm) diameter
Courtesy of the artist

Macetero 3, 2005
Painted or chromed iron, plastic polyvinyl
11.8 x 17.7 in. (30 x 45 cm) diameter
Courtesy of the artist

Macetero 4, 2005
Painted or chromed iron, plastic polyvinyl
15.7 x 34.4 in. (40 x 87.5 cm) diameter
Courtesy of the artist

Claudia Washington and Harry Washington
Ikono Chair, 2010
Laurel wood, metal structure, white-powder coat paint,
PVC string
30.7 x 29.5 x 33.4 in. (78 x 75 x 85 cm)
Courtesy of The Carrot Concept

Estúdio Guto Requena
Tea Hug, 2013
Wool
6.6 x 11.2 ft. (2 x 3.42 m)
Courtesy of Tai Ping

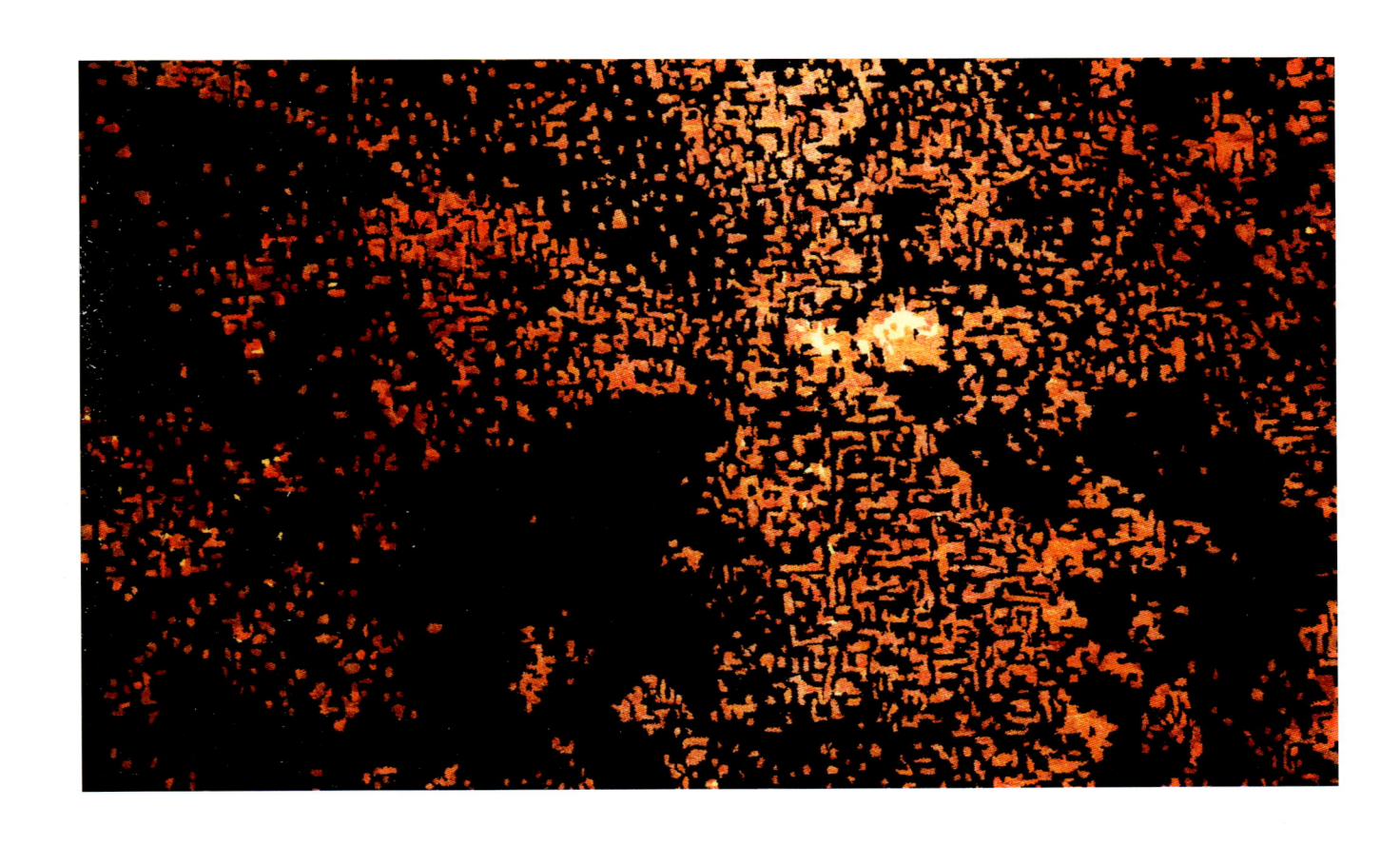

Ariel Rojo
Foco Rojo, 2012
Hand-tufted silk, wool
110.2 x 66.9 in. (2.8 x 1.7 cm)
Courtesy of Marion Friedmann Gallery and Obadashian
Photo: Felix Friedmann Photography

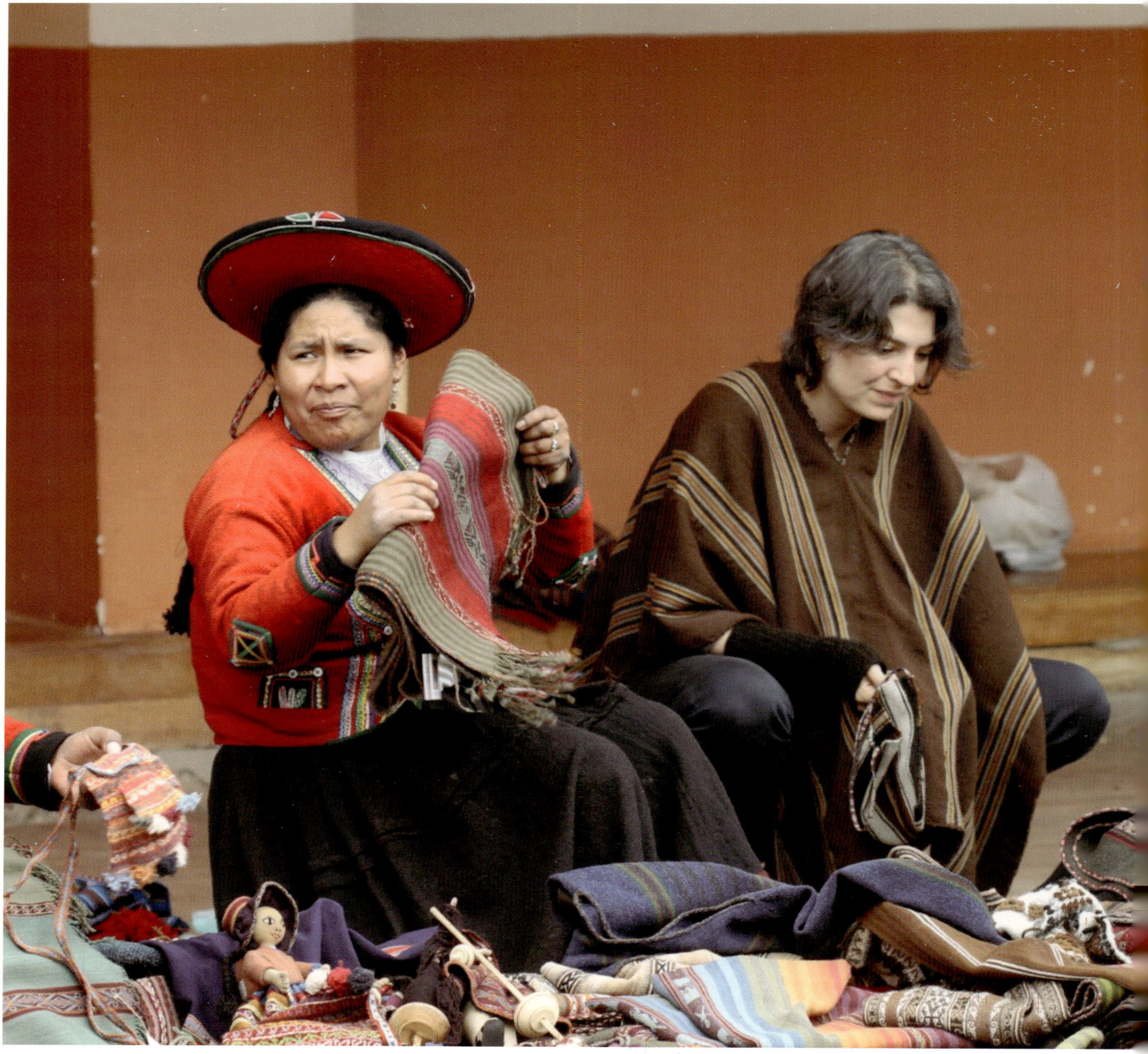

Marcella Echavarría
Mis Ojos Lo Tocarán, 2014
High-resolution digital video (H.264)
8 mins.
Video by Dia Felix

Focus:
HAVANA

Coco Fusco
The Empty Plaza / La Plaza Vacía, 2012
Single-channel video
11:52 mins.
Courtesy of the artist and Alexander Gray Associates, New York

Carlos Garaicoa
Fin de Silencio/Suelos Contrastados, 2010
Video installation; mini DV transferred to DVD
15:45:08 mins.
Courtesy of Galleria Continua

Carlos Garaicoa
Fin de Silencio / Suelos Colores, 2010
Video installation; mini DV transferred to DVD
15:45:19 mins.
Courtesy of Galleria Continua

Carlos Garaicoa
Cancha, from the series *Fin de Silencio II*, 2012
Wool, mercurized cotton, trevira-cs, cotton, acrylic
6.9 x 9.5 ft. (2.10 x 2.90 m)
Courtesy of Galleria Continua

Carlos Garaicoa
La Lucha, 2010
Cotton, wool, Lurex (aluminium), trevira-cs
4.6 x 19 ft. (1.41 x 5.79 m)
Courtesy of Galleria Continua

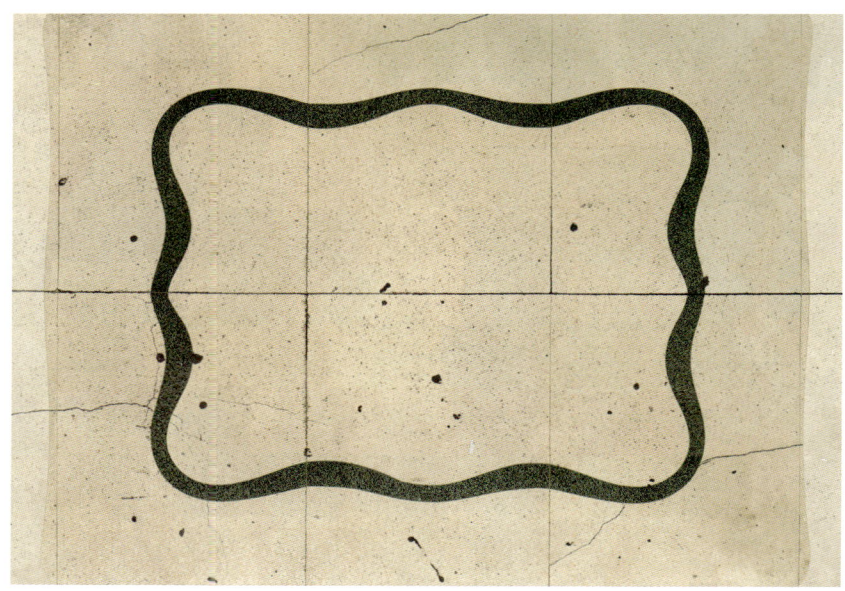

Carlos Garaicoa
El Pensamiento, 2010
Wool, mercurized cotton, trevira-cs, cotton, acrylic
9.4 x 15.7 ft. (2.86 x 4.78 m)
Courtesy of Gallery Continua

Carlos Garaicoa
El Globo, from the series *Fin de Silencio II*, 2012
Wool, mercurized cotton, trevira-cs, cotton, acrylic
9.5 x 11.8 ft. x .5 in. (2.90 x 3.60 m x 1 cm)
Courtesy of Galeria Luisa Strina

Ernesto Oroza
Centro Habana, from the series *Architecture of Necessity*, 2005
Archival pigment print
18 x 24 in. (45.7 x 61 cm)
Courtesy of the artist

Ernesto Oroza
Luyanó, from the series *Architecture of Necessity*, 2012
Archival pigment print
16 x 24 in. (40.6 x 61 cm)
Courtesy of the artist

Ernesto Oroza
Alamar, from the series *Architecture of Necessity*, 2005
Archival pigment print
24 x 18 in. (61 x 45.7 cm)
Courtesy of the artist

Ernesto Oroza
Centro Habana, from the series *Architecture of Necessity*, 2006
Archival pigment print
18 x 24 in. (45.7 x 61)
Courtesy of the artist

Estudio Cabeza
Lace cloth set of chairs (right, central, and left-side versions)
2008
Perforated, folded, and welded-aluminum sheet, paint
Left and right chairs: 17.3 x 24.4 x 16.5 in. (44 x 62 x 42 cm)
Central chair: 31.9 x 17.3 x 24.4 in. (81 x 44 x 62 cm)
Courtesy of the artist
Photo: Mariela Rivas

José Castrellón
Erick, Nazareno from the series *Priti Baiks*, 2010
Archival pigment print
24 x 24 in. (61 x 61 cm)
Courtesy of the artist

José Castrellón
Abdelin, El Valle from the series *Priti Baiks*, 2012
Archival pigment print
24 x 24 in. (61 x 61 cm)
Courtesy of the artist

José Castrellón
Chimbilin, Cermeño, Capira, from the series
Priti Baiks, 2010
Archival pigment print
24 x 24 in. (61 x 61 cm)
Courtesy of the artist

José Castrellón
Nabil, Mariasoto, Colon, from the series
Priti Baiks, 2011
Archival pigment print
24 x 24 in. (61 x 61 cm)
Courtesy of the artist

Liliana Angulo Cortés
Project Quieto Pelo, 2009
Photographs, video, sound interviews
Dimensions variable
Courtesy of the artist

Les Crayons Noirs & Flip
Flip Felipe Yung Signature from the *Bombe* series, 2011
Limoges porcelain, platinum-plated artwork
7.9 x 2.8 in. (20 x 7 cm) diameter
Courtesy of Antoine Caboué
Photo: Nicolas Barbieux

Les Crayons Noirs & Herbert Baglione
Herbert Baglione Signature from the *Bombe* series, 2011
Limoges porcelain, platinum-plated artwork
7.9 x 2.8 in. (20 x 7 cm) diameter
Courtesy of Antoine Caboué
Photo: Nicolas Barbieux

Les Crayons Noirs & Sesper
Sesper Signature from the *Bombe* series, 2011
Limoges porcelain, platinum-plated artwork
7.9 x 2.8 in. (20 x 7 cm) diameter
Courtesy of Antoine Caboué
Photo: Nicolas Barbieux

Les Crayons Noirs & Thais Beltrame
Thais Beltrame Signature from the *Bombe* series, 2011
Limoges porcelain, platinum-plated artwork
7.9 x 2.8 in. (20 x 7 cm) diameter
Courtesy of Antoine Caboué
Photo: Nicolas Barbieux

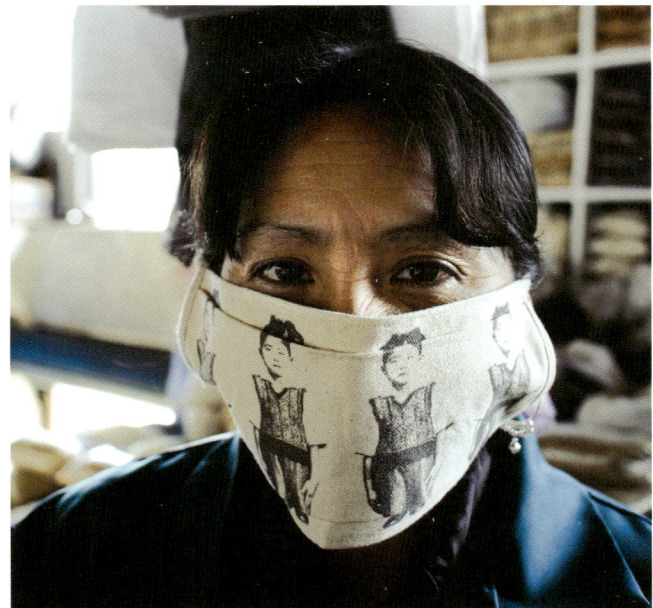

Lucia Cuba
Informed consent: Meta-pieza, from the series *Artículo 6: Narratives of gender, strength and politics,* 2012-14
Cotton canvas, transparent thread, digital printing, machine sewing
10.2 x 5.1 in. (26 x 13 cm) each
Courtesy of the artist

Lucia Cuba
Artículo 6, from the series *Artículo 6: Narratives of gender, strength and politics,* 2012-14
Cotton canvas, thread, digital printing, hand and machine sewing
Pollera: 31.9 x 29.1 in (81 x 74 cm)
Blouse: 19.7 x 26 in. (50 x 66 cm)
Courtesy of the artist
Photo: Erasmo Wong Seoane

Lucia Cuba
Mitad Persona, from the series *Artículo 6: Narratives of gender, strength and politics*, 2012-14
Cotton twill, embroidery thread, digital printing, hand and machine sewing
Pollera: 33 x 29.1 in. (84 x 74 cm)
Blouse: 19.7 x 26 in. (50 x 66 cm)
Courtesy of the artist
Photo: Erasmo Wong Seoane

Lucia Cuba
Juntos, from the series *Artículo 6: Narratives of gender, strength and politics*, 2012-14
Cotton canvas, thread, digital printing, hand and machine sewing
Pollera: 31.9 x 37.8 in. (81 x 96 cm); vest: 20.5 x 20.9 in. (52 x 53 cm); jacket 20.9 x 22.4 in. (53 x 57 cm)
Courtesy of the artist
Photo: Erasmo Wong Seoane

Lucia Cuba
El Sampler, 2012-ongoing
Cotton canvas / Tocuyo, hand embroidery, painting, weaving,
screen print, block printing, sewing
32.7 x 37.8 in. (83 x 96 cm)
Courtesy of the artist

Design Da Gema
Stray Bullet Chair, 2011
Polypropylene chair, stainless steel eyelets
31.9 x 23.6 x 47.3 in. (81 x 60 x 120 cm)
Courtesy of the artist
Photo: Robson Curvello

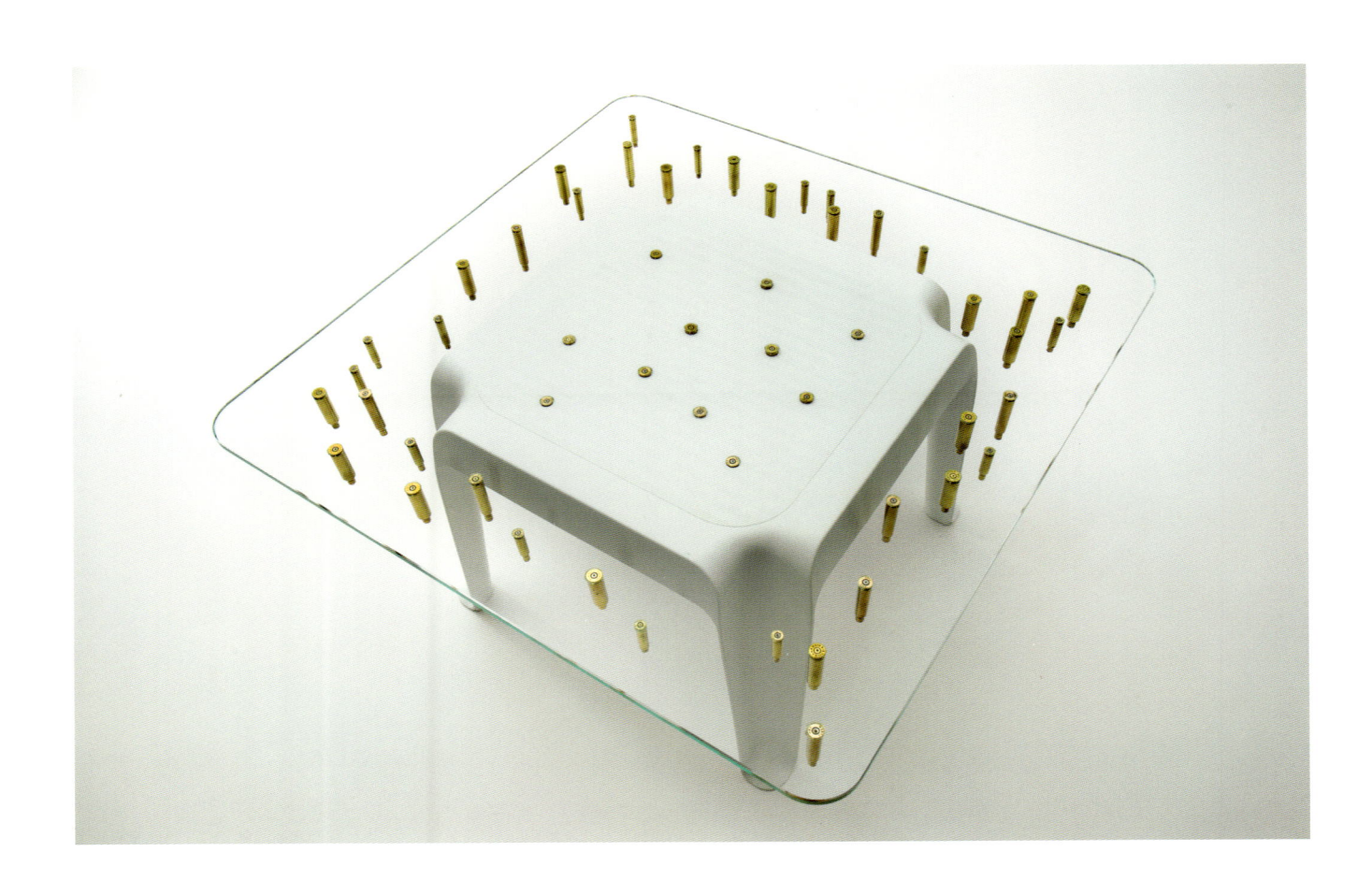

Design Da Gema
Bulletproof Side Table, 2013
Polypropylene monobloc side table, used bullet shells, glass
27.6 x 27.6 x 16.1 in. (70 x 70 x 41 cm)
Courtesy of the artist
Photo: J.J. l'Heritier

Gilberto Esparza
Moscas, from the series *Parásitos Urbanos,* 2007
Cell phone motors, copper thread, electronics
.2 x .4 x .5 in. (4 x 10 x 12 mm) each
Courtesy of the artist

Gilberto Esparza
ppndr-s, from the series *Parásitos Urbanos*, 2007
Toy motors, galvanized wire
7.9 x 7.9 x 6 in. (20 x 20 x 15 cm)
Courtesy of the artist

Gilberto Esparza
mrñ, from the series *Parásitos Urbanos*, 2007
Motor, nylon thread, computer speakers, acrylic, micro-controller
17.8 x 7 x 5.9 in. (45 x 18 x 15 cm)
Courtesy of the artist

Gilberto Esparza
clgd, from the series *Parásitos Urbanos*, 2007
Motors from toys, PVC pipes, aluminum micro-controllers,
ultrasonic sensor
17.8 x 7 x 5.9 in. (45 x 18 x 15 cm)
Courtesy of the artist

Gilberto Esparza
dblt, from the series *Parásitos Urbanos*, 2007
Stainless steel, acrylic, aluminum, micro-controller,
small motor from toys, ultrasonic sensors, rubber
17.7 x 11.8 x 3.9 in. (45 x 30 x 10 cm)
Courtesy of the artist

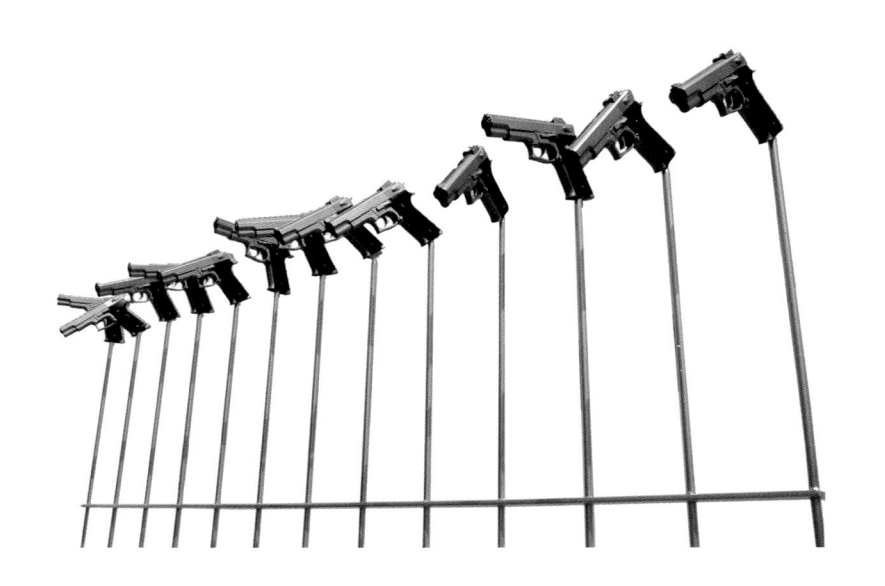

Marcio Kogan and Isay Weinfeld
Gradil, from the series *Happy Land Vol. 2,* 2004
Gun replicas, steel
Dimensions variable
Courtesy of Studio MK27 and Isay Weinfeld

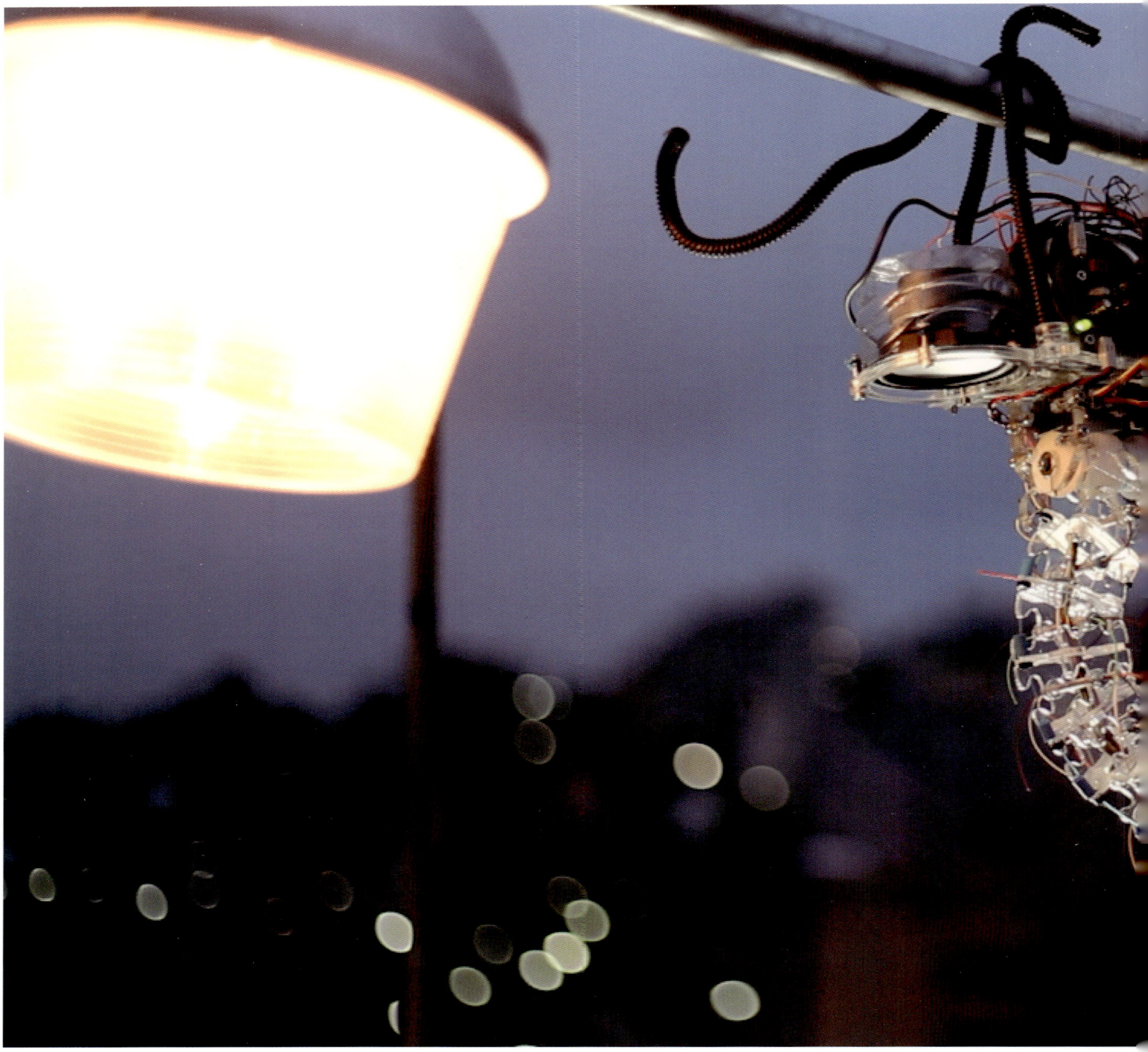

Gilberto Esparza
Urban Parasites, 2014
Video HD 1080p
35 mins.
Courtesy of the artist

Pepe López
Supermarket cart series, 2007
Mini DV
7 mins.
Courtesy of the artist

Ministerio de Cultura de Colombia and El Vicio Producciones
Capítulo 4 La conquista del espacio: Arte Público from the
series *Plástica*, 2005
Video; 24:22 mins.
Courtesy of Ministerio de Cultura de Colombia and Fundación
Patrimonio Fílmico Colombiano

Projeto Morrinho
TV Morrinho apresenta…, 2004
Video; 6 mins.
Director: Fabio Gavião
Courtesy of the artists

Pedro Reyes
Guitarra, 2013
Instrument made from destroyed weapons
38.2 x 13.7 x 3.1 in. (97 x 35 x 8 cm)
Courtesy of the Tiroche DeLeon Collection and Art Vantage
PCC Limited

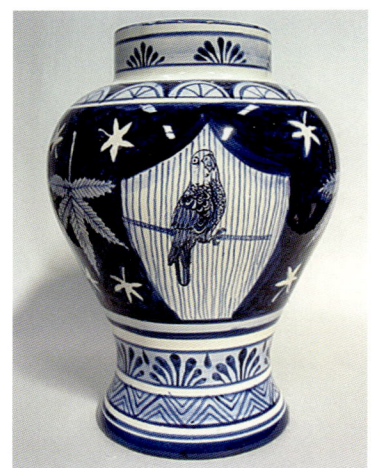

Eduardo Sarabia
A thin line between love and hate #90, 2005
Hand-painted ceramic vase, silkscreen box
Vase: 14.3 x 12 in. (36.2 x 30.5 cm) diameter
Box: 14 x 18 x 14 in. (35.6 x 45.7 x 35.6 cm)
Courtesy of the artist and I-20 Gallery, New York
Photo: Cary Whittier

A thin line between love and hate #38, 2005
Hand-painted ceramic vase, silkscreen box
Vase: 12 x 8.5 in. (31.8 x 21.6 cm) diameter
Box: 13 x 16 x 12 in. (33 x 40.6 x 30.5 cm)
Courtesy of the artist and I-20 Gallery, New York
Photo: Cary Whittier

A thin line between love and hate #19, 2005
Hand-painted ceramic vase, silkscreen box
Vase: 12 x 7.5 in. (30.5 x 19.1 cm) diameter
Box: 12.5 x 15 x 12 in. (31.8 x 38 x 30.5 cm)
Courtesy of the artist and I-20 Gallery, New York
Photo: Cary Whittier

Eduardo Sarabia
A thin line between love and hate, 2005
Hand-painted ceramic vase, silkscreen box
Installation view, I-20 Gallery, New York
March 10-April 22, 2006
Courtesy of the artist and I-20 Gallery, New York
Photo: Cary Whittier

Rodolfo Agrella
Born in Caracas, Venezuela, 1984; lives and works in Caracas, Venezuela / New York, USA

My work is informed by a deep understanding of the tropics, especially from the region in Venezuela where I live. This relates to our homeland and traditions, and each object I design is imbued with multiple connections and emotions. My goal is to inspire a reflective process in each person who uses what I create. As an architect, I use what I have learned from other disciplines. By manipulating scale while remaining faithful to structure, geometry, and function, I seek to activate our sensory systems, which is a vital part of what I develop. In each object, process, or project I work on, there are references to my ancestors, as well as to everyday aspects of my culture and environment.

Rodrigo Almeida
Born in Sorocaba, Brazil, 1975; lives and works in São Paulo, Brazil

I work at the intersection of an object's appearance (its aesthetics), and the demands of its construction (the process). It is important for an object to communicate, to demonstrate its place in time, representative of its culture. Everything is a hybrid, and miscegenation—the intermingling of races—is an important theme. Structures are also important. I work mostly with visible structures, overlapping different layers of materials, creating a tension between the flexible and inflexible. Flexible materials bend, crumple, and interlace the structures in a natural movement, as if matter was casually thrown at the structure. This poetic game is the result of my perception and understanding of Brazilian cultural processes.

Artecnica / Design with Conscience
Tord Boontje, born in Enschede, Netherlands, 1968; lives and works in London, England; Cooperativa de Trabalho Artesanal e de Costura da Rocinha Ltda. (Coopa-Roca), founded by Maria Teresa Leal, 1987, located in Rio de Janeiro, Brazil; Artecnica, founded by Enrico Bressan and Tahmineh Javanbakht, 1986, located in Los Angeles, USA

Artecnica's vision is to introduce into the world's artisanal communities two essential components: the designer and the project producer. A designer like Tord Boontje can dovetail the talents of artisans with the needs of the international market. Artecnica, as the project producer, oversees the art direction, logistics, and marketing necessary to develop a competitive product that will encourage the survival of indigenous craft. Design with Conscience, a program founded by Artecnica in 2002, matches internationally recognized designers with artisans in underdeveloped communities, invigorating commerce and assisting surrounding communities.

The Come Rain, Come Shine *chandelier was designed by Tord Boontje in London and manufactured in Brazil by Coopa-Roca, a women's cooperative based in Rocinha, Rio de Janeiro. Coopa-Roca generates business opportunities by increasing the production of goods by women in the Rocinha community while promoting the preservation of craft traditions.*

Alessandro Balteo Yazbeck and Media Farzin
Alessandro Balteo Yazbeck, born in Caracas, Venezuela, 1972; lives and works in Berlin, Germany; Media Farzin, born in San Diego, California, 1979; lives and works in New York, USA

Since the mid-nineties, Alessandro Balteo Yazbeck has developed a hybrid practice that incorporates the activities of a researcher, archivist, historian, curator, and designer. Media Farzin has written extensively on contemporary art as a critic and art historian, and is currently completing a doctoral dissertation on the books and performances of French Los Angeles–based artist Guy de Cointet.

Since 2007, Balteo Yazbeck and Farzin have been collaborating on archival and historic research into chronological coincidences, the histories of cultural diplomacy, and the modernist artifacts of the Cold War era. The installation Eames-Derivative (small version) *narrates a three-decade-long story of socioeconomic power structures and modern design. The sculptural component comprises custom-made slotted cards that depict now-outmoded computer technology. The cards are a "remake" of the* Computer House of Cards, *produced by the Eames office in 1970 for IBM's pavilion at the Osaka World's Fair. Much of the Eames' iconic work for IBM, which was intended to promote a friendly image of computers to the public, laid the groundwork for the omnipresence of digital technology today. The fragility of* Eames-Derivative's *technological house of cards invokes both the dominant influence of modern technology and the volatility of today's most vital financial systems. The installation also includes five vintage IBM magazine ads from the 1950s, which illustrate the company's deliberate emphasis, through the language of advertising, on the importance of its products as the enabling technology for the growing US military-industrial complex as well as the global financial system.*
Photos: Ethan Carrier/def image

Cecilia León de la Barra
Born in Mexico City, Mexico, 1975; lives and works in Mexico City, Mexico

I have been working as an independent designer and collaborating with other recognized designers and architects since 2000. My ideas come from constant research and the observation of everyday life, which I use and document for inspiration and then transform into new objects. My designs are inspired by the forms, color, and techniques of traditional folk arts and popular culture, which I translate into innovative and fresh designs. In 2010, I curated the design exhibition HECHO A MANO: Nuevos Procesos Colaborativos de Diseño (HANDMADE: New Collaborative Design Processes) at Casa del Lago, Mexico City, where I showed the work of Mexican designers who collaborated with local artisans and communities. In 2014, with Jorge Gardoni, I co-curated Copies: Transformation and Development in Creative Processes, at Archivo Diseño y Arquitectura in Mexico City.

Pedro Barrail
Born in Asunción, Paraguay, 1964; lives and works in Asunción, Paraguay

The brilliant observation that "Man invents words to lie to himself..." was made by the Paraguayan/Spanish poet Josefina Pla. Her words reflect our capacity to create "fictions" that guide us to our own "truth." As such, I am driven to ask questions and make observations about society's behaviors by means of design, art, and architecture. I do this without passing judgment, commenting on only what affects me, and viewers draw their own conclusions about the work. The questions I ask define the discipline and medium used in my responses. Since everything is valid, what will be most appropriate for the subject at hand? My series of furniture with indigenous pyrography initiated a dialogue between contemporary design, academic history, and indigenous design that is based in tradition, ingenuity, and intuition. We developed the tattoo designs during conversations with the master craftsmen of the Pai Tavytera tribe—we began by cross-pollinating via an exchange of information, and the resulting images capture quotidian realities and comment on issues of mass consumption. Engraved with fire, these works also represent the conflict between ecology and commerce, since tribal members, alleged guardians of the ecosystem, must use large amounts of vegetal coal to burn their designs, to register their reality, and to sell themselves. Everything is commerce.

Angello García Bassi
Born in Caldera, Chile, 1985; lives and works in Santiago, Chile

I am an advertising graphic designer and Cubotoy is a personal project that I developed to explore the Artoy cultural movement. Experiments with drawings were my points of departure; with scissors I then introduced the third dimension and turned the drawings into sculptures. The Cubotoy characters are part of an imaginary world of heroes and villains. They are visual and tactile, and various meanings can be extracted from their forms. I design, sculpt, and produce each original figure, and viewers may construct, convert, or reconsider my characters.

Fabián Bercic
Born in Buenos Aires, Argentina, 1969; lives and works in Buenos Aires, Argentina

My work has an industrial and impersonal aspect, although my process relies on that which is handmade: I personally model the figures, make the molds, transform them into polyester resin, and polish them (and because of this, production is a lengthy process). My work is related to the physical experience of doing, with the application of discipline and concentration. I don't have assistants, and I don't believe in technical shortcuts. I pay attention to detail, and I have a deep admiration for the trades. I care deeply about the way in which certain contemporary visual elements can be conjugated with profound experiences related to social and religious traditions.

Mana Bernardes
Born in Rio de Janeiro, Brazil, 1981; lives and works in Rio de Janeiro, Brazil

Mana Bernardes is a designer, poet, multimedia artist, and art therapist who is best known for her jewelry made of discarded plastics and other materials. A desire to recreate her Jóias Cotidianas (Everyday Jewels) on a larger scale led to her collaboration with Airton Pimenta (illuminator and owner of Lightworks) and Zeca Cury (woodworker and owner Oficina de Marcenaria). During meetings (and dives) in Rio de Janeiro, São Paulo, and Ubatuba, the collective created Móbiluz, a limited edition of mobiles that are ethereal, subtle, translucent, and lightweight. Each object is made of laminated wood, LED lighting, and industrial scraps of iridescent sequins. The Móbiluz fixtures are a contemplative objects that can be adjusted manually to create different shadows and moods.

Guillermo Bert
Born in in Santiago, Chile, 1959; lives and works in Los Angeles, USA

As a visual artist, I am fascinated by the concept of encrypting messages and embedding ideas beneath the "skin" of the piece. Beginning with the series Bar Codes: Branding America, I used high-tech devices to question the price of societal values—such as democracy and justice—by blurring the line between culture and commodities. My current project, Encoded Textiles, extends earlier motifs into work that engages a new generation of bar codes and indigenous symbol systems through textile arts. I first noticed that QR codes, like those used to tag airport luggage, share remarkable similarities to the textiles of the Mapuche peoples of my home country in Chile. From this observation, I began a multilayered project which, to date, has involved collaboration with Mapuche, Navajo, and Zapotec weavers.

Carlos Bobonis
Born in San Juan, Puerto Rico, 1979; lives and works in New York, USA

My approach toward design has always been a process of discovery—trying to understand the complexities of a new object, while executing a balance between function, looks, and feel. Each product that I make presents different challenges conditioned by the scope of the project, its materials, and the method of fabrication. Much about my design approach is the elimination of unnecessary details, creating simple forms that strike elegance and simplicity. Computer-aided design (CAD) and digital fabrication have been important tools in the development of my designs, helping me to quickly visualize ideas while creating precise models for testing and improvement. But while technology has been a fundamental tool for productivity, I find it incredibly valuable to establish new relationships with skilled craftsmen. Their material knowledge and fabrication skills are a great source of creativity that helps me deliver a better and more refined product.

I carefully follow global design trends, constantly seeking new and interesting ideas, but always looking to find inspiration in the culture of my native Puerto Rico. The people, the food, the environment, the architecture, the music and the products that are commonly used, all highly influence my view on design. I look for the defining characteristics in the objects that we use in the Caribbean, in order to understand the practical and cultural values they carry. These observations shape the products that I create. So while I continue to design new objects, they are sure to be "stained by the plantain."

Vladmir Garcia Bonilla
Born in Mayagüez, Puerto Rico, 1976; lives and works in San Juan, Puerto Rico

The Meteoro series is a contemporary, versatile, and practical planting system. Each unit is conceived as a space-defining element that, when arranged in groups, performs as a family of complementary furnishing items to bring nature and beauty to the interior of urban buildings with limited outdoor space. Diverse in size and formal configuration, each vessel opens a dialogue with space through geometry, color, and function to enhance the plant's textures, patterns, and shades. Meteoro pays homage to the residential steel planting ornaments characteristic of the Puerto Rican mid-century modern house patio décor. The design embraces its formal and material language, but expands its functionality and manufacturing capabilities to propose a fresh, contemporary tropical aesthetic.
Photo: Miguel Villalobos

Diana Cabeza (Estudio Cabeza)
Born in Buenos Aires, Argentina, 1954; lives and works in Buenos Aires, Argentina

The immeasurable South American landscape challenges me to set limits and demarcate a territory. My designs are based on my interest in the human body—male and female bones and muscles adjusting to a space, and leaving a trace in their absence. It is this space of contact that I wish to apprehend and materialize. I approach the urban or landscape scale by designing units of association, designs that integrate the expansive skin of the city with their human users. I think in terms of "use" and not of "object," thinking of design as a verb—relax, take refuge, reunite—and from an anthropological point of view. My process is nurtured by travels throughout my country, photographic surveys of sites that, through their cultural, geographic, or social content, nourish my intuition and shelter my thoughts under the umbrella of "dwelling." I design in order to inhabit the natural and urban landscape, but at the same time, to play a game of mirrors: the landscape inhabits me.

Raul Cabra (Oax-i-fornia)
Born in Caracas, Venezuela, 1964; lives and works in Oaxaca, Mexico

Directed by Raul Cabra, Oax-i-fornia emerged as an academic program for the California College of the Arts (CCA) in San Francisco, its main goal being to investigate new methodologies for the use of design and creativity as tools for social change and cultural engagement. As a creative endeavor, Oax-i-fornia belongs to a class of collaborative efforts around the world, both academic and professional, where intercultural exchange shapes the productive process. It is a shared space of creative making rather than a designer-producer relationship (in which the designers design, and the artisans make). Collaborations are an experience of learning: artisans bring their mastery of craft and materials, while students bring their curiosity and experimentation—a luxury that most artisans, under commercial demands, rarely have. In this relationship, neither of the two groups is ever fully in charge of the process. It is through the concept of play that cultural differences become secondary to a joint process of "making together." Participants must rely on their strengths as makers, knowledge, and each other, as they attempt to conquer the challenges at hand. It is precisely the nature of this shared responsibility that is at the heart of Oax-i-fornia. As a result, the objects that emerge from the collaboration oscillate between worlds, a dynamic mixture of tradition and experimentation.

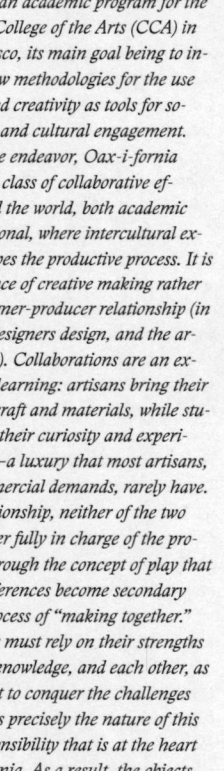

The Carrot Concept
Roberto Javier Dumont, born in San Salvador, El Salvador, 1979; José Roberto Paredes, born in San Salvador, El Salvador, 1974; Claudia Washington, born in San Salvador, El Salvador, 1976; Harry Washington, born in San Salvador, El Salvador, 1981; live and work in San Salvador, El Salvador

The idea was simple: to succeed in the global market, it was essential that we join forces and work together. By sharing ideas and pooling resources, we created the critical mass needed for El Salvador to compete in the international market and establish a stronger local design and production community. Having a physical presence in San Salvador—a home for design with a wide-open door—was crucial to fostering creativity as the face of design in El Salvador. The Carrot Concept is a physical space: a gallery, workspace, shop, and a café that serves as a common home for art and design. This is where we work, connect, and share ideas, and where we are inspired by nature while surrounded by great people. It is a venue for visitors to relax, explore the design process, and purchase Salvadoran products. This concept has a clear objective: to transform Salvadoran design into a disciplined and systematic method for developing projects. As a consequence, quality is improved, value is enhanced, and production time can be reduced. Another objective is the expansion and elevation of local manufacturing by involving producers in the design process. Our goal is to bring design into the lives of the public through education, work, and social interaction.

Leo Capote
Born in São Paulo, Brazil, 1981; lives and works in São Paulo, Brazil

For nearly sixteen years, I have been searching for alternative uses for objects that are made for other purposes. Industrialized objects perform specific functions and are designed based on ergonomic principles—they adhere to technological and formal requirements, and are made of various materials, different finishes, and produced by a variety of manufacturing processes. These objects become raw material for me. They lose their original function and are transformed to serve another system and perform different functions. This is my way of thinking about objects.

José Castrellón
Born in Ciudad de Panama, Panama, 1980; lives and works in Ciudad de Panama, Panama

My sensibility as an artist comes from the transformational forces of society, and as a photographer, I identify with cultural changes and the impact they have on different places. I am attracted to the cultural influence of others and physical changes in urban or rural spaces brought about by commercialism and urban construction. I am drawn to anything that generates change—in people or their way of life. My goal is to document cultural modifications and gauge the way in which people evolve within their societies. I see my work as a poetic testament that captures the vestiges of cultures and the impact of transformational events.

Chiachio & Giannone
Leo Chiachio, born in Buenos Aires, Argentina, 1969; Daniel Giannone, born in Cordoba, Argentina, 1964; live and work in Buenos Aires, Argentina

Ours is a collaborative process-based method, a way in which we can expand the boundaries of our work. We have recently focused on embroidery as a technical process for developing images. Embroidery is a traditional technique associated with women. In view of this, we feel as though we have resuscitated a handcrafted art form and reconfigured it for the dual practice of a male couple. We also wish to show that two men can access this world with a sense of freedom, as two children playing. We are interested in working with simple materials—primary school art supplies, such as glitter, flexible fabric, cardboard, and colored pencils—as well as domestic materials, such as thread, cloth, and buttons, for a kind of transformative embellishment. Self portraiture is an integral part of all of our work, and then the image of Piolin (our pet dachshund) began appearing as another character. The scenarios in which we situate ourselves in our images arise from our research on legends and myths of different cultures.

Álvaro Catalán de Ocón
Born in Madrid, Spain, 1975; lives and works in Madrid, Spain

Plastic bottles embody a contradiction: they are intended to have a short lifespan but are made of a material that takes an extremely long time to decompose. Catalán de Ocón decided to give PET bottles a second life by transforming them into a series of lamps that combine one of the most industrial products on earth with one of the most traditional artisanal techniques found in every culture: the textile tradition. The concept behind the lamps is simple: the body of the bottle is cut into vertical strips along the lines of the mold used in its manufacture. The strips, which remain attached to the neck of the bottle, act as the structure upon which other materials are woven. The neck of the bottle connects the lampshade to the lamp's electrical components. In August 2012, the studio organized a workshop in Bogotá in collaboration with Artesanías de Colombia, artisans from the Cauca region who have been displaced by the guerrilla war in Bogotá. The artisans applied their traditional basket weaving techniques onto plastic bottles using their own paja de tetera *fiber tinted with natural pigments.*

Liliana Angulo Cortés
Born in Bogotá, Colombia, 1974; lives and works in Bogotá, Colombia

As an artist in Colombia, I have been committed to challenging racial politics, as conceived by both the oppressors and the oppressed, focusing on African diaspora populations, particularly in the Americas and Caribbean. My work refutes the limitations of identity in national narratives and of power relations within these discourses. It challenges imposed hierarchies, disputing the ideas of a disembodied universality. I use and create fractures in the Eurocentric, colonial, racist, and classist order. I present stories of resistance and radical thinking about freedom as the submerged history of the oppressed, in an attempt to articulate social problems, engaging critically with issues of ethnicity, sexuality, gender, class, or race. I focus on cultural practices outside traditional artistic disciplines and the art market, to challenge settings of white privilege that unilaterally reinforce an "Art World" founded on exclusion and the extension of privileges given to a supposedly "high culture." I believe in the artist as a public intellectual. My practice involves different roles—researcher, creator, educator, distributor, administrator, and curator—and diverse media combining interventions, installation, performance, video, photography, and language, among others.

Tais Costa, Davi Deusdará, Érica Martins, Rafael Studart
Tais Costa, born in Ceará, Brazil, 1983; Davi Deusdará, born in Ceará, Brazil, 1985; Érica Martins, born in Ceará, Brazil, 1984; Rafael Studart, born in Ceará, Brazil, 1983; live and work in Fortaleza, Brazil

As Brazilian architects, we were extremely excited to take on the challenge of designing public furniture. At its core, the concept of the U Rock Chair is a contemporary take on the way we experience public spaces, where different users coexist in a rich, colorful, and peaceful fashion. U Rock complements this way of thinking, generating a lasting emotional connection with its users, inviting them to come back, move around a bit, and keep rocking. The most important description of this chair is "moveable." You can choose to sit straight in a comfortable and beautiful chair, or flip it over to rock out in a new interpretation of the classic rocking chair. Light, stackable, and easy to carry, it is design-friendly for all ages. The chair is made from recycled PET bottles that are collected in specially identified containers in Battery Park in New York City. The park visitors are directly responsible for their future seats through a connection with design and recycling processes. This creates an emotional bond between U Rock and its users even before production, increasing the feeling that the chairs belong to everyone.

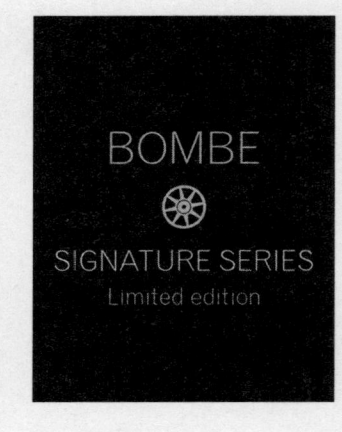

Les Crayons Noir
Herbert Baglione, born in São Paulo, Brazil, 1977; Thais Beltrame, born in São Paulo, Brazil, 1976; Alexandre Cruz (Sesper), born in São Paulo, Brazil, 1973; Felipe Yung (Flip), born in São Paulo, Brazil, 1978; live and work in São Paulo, Brazil

Created by Antoine Carboué, from the publishing house Les Crayons Noirs, in collaboration with the Brazilian collective La Famiglia, Bombe is a series of artisanal objects fashioned in porcelain from Limoges, France—an original collection of pieces in a numbered and limited edition of sixty. With Bombe, we brought together two distinct universes: street art and fine art—with a surprising combination of freedom, creativity, and transgression. Bombe is created by fusing the graffiti writer's famous tool—spray paint, or translated into French slang, bomb—with kaolin, the unique material used to create porcelain. We wanted to blend a modern tool linked to artistic expression with a traditional and fine material, as well as a certain savoir-faire and art de vivre. With Bombe, we hope to promote a close collaboration between the Brazilian artists of La Famiglia and the French artists of Les Crayons Noirs, in order to create an object that will be part of the reinvestigation of Brazilian art and the renewal of porcelain craft. This intercultural approach has inspired our concept.

Abraham Cruzvillegas
Born in Mexico City, Mexico, 1968; lives and works in Mexico City, Mexico

I often combine diverse objects—leftovers from contradictory contexts—together in one work. This represents an economic clash of things on top of each other: organic matter, industrially made or handmade. These elements might be made in Taiwan, Marrakesh, New York, Paris, or Mexico City. They possess an internal system, and I preside over them coming together, as a voyeur of their relationships. There might be conflict or physical or conceptual instability to coexist, but there is also love, hate, power, and sometimes friendship. In effect, it is the same for all of us: at times we must accept our own contradictions in order to develop and maintain alliances—or not. In my long-standing project, Autoconstrucción, *I drew inspiration from the eclectic and improvisatory environment of my childhood home in Pedregales de Coyoacán, an area of Mexico City that was initially inhabited by migrants who moved in and set up squatter settlements in the 1960s. Like many of their neighbors, my parents built their house themselves, modifying it over many decades—a process I refer to as* autoconstrucción, *or self-constructing.* Autoconstrucción *operates as a metaphor for individual identity and the identity of a place existing in a state of flux, unfinished. It relates to ideas of "survival economics"—how scarcity can lead to recycling and solidarity as opposed to consumption and individualism.*
Photo: Kurimanzutto, Mexico City

Lucia Cuba
Born in Lima, Peru, 1980; lives and works in Quebec, Canada

My work involves strong political content and constitutes a critical approach to fashion design and the construction and exploration of garments as performative and political devices. I am interested in broadening the understanding of the role of fashion-design objects, from the purely functional or aesthetic, outward toward social, ethical, and political perspectives. I seek to harness the agency of clothes and question the established language of fashion as experienced today. As a scholar of public health and psychology, I am particularly interested in addressing issues of body, gender, and biopolitics through the construction of garments that act as critical devices. My work combines fashion, art, and activism.

DFC (Distrito Federal Casa)
Mauricio Paniagua, born in Guatemala City, Guatemala, 1969; Tony Moxham, born in Sydney, Australia, 1971; live and work in Mexico City, Mexico

All DFC designs, aside from our wall coverings (which are created with Flavor Paper, a Brooklyn–based firm) are 100 percent handmade in Mexico. From the start—especially as newcomers wanting to prove ourselves in our new home—we knew it was important to work locally and incorporate Mexican culture and history. We began by traveling and making contact with artisans throughout the country. In this way, we built a small team of trusted and incredibly talented craftspeople who produce our work. For certain projects, we often research locations known for specific techniques and seek out the best craftspeople. From our experience, it's important to work with a team that is not only technically skilled, but also interested in learning and changing, while preserving traditional skills and techniques. We believe that for "artesania," as we call it, to evolve, the people who create it must be willing to adapt. We introduce artisans working in different techniques to each other's work, and we often create projects that combine the work of artisans in different fields.
Photo: Marco Ovando

Marcella Echavarría
Born Medellín, Colombia, 1972; lives and works in New York, USA

My life's journey is about building bridges, weaving invisible threads, and translating emotion into words and images. My passion is drawing from forgotten cultures, talent, tradition, and meaning—always with a purpose in mind—to improve the lives of artisans and contribute to preserving their centuries-old heritage. I achieve these goals in different ways: writing stories for various publications worldwide, photographing, conceptualizing collections and, especially, creating thriving brands with content and meaning. My work straddles two worlds: branding and development, north and south.

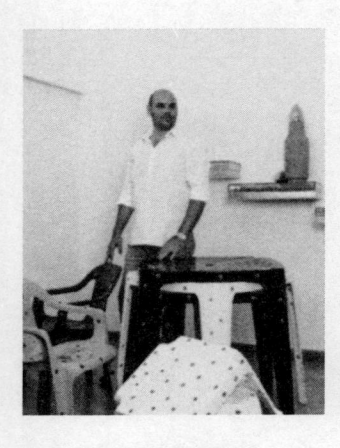

David Elia (Design da Gema)
Born in Rio de Janeiro, Brazil, 1982; lives and works in Monte Carlo, Monaco

The concept behind Design da Gema comes from the spontaneity and resilience of the Cariocas, as the natives of Rio de Janeiro are known. A design studio and small production unit, Design da Gema is based in Monaco and Rio de Janeiro. Coastal and mountainous, with rich contrasts between urban and jungle landscapes, Rio de Janeiro is a deeply creative place that inspires artists and energizes its inhabitants. Design da Gema was conceived between a samba and the open-air bazaars of Rio's city center, where the materials of original artifacts displayed are as improbable as they are graphic. Repurposing is almost a way of life in Brazilian and Carioca culture, and diverse objects can be reconstructed and re-adapted, giving them a second life. Consequently, I make use of upcycling, the process of converting waste materials or useless products into new materials or products. The Carioca spirit represents the ability to cope with everything at once, which is what I convey in my designs. City life is my main source of inspiration. By observing what surrounds me, I frame my artwork and transcend everyday perception. Everything is a pretext for creation, and takes shape in an unexpected way.

Sebastian Errazuriz
Born in Santiago, Chile, 1977; lives and works in New York, USA

I question the paradigms that structure our daily routines by creating original representations of new possibilities that interrupt our conceptions of normality, transform meaning, and invite viewers to imagine life differently. Through an interdisciplinary art/design practice, the artworks I create incorporate elements of functionality while my designs might include sculptural, existential, or political aspects that are traditionally associated with the arts. I believe that all artists have a social responsibility, and I create artworks that are purposely designed to function—to force the viewer to see and feel realities that they might not want to experience. Each work embodies an original idea that is stripped to its simplest iconographic image and intended to create maximum effect with minimal interventions and resources.

Gilberto Esparza
Born in Aguascalientes, Mexico, 1975; lives and works in Guanajuato, Mexico

In my work I research technological developments and their impact on individuals, the urban environment, society, and nature. The projects that come out of this research reflect the speed at which the environment is changing. Organisms must adapt in a symbiotic way to rapid changes, and we humans can help the process. By using recycling technology, we can transform our relationship with nature.

Carla Fernández
Born in Coahuila, Mexico, 1973; lives and works in Mexico City, Mexico

My hometown is very close to Laredo, Texas, and like my mother and many others in northern Mexico, I shopped at malls or Salvation Army stores across the border in the United States. My father was the director of museums at the Instituto Nacional de Antropología e Historia, and we traveled all over Mexico. I spent hours looking at the clothes worn by the local people and would buy similar clothes, when I could find them, at the outdoor markets, incorporating them into my regular wardrobe. Indigenous people continue to follow the same design traditions that existed in precolonial America: using squares, lozenges, and rectangles. Their geometric designs connected my two areas of study—fashion design and art history, especially the work of artists from Constructivist and Futurist avant-garde movements. Through this lens I discovered indigenous dressmaking, studying it not as a "primitive" object, but in terms of artistry and process. My dream of working with indigenous communities came true when I was asked to teach dressmaking at traveling craft-design schools in a program launched by the Institute of Folk Cultures of Mexico's Consejo Nacional para la Cultura y las Artes (National Council for Culture and Arts), known as Conaculta. That same year, I opened my own fashion design workshop, Taller Flora, to develop designs based on my research.

Eddie Figueroa Feliciano
Born in San Juan, Puerto Rico, 1978; lives and works in San Juan, Puerto Rico

As a Caribbean designer, I use local references and convert them into objects. Collections develop from experimentation and a dialogue concerning traditional craftsmanship, architecture, and our cultural. Globalization creates homogenization and the appropriation and commodification of cultures by market forces in search of trends and new products. This results in the loss of many of the diverse characteristics in design, in many geographical regions. I try to address this problem in the design process by consciously selecting and using local materials and technologies that are typically from Puerto Rico.

Coco Fusco
Born in New York City, USA, 1960; lives and works in New York, USA

The Empty Plaza / La Plaza Vacía *is a single-channel video. Inspired by the organized public protests in the Middle East beginning in 2011, the artist took note of the communal spaces around the world being utilized and, in contrast, those left empty. The empty Plaza de la Revolución in Havana, Cuba, becomes the protagonist in her meditation on public space, revolutionary promise, and memory. Intermittent close-range views bring the Plaza's architecture into focus; long takes documenting Fusco's passage through the vacant square are punctuated by vintage archival footage depicting scenes from postrevolutionary Cuba. Throughout the duration of the video, a Spanish narration, written by acclaimed Cuban journalist Yoani Sánchez, describes what appears—and does not appear—in view. Also on exhibit are film stills from* The Empty Plaza. *Cinematic in impact, the images are dominated by a broad horizon line as the large sky and the vast civic plaza are nearly equalized.*

"The absence of public in some plazas seemed just as resonant and provocative as its presence in others," Fusco recalls. "Cuba's Plaza de la Revolución is one such place—a stark, inhospitable arena, where all the major political events of the past half-century have been marked by mass choreography, militarized displays, and rhetorical flourish. I decided to create a piece about that legendary site—an empty stage filled with memories, through which every foreign visitor passes, while nowadays many, if not most, Cubans flee."

Carlos Garaicoa
Born in Havana, Cuba, 1967; lives and works in Madrid, Spain / Havana, Cuba

I take a multidisciplinary approach to issues of culture and politics, particularly Cuban, through the study of architecture, urbanism, and history. My main subject and inspiration have always been the architecture of the city of Havana and the Cuban way of life, but there are also parallels with many other cities that I visit, which also inspire me. My work includes installation, video, photography, sculpture, drawings, and even pop-up books.

Anabella Georgi
Born in Caracas, Venezuela, 1975; lives and works in Berlin, Germany / Caracas, Venezuela

My design has its own language and identity. The graphic and the three-dimensional join to reflect my environment, which is full of contrasts, rhythms, light, and color. Various materials combine the industrial with craft, and the line between chaos and order defines the language of the pieces. I use my objects to communicate the sensation of living in Latin America.

Glimpt
Mattias Rask, born in Göteborg, Sweden, 1985; Tor Palm, born in Halmstad, Sweden, 1985; live and work in Göteborg, Sweden

We spent the autumn of 2012 in Peru working and learning from the crafts cooperative Artesanos Don Bosco—a continuation of our work with craftsmen and craftswomen from different countries. The organization provides craftsmanship training, and after five years of training, most of the artisans work in the organization's cooperative. The courses are primarily related to different ways of working with wood—including furniture making, decorations, carving pictures, and housing construction. We decided we wanted to develop a more modern series of furniture, and after visiting several villages and different cooperatives in the Andes, we finally settled on the village of Yungay, where there was a little cooperative that worked with furniture making. During our visits, we were impressed by their very high standards of craftsmanship and, above all, by the skill of the people who carved pictures in wood. The collaboration resulted in the production of a series of coffee tables called Prehistoric Aliens. *The name was inspired by Peru's fantastic cultural heritage, which can seem very mystical and ancient to our Western eyes. The small coffee tables are almost like small spaceships that have just landed, with their leader, the robot.*

gt2P (Great Things to People)
Eduardo Arancibia, born in Santiago, Chile 1980; Victor Imperiale, born in Puerto Varas, Chile, 1986; Guillermo Parada, born in Santiago, Chile, 1981; Tamara Pérez, born in Diriamba, Nicaragua, 1981; Sebastian Rozas, born in Santiago, Chile, 1978; live and work in Santiago, Chile

We are a studio involved with architecture, art, and design projects. We are engaged in a continuous process of research and experimentation in digital crafting, promoting new encounters between contemporary technologies and the richness of the local, expressed in traditional materials and techniques. We seek to systematize knowledge and observation, whether of natural, artificial, geometric, or spatial phenomena, through generative algorithms. Parametric design is a tool to guide the planning of our projects, enabling the integration of design, development, and production. We have also discovered an artistic dimension that connects us with our cultural heritage, through the incorporation of traditional experience and knowledge that feed and qualify the generative algorithms, or DNA, that we create. Revealing the surprise of manual processes and local materials is a way to value who we are through what we do.
Photo: Cristobal Palma

Thierry Jeannot
Born in Beauvais, France, in 1963; lives and works in Mexico City, Mexico

Based in Mexico for the last twenty years, Thierry Jeannot focuses on generating high added value to recycled materials, with an interest in traditional-technique crafts and craftspeople. He first began working with a range of unconventional materials in the 1980s, both for fashion designer Thierry Mugler in Paris, as well as on his own projects. Jeannot engages paradox and contrast in his work, transforming discarded matter that is generally viewed as a scourge into sophisticated designs. PET bottles—from store shelves, the trash, or the street—are crafted into one-of-a-kind chandeliers as opulent as crystal, yet constructed from hundreds of plastic containers, meticulously selected, cut, and reassembled as an exceptional and unique piece. He follows a design philosophy where the design and production processes are never separated. A coffee table is constructed through marrying scrap materials with sophisticated handcrafted bronze parts, and gold and silver leaf with burnt wood. Jeannot likes to maintain a strong connection to history and the decorative arts, though at the same time the resulting design-art pieces question established symbols of luxury and our preconceptions of the value of materials.

Lattoog Design
Leonardo Lattavo, born in Rio de Janeiro, Brazil, 1970; Pedro Moog, born in Rio de Janeiro, Brazil, 1970; live and work in Rio de Janeiro, Brazil

All Lattoog products are conceived, designed, and produced to join the rational aspects of high technology with the poetry and subjectivity of art objects. Behind our brand are the forces that bind us as partners, and we bring together our complementary academic backgrounds and pluralistic experiences to offer innovative furniture design and architecture. We launched our first furniture collection in São Paulo in 2005, one year after we established our partnership, and the results are functional objects that combine harmonious, sinuous, and organic lines with geometrical forms, while retaining the cultural elements so important to Brazilian culture. We are inspired by daily life in the old historical neighborhood of São Cristovão—its flowery ceramic tiles on walls and tabletops, the iron gates transformed into furniture—and the celebrated wave designs on Copacabana and Ipanema sidewalks. In our Viralatas *series (Mongrel), is an example of hybrid furniture: two pieces unite to make a third, at once different from the others. This is a reminder of the racial mixture that is Brazil, which contributes to its rich artistic and cultural fabric.*

Jorge Lizarazo (Hechizoo)
Born in Bogotá, Colombia, 1968; lives and works in Bogotá, Colombia

Hechizoo is a place where textiles from natural fibers, copper wire, brass and tin, and leather are developed. The old mixes with the new, tradition with technology, reinterpreting our origins through textile designs. Hechizoo textiles tell a story. It begins with the selection of materials from different parts of Colombia and the rest of the world. It continues with the many hands that produce and provide the raw materials, and concludes with the weavers and artisans who transform the materials and our ideas into textile fibers. Hechizoo is like a tour of Colombia in all its biodiversity—the colors, textures, and inhabitants.

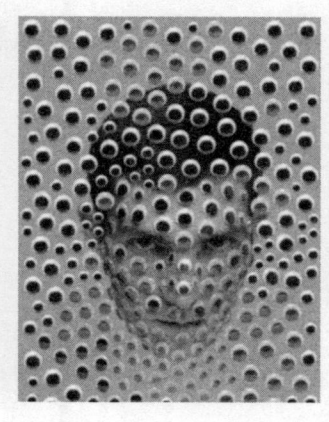

Pepe López
Born in Caracas, Venezuela, 1966; lives and works between Caracas, Venezuela / Paris, France

The development of my artistic work is the result of continuous observation of my urban environment. I project my experiences as a consumer, citizen, and inhabitant of the planet in each series of work, bringing together multiple sources of conceptual and aesthetic experiences. My images and objects are spaces where we might look into ourselves, as well as a window into contemporary society. I think of my work as a magic mirror, in which you see the reflection of others when looking at yourself.

MáximaDuda
Anabella Georgi, born in San Cristóbal, Venezuela, 1975; lives and works in Caracas, Venezuela / Berlin, Germany; Mária Antonia Godigna, born in Caracas, Venezuela, 1973; lives and works in Caracas, Venezuela

Various crafts in Venezuela are disappearing under pressures and influences from outside of the country. We believe that "design" as a tool must be used to ensure that our ethnic and artisan communities survive and are able to create new products for the contemporary market. Within this context, our plan has been to focus on preserving and sustaining indigenous Venezuelan craft—fused with the rainforest—which in turn reaffirms the essential values of our culture and traditions. The MáximaDuda design lab allows for the exchange of knowledge, skills, and creativity.

Bernardo Mazzei
Born in Caracas, Venezuela, 1957; lives and works in Caracas, Venezuela

I have always had great respect for other design traditions: the principles of Bauhaus, Italian, and Scandinavian design, and the idea of using aluminum profiles in furniture has always been attractive to me. Why aluminum? It is a formidable metal that is perfect for the rigors of contemporary living: light, recyclable, as noble as wood, impervious to rust, and very appealing. The simple fact that airplanes cannot fly without it lends a romantic aspect to this ubiquitous metal. I also celebrate the influence of popular culture in the history of furniture, and this celebration is evident in pieces like Anauco Aalto, a contemporary reinterpretation of a precolonial Venezuelan chair from the Cumanagoto people. Polished aluminum replaces wood, and rawhide is woven in a manner similar to how Alvar Aalto and other modernists used weaving in the mid-twentieth century. The results are sleek and elegant pieces of indoor/outdoor furniture that function brilliantly, even in public spaces.

Vik Muniz
Born in São Paulo, Brazil, 1961; lives and works in Rio de Janeiro, Brazil

Many people know of Smithson's Spiral Jetty, but how many have actually seen it? For most, the gargantuan work is no larger than a page in a book or magazine. How many people have actually seen the surface of a nearby planet, witnessed open-heart surgery, or children sprayed with napalm? Mediated knowledge comes with strings attached: It substitutes the opacity of not seeing for the transparency of seeing through. The Black Forest of myth has been replaced by a crystal garden of holographic distortions. We're equally blinded by our ability to see through everything. The woman who stands on top of Spiral Jetty cannot see it any better than the woman who gazes at it in a book. My work attempts to define the levels of these mediations as if they were a landscape itself. Like a nineteenth century easel painter, I try to render the scenery of signs, trying to depict things, as an Impressionist would insist, as I see them. The landscape has changed, but the role of the artist remains the same: to shed light on the complex relationship between the mind and phenomena.

Nada Se Leva
André Bastos, born in Porto Alegre, Brazil, 1962; Guilherme Leite Ribeiro, born in Rio de Janeiro, Brazil, 1968; live and work in São Paulo, Brazil

Our partnership seeks to explore colors, texture, contours, and materials to the fullest, through our two areas of expertise fashion and graphic design. Our first collection was lauded for its sensitive yet daring recovery of the Brazilian baroque, an irreverent take on the opulent and ornate art of the period—black-outlined mirrors, ruby-colored side tables, and portable chandeliers that fold flat. In revisiting the past, we recognize that in life there are things that you "can't take with you," although everything is there to be revisited, rethought, reapplied. Our primary objective as Nada Se Leva is to draw from the heritage of the past and apply it using today's technology. Whether it is our fun mini-stools or transformative floor lamps, we have focused on fine craftsmanship applied to sensibly designed pieces made of fine woods, aiming to re-create the simplicity of design developed by our Brazilian predecessors such as Tenreiro, Lucio de Carvalho, and Zanine Caldas. We also seek out new materials and techniques to develop our work, such as laser-cut acrylic and digitally stamped Formica, all with a deeply rooted sense of humor.

Maria Nepomuceno
Born in Rio de Janeiro, Brazil, 1976; lives and works in Rio de Janeiro, Brazil

My art education began with painting, but I eventually veered toward sculpture, especially when I began studying industrial design and working with materials such as acrylic, wood, latex, plaster, ceramics, and others. During my pregnancy, I began to incorporate ropes into my work, a metaphor for the umbilical cord, and beads, which represent cells. To connect these different materials, I developed my own handmade sewing technique, thereby connecting my work with my indigenous and African ancestry. For the past few years, I have been using sculpture to establish a relationship between body and nature, the micro- and macrocosm—weaving memories of backgrounds and experiences, and promoting encounters with the past, present, and future. In this way, my work also relates to a suspended time, an eternal moment of contemplation of life's cycles and infinity, always suggesting the integration between man and nature.

Edgar Orlaineta
Born in Mexico City, Mexico 1972; lives and works in Mexico City, Mexico

My work focuses on the minutiae of everyday life, employing objects and ideas and transforming them into sculptural forms. I reconfigure modernist design, architecture, and historical and cultural symbolism into hybrid forms, in which modernist ideals and cultural perspectives collide. I try to approach objects in an analytical way, searching for their historical contradictions. In this way, I reach formal and conceptual conclusions that both celebrate and criticize the matter at hand. Ultimately I try to draw attention to the transformative powers of the everyday.

Ernesto Oroza
Born in Havana, Cuba, 1968; lives and works in Aventura, USA

My work involves a series of research projects concerning relationships between vernacular practices and the typologies of architectural and design objects. My main goal is to understand and engage with material culture and production processes, particularly new practices that come out of urban areas resistant to official or established protocols. I am interested in texts, structures, functional objects, spaces, and methods for the dissemination of my research using similar tactics of vernacular practice to activate and invent. In general, my work is diagrammatic, an effort to map the dynamic models of new relationships that vernacular practices develop and regenerate within their contexts.
Photo: Glexis Novoa

Liliana Ovalle (in collaboration with Colectivo 1050º)
Born in Mexico City, Mexico, 1977; lives and works in London, UK

Everyday objects can offer a space for reflection. As a designer, Ovalle is particularly interested in how different idiosyncrasies are translated in material culture and how the world of things represent not only the context of where they come from, but the beliefs and systems of the people behind them. In her work, Ovalle pays special attention to inquiring themes such as the "incomplete" and the "unrehearsed" observed in the urban context. The collaboration with Colectivo 1050º brings together Ovalle's aesthetic explorations with the richness of vernacular pottery from Oaxaca. The exchange, while sensitive to the heritage and context of the ceramics, delivers a contemporary result where both tradition and design feed into each other.

Colectivo 1050º was founded by Kythzia Barrera in Oaxaca, Mexico in 2010. It creates contemporary ceramics inspired by traditional cultures but finely adapted to modern life. 1050º is the temperature at which tradition and modernity merge, and urban designers and women potters in rural Mexico work together, hand in hand, through collaborative design methods. Their production aims to reduce environmental impact through the combination of traditional processes and alternative technologies. Above all, Colectivo 1050º helps to create real job opportunities that support the economic development of indigenous women in the poorest villages in Oaxaca. This collaboration was possible thanks to the craftsmanship of Elia Mateo (1980), Angelina Mateo (1966), Macrina Mateo (1969), Alberta Mateo (1963), and Dorotea Mateo (1953). The Mateo family lives and works in Tlapazola, Oaxaca.

Rolando Peña
Born in Caracas, Venezuela, 1942; lives and works in Caracas, Venezuela

I see the arts as a commitment to life—a philosophy—and I express myself by integrating dance, theater, cinema, video, photography, installation, architecture, and design. Art is participation, a way to touch people in the deepest recesses of their souls, brains, and hearts. It is catharsis and has to shake people, orient them, point out the best and worst of our society, the best and the worst of each of us: that is my credo. I became involved in the art world during the late 1950s through theater, dancing, happenings, and performances, and as a result, the union of art, science, and technology became an ongoing leitmotif in my work. I see my chosen subject—oil—as a concept, an energy that is positive and negative, depending on what we make of it. As an artist, I'm committed to creating awareness, denouncing the ecological disasters caused by oil's misuse. I hope to affect people's consciousness on this critical issue. Heroism is understanding everyday events and turning them into art.

Eduardo Portillo and María Eugenia Dávilla
Born in Jajó, Venezuela, 1966; María Eugenia Dávilla, born in Mérida, Venezuela, 1966; live and work in Mérida, Venezuela

We are interested in representing experiences in materials and processes that bear the imprint of people and places, and reveal the relationships between people and their environments. When we decided to work with silk, we were compelled to travel to China and India to study and research their age-old practices of sericulture. Our experiences were crucial to our training. We have always been passionate about knowledge, experimentation, and especially its reinterpretation within our own place and culture, in Mérida, in the Venezuelan Andes. We also work with local materials, such as cotton and alpaca from Peru and Bolivia, fiber from the moriche and chiqui-chique palm trees of the Orinoco River Delta and Amazon region, as well as dyes from the indigo plant. For us color is crucial. Our interest in color starts at its very foundations: how it is obtained, where it is found in nature, in objects, in people. Through color we discover the way to follow each project.

Projeto Morrinho
Founded in Rio de Janeiro, Brazil, in 1998

Projeto Morrinho is a social and cultural project based out of the Vila Pereira da Silva favela (Pereirão) in the Laranjeiras neighborhood of Rio de Janeiro, Brazil. Morrinho (little hill), which was started by local youth in 1998, is a 320 square meter model of the city constructed from bricks and other recycled materials. It began as a game played by local children in order to escape from the realities of violence and corruption that surrounded them and their community. Within this miniature urban world of Morrinho, participants act out a role-playing game with the numerous LEGO block dolls that inhabit the model, re-creating life in Rio's favelas. The young creators of Morrinho began to create stories of the daily life of the community, which eventually became short films. The exhibitions of replicas of Morrinho in galleries and museums have been very well received by the public, and is related to the curiosity that we have about the favelas. In an anthropological sense: what do people do in favelas? How do they survive? What do they have to say about themselves and the world? Answering these questions has been one of the things Project Morrinho has tried to accomplish.

Re(D)
Deborah Castillo, born in Caracas, Venezuela, 1971; lives and works in Caracas, Venezuela / New York, USA; Carolina Tinoco, born in Caracas, Venezuela, 1972; lives and works in Paris, France

As part of the Re(D) project, we intervened in and reevaluated designs from the past. Redesign is part of our vision. We also seek to re-create, reinvent, renew, reuse, and recycle notions that are part of contemporary culture. Our manual and mechanical interventions on Panton chairs resulted in objects that blur the lines between art, architecture, and design. Re(D) points to the ways in which urban growth and mass production can be dehumanizing. The application of graphics to three-dimensional forms shakes up the concept of mass production and multiples. It reorders the unit, placing it within a kind of chaos, blending chaos as survival that is unique to Latin American urban aesthetics.

Guto Requena (Estudio Guto Requena)
Born in Sorocaba, Brazil, 1979; lives and works in São Paulo, Brazil

At Estudio Guto Requena, we shape memories trough the experimental use of digital technologies. Our practice includes a variety of design scales—small objects, interiors, buildings, and even cityscapes. We look for answers to questions of sustainability, identity, memory, interaction, hybrid realities, and flexibility. In doing so, we draw on Brazilian contemporary design, seeking to create a methodology associated with research. The goal is in fact the process itself, not just the final result. We follow three main lines of creativity and production: theory (consulting, lectures, workshop research), individual projects (furniture, interiors, scenography, architecture), and mass media (design shows for television and the Internet).

Pedro Reyes
Born in Mexico City, Mexico 1972; lives and works in Mexico City, Mexico

I seek to address the interplay between physical and social space through my work, making tangible the invisible geometry of our personal relationships. In doing so, I explore the ways in which a space is capable of allowing individual moments of liberation or activating groups of people. My notion of sculpture examines the cognitive contradictions of modern life, and the possibility of overcoming our particular crises by increasing our individual and collective degree of agency.

Daniel Reynolds
Born in Caracas, Venezuela, 1961; lives and works in London, UK

My porcelain pieces reference the age-old practice of reinterpreting existing objects in different, sometimes unexpected materials. The ancient Chinese did this to great effect when re-creating, in fine porcelain, much older vessels originally made in bronze, wood, or basket ware. Features of the original materials such as bronze rivets or wood grain were often faithfully reproduced in the porcelain object, resulting in an unexpected playfulness and humor being imparted to the new pieces. In the modern vernacular, various kinds of plastic objects are produced for mass consumption, borrowing the look of traditional fine porcelain. I am particularly interested in the aspect of preserving these ephemeral, disposable contemporary objects—made from polystyrene (stacking picnic plates), rubber (hot-water bottle) and coated card (milk carton)—in a classic imperishable material such as porcelain. With Andy Warhol and Jasper Johns as direct early influences on my work, the industrial design of these pieces is brought into sharp focus by the change in perception that casting them in porcelain brings. Here the traditional techniques of handmade contemporary studio ceramics are applied to the reinterpretation of throwaway objects of industrial mass production.

Jorge Rivas
Born in Caracas, Venezuela, 1964; lives and works in Los Angeles, USA

Furniture can tell stories, and my work seeks to involve the user in my creative universe, which is linked to Venezuelan material tradition and modern design. Designs are inspired by the past and projected into the future, and I seek to establish a dialogue between different moments and aspects of material culture, history, art, and society. My references include pre-Columbian cultures, the art of the colonial period in Latin America, Venezuelan design of the mid-twentieth century, geometric abstraction, and modern design. In all my pieces, there is a careful study of geometry, proportion, and the relationship between the whole and its parts. I also believe that the materials and manufacturing techniques are essential parts of each project. Although I have used a range of materials, wood is my preferred medium. I generally choose varieties of wood available in Latin America for their colors and grains, which are specific to tropical species. My furniture is inextricably linked to its production environment and to traditional craftsmanship, especially the artisans and the communities where it is manufactured.

Ariel Rojo
Born in Mexico City, Mexico, 1976; lives and works in Mexico City, Mexico

Ariel Rojo is a designer whose studio is dedicated to enhancing the quality of life through design solutions. Conscience, social responsibility, and humor are the key ingredients of Rojo's design philosophy. With each of his projects, Rojo questions the way it will be perceived, and seeks to provoke a smile or a moment of reflection for the user. Ariel began his career designing motherboards for oil platforms. Today Ariel Rojo studio maintains an international practice, with clients in Latin America, Europe, the United States, and the Middle East. The rug Foco Rojo *(made for the Marion Friedmann Gallery in London) reflects the state of "alertness" of Mexico City. With a population of 25 million, its metropolitan area is one of the most populated in the world; insecurity, corruption, and crime fuel distress there. However this alertness is also characterized by a quick-wittedness and energy that triggers enormous power, stimulating positive change and creativity. Each light in the rug represents an idea born every minute in Mexico and conveys that Mexico is on the verge of something unique and new.*

Eduardo Sarabia
Born in Los Angeles, USA, 1976; lives and works in Guadalajara, Mexico

As a teller of stories, Sarabia develops his works through a travel-intensive, research-based process in which the histories and mythologies of various communities are mined in order to unveil how our understanding of the world is constructed through fact and fiction. Working in drawing, painting, sculpture, video, and installation, Sarabia deconstructs the clichés and stereotypes that result from tense moments of cultural contact, instead depicting textured narratives informed by the movement of bodies, capital, and materials—both licit and illicit—across geographies and undefined terrains. The works showcased in New Territories *were also featured in* Eduardo Sarabia, *the artist's first museum survey, organized by the Instituto Cultural Cabañas and guest curated by Cesar Garcia, Director/Chief Curator of The Mistake Room. The exhibition included installations that explored a range of themes tied to the peoples of Mexico's Yucatan peninsula: drug trafficking and its impact on popular culture, the quest for Pancho Villa's hidden treasure, the world of spirits and shamans, and ancient Mayan myths about the end of our current era. Through Sarabia's work, we come to understand how our individual perspectives of the world are tied to broader social processes, and how our dreams, desires, and fears are assembled not by only our own lives and imaginations but also by forces in other lands, real and imagined.*

Alejandro Sarmiento
Born in General Villegas, Argentina, 1959; lives and works in Buenos Aires, Argentina

As an industrial designer, I am interested in working with standard materials, as well as industrial refuse, considering possibilities for using and reusing materials for generating new products. My projects cover a broad range—from exploration and experimentation of materials to design and product development—and I consider human energy to be integral for production, as a way of reducing the use of industrial machines and their energy consumption. I believe there are many reusable resources that can be obtained at a very low cost (sometimes virtually nothing), allowing new products to be made from old as they reenter the market through reuse.

Satorilab
Alejandro Sarmiento, born in General Villegas, Argentina, 1959; Luján Cambariere, born in Buenos Aires, Argentina, 1971; live and work in Buenos Aires, Argentina

The Satorilab workshops are collective practices, negating ego and individual authorship. We see design as a tool, rather than as a fashion or style, and in countries such as Argentina, with few major industries or technologies, establishing new links between design professionals and vulnerable populations or communities of artisans can be of great benefit to all. We are interested in raising awareness of the amount of waste material that can be repurposed into new designs, and we strive to go one step further to create an increased sense of awareness of these virtually invisible populations.

Studio MK27 (Marcio Kogan)
Born in São Paulo, Brazil 1952; lives and work in São Paulo, Brazil

Studio MK27 was founded in the early 1980s by architect Marcio Kogan. The firm, which is made up of more than twenty architects, is known primarily for the formal simplicity of its residential and commercial projects. However, Studio MK27 has also participated in furniture design and fine arts projects in collaboration with other artists and designers such as Isay Weinfeld, Manuela Verga, and Paola Boatti. In its project with Weinfeld, Happyland *and* Happyland Vol. 2, *the studio critiqued the violence, kidnappings, traffic accidents, and lack of urban planning endemic to the greater São Paulo area. The series* Prostheses *and* Innesti, *produced in collaboration with Verga and Boatti, represents a mindfulness of the wealth of ingenuity displayed in anonymously constructed works, which are then modified by discrete interventions meant to evoke an effect of contrasts, prolong their lifespan, and offer new meanings and materiality.*

Studio Swine
Alexander Groves, born in England, 1983; Azusa Murakami, born in Japan, 1984; live and work in Shanghai, China

Central to Studio Swine's practice is the notion of place-making and research-led design that is the product of a region and its culture, crafts, and resources. Swine believes that desire is the greatest agent of change and, to this end, explores design through material innovation and creating new sustainable systems while placing an equal importance on aesthetics. Cofounded by Japanese architect Azusa Murakami and British artist Alexander Groves, Studio Swine operates across a wide range of disciplines, working with clients such as Veuve Clicquot, Heineken, Unilever, and those who seek imaginative and visionary ways of developing their brand messages, whether through product, interiors, or unique commissions.

Zanini de Zanine
Born in Rio de Janeiro, Brazil, 1978; lives and works in Rio de Janeiro, Brazil

My parents taught me at a young age to value my Brazilian heritage through encounters with Brazilian culture. I conduct research and apply age-old techniques of traditional Brazilian carpentry in my work, a legacy from my father. I regularly work with hand tools such as the adz, chisel, and bucksaw, and the wood I use mostly comes from old homes, now demolished, or farms built decades ago. Certain species of wood are of great beauty and strength: ipê tobacco, peroba do campo, maçaranduba, gonçalo alves, roxinho, and the rare and noble jacarandá. I work with six highly skilled carpenters making one-of-a-kind pieces or in a limited quantity owing to the scarcity of these types of wood. I also inherited a healthy curiosity from my father, and this lead me to work with other materials such as plastic, methacrylate, upholstery, stainless steel, COR-TEN steel, and glass. I experiment with new technologies, such as injection materials, all the while looking for rich textures and colors that excite me. Another aspect of my work is the subversive reuse of objects and materials. Brazil's large indigent population has learned to improvise and recycle in fantastic ways, and I try to portray their efforts with integrity. In fact, my goal is to present the range of positive features along with the defects found in this vast and curious country known as Brazil.

vacaValiente
Founded in 2006; based in Buenos Aires, Argentina

As a design lab from Argentina, a country of vast cattle ranches, it is perhaps not surprising that we work with recycled leather and that our name means "brave cow." Many of our forms are reduced to a minimalist geometry, the result of research into techno-morphology. We explore the relationship between form and structure based on specific laws of nature. Through this design strategy, we celebrate eco-sustainability, functionality, efficiency, and beauty. Some products have a strong symbolic identity, related to essential social practices in contemporary life, a few of which now seem in danger of extinction: writing from the heart, keeping a diary, or cooking for friends. Designs by vacaValiente are innovative not only in form, but also in the functions they propose. This attitude means designing from the strengths and material sense of an idea, and adapting the material and technology to the design.

Selected Bibliography

Acha, Juan. *Introducción a la teoría a de los diseños.* Mexico City: Editorial Trillas, 1988.

Ades, Dawn. *Art in Latin America: The Modern Era, 1820–1980.* New Haven: Yale University Press, 1993.

Albornoz, César, and Claudio Rolle. *1973: la vida cotidiana de un año crucial.* 1. ed. Santiago de Chile: Planeta, 2003.

Alvarez, Manuel. *Surgimiento del diseño en Mexico, Cuadernos de Diseño.* Universidad Iberoamericana, Mexico City, 1981.

American Institute of Architects. *Cities as a Lab: Designing the Innovation Economy Local Leaders Report.* Washington, DC: AIA, 2013.

Anderson, Benedict. *Imagined Communities: Reflections on the Origin and Spread of Nationalism.* London; New York: Verso, 1991.

Ankele, Gudrun, Daniela Zyman, Francesca von Habsburg, and Paulo Herkenhoff. *Los Carpinteros: Handwork—Constructing the World.* New York: Distributed Art Publishers, 2010.

Ariet, Maria del Carmen. *Documentos sobre Diseno y Calidad de Productos del Comandante Che Guevara.* La Habana: Centro Che Guevara, 2006.

Armas, A.A. *Diseno grafico en Venezuela.* Caracas: Maraven, 1985.

Bauman, Zygmunt. *Liquid Modernity.* London: Polity, 2008.

Bermúdez, Jorge R., *Clara Porset: diseño y cultura.* Havana: Editorial Letras Cubanas, 2005.

Bonsiepe, Gui. *Teoría y práctica del diseño industrial: elementos para una manualística crítica.* Barcelona: Gustavo Gili, 1978.

Bonsiepe, Gui. *Design, Cultura e Sociedade.* São Paulo: Blucher, 2011.

Borges, Adélia. *Design and Craft: The Brazilian Path.* São Paulo: Terceiro Nome, 2011.

Boutique: recuento de una exposición. Mexico City: Museo de arte Carillo Gil, 2003.

Byrd, Antawan I. *Art Cities of the Future: 21st Century Avant Gardes.* London: Phaidon Books, 2013.

Canclini, Néstor García. *Culturas híbridas: estrategias para entrar y salir de la modernidad.* México: Grijalbo, 1990.

Chaparro, F. *Diseno Grafico. Informe de Autoevaluacion del Programa Curricular.* Boyaca: Universidad Nacional, 2005.

Contemporary Brazilian Furniture. Rio de Janeiro: FGV Projetos e Aeroplano Editora, 2013.

Ramírez, Mari Carmen, Héctor Olea, and Tomás Ybarra-Frausto. *Resisting Categories: Latin American and/or Latino?* 1. Critical Documents of the 20th-Century Latin American and Latino Art. New Haven: Yale, 2012.

Cruz-Diez, Carlos, and Edgar Cherubini Lecuna. *Cruz-Diez en Blanco y Negro, exh. cat.* Paris: Cruz-Diez Foundation, 2013.

Cuadot, Felicita. *Estudios de las capacidades estatales del diseño en Cuba.* La Habana: documentos ONDI, 1983.

Cuba Arte Contemporaneo. New York: Overlook Duckworth, 2012.

Cushing, L. *Revolucion!* Cuban Poster Art. San Francisco: Chronical Books, 2003.

De cambios e intercambios / Import Export. Mexico City: Museo Franz Mayer and the British Council, 2006.

De Zanine, exh. cat. Rio de Janeiro: MeMo—Mercado Moderno Gallery, 2012.

Drysdale, Eric. *The Afro-Brazilian touch: the meaning of its artistic and historic contribution.* São Paulo: Tenenge, 1988.

Dunn, Christopher. *Brutality Garden: Tropicália and the Emergence of a Brazilian Counterculture.* Chapel Hill: University of North Carolina Press, 2001.

El diseño de Clara Porset: inventando un México moderno. Mexico City: Museo Franz Mayer, Difusión Cultural UNAM, 2006.

El Museo's Bienal: The (S) Files 2011. New York: El Museo del Barrio, 2011.

Escobedo, Alpha. *Teresa Margolles: Frontera, exh. cat.* Kassel: Kunsthalle Fridericianum, 2011.

Esté, Aquiles. *DGV 70.80.90: diseño gráfico en Venezuela.* Caracas: Centro de Arte La Estancia, 1996.

Fernandez, Silvia, and Gui Bonsiepe. *Historia del diseño en América Latina y el Caribe: industrialización y comunicación visual para la autonomía.* São Paulo: Editora Blücher, 2008.

Flores, Oscar Salinas. *Clara Porset: una vida inquieta, una obra sin igual.* Mexico City: Universidad Nacional Autónoma de México, Facultad de Arquitectura, 2001.

Gruzinski, Serge. *El pensamiento mestizo.* Barcelona: Paidós, 2000.

Hanor, Stephanie. *TRANSactions: contemporary Latin American and Latino art*. La Jolla, CA: Museum of Contemporary Art San Diego, 2006.

Huizinga, Johan. *Homo Ludens: A Study of the Play-Element in Culture*. Boston: Beacon Press, 1971.

Kaufman, Ned. *Pressures and distortions: city dwellers as builders and critics: four views*. New York: the Research Program of Rafael Vinoly Architects, 2011.

Kertzer, Adriana. *Favelization: The Imaginary Brazil in Contemporary Film, Fashion and Design*. New York: Cooper-Hewitt, National Design Museum, 2014.

Kim, Ami. *As Cute as It Gets: Kawaii Aesthetics of Japanese Contemporary Visual Culture and Art*. PhD dissertation, New York: New York University, forthcoming 2015.

Lantarón, Rubén del, and Maribel Despaigne. *Bienal de La Habana para leer: compilación de textos*. Valencia: Universitat de València, 2009.

Lima, Zeuler. *Lina Bo Bardi*. New Haven: Yale University Press, 2013.

Maldonado, Tomás. *Disegno industriale: un riesame*. Milan: Feltrinelli, 1991.

Martín-Barbero, Jesus. *Communication, Culture and Hegemony: From the Media to Mediations*. Translated by Elizabeth Fox and Robert A. White. Newbury Park: Sage Publications, 1993.

Mata, Chicho. *El hombre de Uchire*. Caracas: Centro de Arte La Estancia, 1996.

Mena, Juan Carlos, and Oscar Reyes. *Sensacional de diseño mexicano*. México: Tricle Ediciones, 2001.

Miller, Daniel. *Material Cultures: Why Some Things Matter*. Chicago; London: University of Chicago Press, 1998.

Miménez, Martiza. *Maderas de Jorge Rivas: innovación en la tradición*. San Joaquín: Casa Alejo Zuloaga, 2004.

Mirkin, Dina Comisarenco, Carmen Cordera Lascurain, Juan Rafael Coronel Ribera, Alejandro Hernández Gálvez, and Anne Elena Mallet Cáardenas. *Vida y Diseño en Mexico, Siglo XX*. Mexico City: Grupo Financiero Banamex, 2007.

Majluf, Natalia, Luis Eduardo Wuffarden, and Elena Izcue. *el arte precolombino en la vida moderna*. Lima: Museo de Arte de Lima and Fundación Telefónica, 1999.

Majluf, Natalia. *Elena Izcue: Lima-Paris, années 30*. Paris: Musée du Quai Branly and Flammarion, 2008.

Navarro, Duran Horacio. *Diseño Industrial 1969 el inicio, en Cuadernos de Arquitectura y Dicencia. Monografia sobre la Facultad de Arqitectura*, no. 4–5. Mexico City: UMAM, 1990.

Niemeyer, Lucy. *Design no Brasil. Origens e Instalação*. Rio de Janeiro: 2AB, 1997.

Noyes, Eliot F. *Organic Design in Home Furnishings*. New York: Museum of Modern Art, 1941.

Olea, Héctor, and Mari Carmen Ramírez. *Inverted Utopias: Avant-Garde Art in Latin America, 1920–1970*. London; New Haven: Yale University Press, in association with The Museum of Fine Arts, Houston, 2004.

Olivares, Rosa. *100 Artistas Latinoamericanos*. Madrid: Exit Publicaciones, 2001.

Oroza, Ernesto. *Statements of Necessity*. Miami: Alonso Art, 2008.

Pedrosa, Adriano, and Rodrigo Moura. *Inhotim*. Belo Horizonte: Instituto Inhotim, 2009.

Pendleton-Jullian, Ann. *The Road That is Not a Road and the Open City, Ritoque, Chile*. Massachusetts: MIT Press Series in Contemporary Architecture Disc, 1996.

Perez U., E. *Identidad y diseño de productos en Venezuela*. Mérida: Universidad de Los Andes, 2005.

Perez U., E. *Promoción del diseño industrial en Venezuela través de una institución cultural*. Caracas: Centro de Arte Estancia, 2005.

Ramírez, Gonzalo. *Enciclopedia del desarrollo colombiano*. Bogotá: Canal Ramírez-Antares, 1973.

Ramírez, Mari Carmen, and Tomas Frausto. *Resisting Categories: Latin American and/or Latino?* 1. Houston: The Museum of Fine Arts, 2012.

Roca, José, and Alejandro Martin. *Waterweavers: The River in Contemporary Colombian Visual and Material Culture*, exh. cat. New York: Bard Graduate Center; London and New Haven: Yale University Press, 2014.

Ruiz, Alma. *Carlos Garaicoa: Capablanca's Real Passion*. Los Angeles: Museum of Contemporary Art, 2005.

Salinas, Fernando, and Roberto Segre. *El diseño ambiental en la era de la industrialización*. La Habana: Centro de Información Científica y Técnica, Universidad de La Habana, 1972.

Salinas Flores, Oscar. *Historia del Diseno Industrial*. Mexico City: Editorial Trillas, 1992.

Samar, Lidia, and Gay Aquiles. *El diseno industrial en la historia*. Córdoba: Ediciones TEC, Centro de Cultura Tecnológica, 2004.

Schwartzman, Allan, Jochen Volz, and Rodrigo Moura. *Through: Inhotim*. Brumadinho: Instituto Inhotim, 2009.

Seton-Watson, Hugh. *Nations and States: An Enquiry into the Origins of Nations and the Politics of Nationalism*. Boulder: Westview Press, 1977.

Taborda, Felipe, and Julius Wiedeman. *Latin American Graphic Design*. Hohenzollernring: Taschen, 2008.

Tulchin, Joseph S., and Elizabeth Bryan. *Cambios en la sociedad cubana desde los noventa*. Washington DC: Woodrow Wilson International Center for Scholars Latin American Program, 2005.

Vasconcelos, José. *La Raza Cósmica: Misión de la raza iberoamericana y notas de viajes a la América del Sur*. Barcelona: Agencia de Librería, 1925.

Vik Muniz: Pictures of Anything, exh. cat. Tel Aviv: Tel Aviv Museum of Art, 2014.

Weiss, Rachel. *To and from Utopia in the New Cuban Art*. Minneapolis: University of Minnesota Press, 2011.

Winkler, Andreas. *Cuba: arte contemporáneo = contemporary art*. New York; London: Overlook Duckworth, 2012.

Ybarra-Frausto, Tomás. *Rasquachismo: a Chicano Sensibility, in Chicano Aesthetics: Rasquachismo*, exh. cat. Phoenix: MARS, Movimiento Artístico del Rio Salado, 1989.

Zamudio-Taylor, Victor, and Isolde Brielmaier. *Objectos en tránsito*. Santo Domingo: Sala Gasco Arte Contemporaneo, 2006.

Articles

Gareth Harris, "From Beirut to Bogotá: Art Cities to Watch?" *New York Times*, September 23, 2013.

Mosquera, Gerardo. "Good-Bye Identity, Welcome Difference." *Third Text* 56 (2001).

Cullen, Manuel, Ernesto Oroza. "Revolución de la Desobediencia." *Hecho en Buenos Aires* 14, no. 161, (December 2013).

Maldonado, Tomas, and Gui Bonsiepe. "Science and Design." Ulm 10/11 (1964): 10.

"An exploration of the Mexican contemporary art scene." *Peepingtom Digest 2: Mexico* (2011).

Williams, Lyneise E. "Heavy Metal: Decoding Hip Hop Jewelry," *Metalsmith* 27, no. 1 (2007).

Fernández, Silvia. "The Origins of Design Education in Latin America: From the hfg in Ulm to Globalization," *Design Issues* 22, no. 1 (Winter 2006).

Fathers, James. "Peripheral Vision: An Interview with Gui Bonsiepe: Charting a Lifetime Commitment to Design Empowerment," *Design Issues* 19, no. 4 (Autumn 2003).

Margolin, Victor. "A World History of Design and the History of the World," *Journal of Design History* 18, no. 3 (Autumn 2005).

Quijano, Aníbal. "Coloniality of Power and Eurocentrism in Latin America," *International Sociology* 15, no. 2 (2000).

Ogata, Amy F. "Creative Playthings: Educational Toys and Postwar American Culture," *Winterthur Portfolio* 39 (Summer–Autumn 2004).

Vallega, Alejandro A. "Displacements: Beyond the Coloniality of Images," *Research in Phenomenology* 41, no. 2 (2011).

Lizette Alvarez, "Economy and Crime Spur New Puerto Rican Exodus," *New York Times,* February 8, 2014.

Michael Kimmelman, "A City Arises with Its Hopes," *New York Times*, May 18, 2012.

This book is published on the occasion of the exhibition *New Territories: Laboratories for Design, Craft and Art in Latin America*, curated by Lowery Stokes Sims, for the Museum of Arts and Design, November 4, 2014–April 6, 2015.

Designed by Leftloft, New York and Milan
Edited by Donna Wingate
Copyedited by Martina D'Alton
Proofread by Chesley Hicks
Produced by Turner at Estudios Gráficos Europeos

Text © the authors
Photos © the artists unless otherwise noted

Copyright © 2014 Museum of Arts and Design and TURNER
Rafael Calvo 42 - 2º
28010 Madrid
+34 91 308 33 36
www.turnerlibros.com

ISBN 978-84-15832-85-0
D.L.: M-21218-2014

Distributed in North America by DAP/artbook.com

All rights reserved. No part of this publication may be reproduced or transmitted in any form or by any means, electronic or mechanical, including photocopy, recording, or any other information storage and retrieval system, or otherwise without written permission from the publisher.

Printed in Spain

Major support for *New Territories: Laboratories for Design, Craft and Art in Latin America* is provided by the Ford Foundation and the Robert Sterling Clark Foundation. Additional support is provided by Karen and Charles Phillips, Furthermore: a program of the J.M. Kaplan Fund, The Venezuelan American Endowment for the Arts, the Consulate General of Brazil in New York, The Louise D. and Morton J. Macks Family Foundation, the Mex-Am Cultural Foundation, and Ch.ACO, Contemporary Art Fair of Chile. Support for the exhibition website is provided by Phillips.